S0-ADF-083

A Concise Dictionary of Foreign Expressions

A Concise Dictionary of Foreign Expressions

B. A. Phythian

BARNES & NOBLE BOOKS
TOTOWA, NEW JERSEY

First published in the USA 1982 by
BARNES & NOBLE BOOKS
81 ADAMS DRIVE
TOTOWA, NEW JERSEY, 07512

ISBN 0-389-20327 0

Printed in Great Britain

Foreword

The origins of modern English, its subsequent international nature, and the history of Britain, have all contributed to the frequency with which foreign words and expressions are found in English. With the passage of centuries, many such importations have lost their foreign identity and feel along with, in many cases, their original spelling or pronunciation, and are now recorded in dictionaries as fully fledged English words. Other importations are still in transit, so to speak: some of them have more than one spelling or pronunciation – their original ones and anglicised ones – and dictionary-makers have differing views about their status. A third group is, however, undeniably foreign, even though words and expressions from this group are sometimes recorded in English dictionaries with a clear (often typographical) indication that they are not yet assimilated into English. The present collection is drawn mainly from this third group, together with a few 'transit' words that still have enough of their original flavour for the general reader to expect to find them here.

Pronunciation

The English language alone contains forty-four different vowel and consonant sounds. Other languages, such as French and German, use sounds which do not exist in English. To have represented, with absolute authenticity, the pronunciation of words from the two dozen languages quoted in this book would have required a huge apparatus of phonetic symbols – quite apart from the fact that there is no general agreement about how Latin is to be pronounced. In the interests of simplicity, therefore, no phonetic symbols are used, and there is no attempt to represent authentically the true sounds of foreign pronunciation. What has been provided is the sort of approximation that most English speakers normally use.

The pronunciation is given in brackets in italics, with stressed syllables printed in capital letters. The reader is advised to pronounce the syllables one by one, and then to run them together.

French is normally pronounced without stresses, but some of the most frequently used French words and expressions have acquired an anglicised stressing, and this is indicated where appropriate.

The following pronunciation scheme has been used:

a	as in sat
ah	,, ,, father
ai	,, ,, air
ar	,, ,, carry
ay	,, ,, ray
e	,, ,, set
ea	,, ,, fear
ee	,, ,, feel
eh	,, ,, fetch
ew	,, ,, few
eye	,, ,, eye
g	,, ,, girl
i	,, ,, sit
j	,, ,, jab
kh	,, ,, loch (i.e. a rolled k)
ṁ	signifies that the preceding vowel is nasalised, the m being pronounced
ṅ	signifies that the preceding vowel is nasalised, the n not being pronounced
o	as in lot
oa	,, ,, oar
oh	,, ,, hole
oo	,, ,, fool
or	,, ,, for
ow	,, ,, now
oy	,, ,, boy
s	,, ,, sat
u	,, ,, pull
uh	,, ,, token
ur	,, ,, fur
x	,, ,, extra
y	,, ,, your
z	,, ,, zoom
zh	,, ,, vision

Note: In German, nouns are written with an initial capital letter. This has been retained for those words which are still felt to be primarily

German. Words which have become more assimilated into English are printed with small initial letters. In cases where there appears to be no common current agreement, both versions are given.

Abbreviations

Arab.	Arabic
Chin.	Chinese
Dan.	Danish
Dut.	Dutch
Finn.	Finnish
Fr.	French
Ger.	German
Heb.	Hebrew
Hind.	Hindustani
Hung.	Hungarian
Ir.	Irish
It.	Italian
Jap.	Japanese
Lat.	Latin
Nor.	Norwegian
Pers.	Persian
Port.	Portugese
Sp.	Spanish
Swa.	Swahili
Turk.	Turkish

A

à bas [Fr.] Down with . . . *(a bah)*

abbé [Fr.] Abbot; in France, anyone entitled to wear ecclesiastical dress, even though he may have no ecclesiastical function. *(a-bay)*

ab extra [Lat.] From outside. *(ab EKS-trah)*

à bientôt [Fr.] Good-bye, I'll see you again soon. *(ab-yaṅ-toh)*

ab initio [Lat.] From the beginning. *(ab-in-IT-ee-oh* or *ab-in-ISH-ee-oh)*

ab oro [Lat.] From the very beginning (tediously). *(ab OH-roh)*

abseil [Ger.] (Make a) descent of a steep face (e.g. rock-face) by using a rope wrapped round the body and either tied to a higher point or looped over it (e.g. a hook) to form a doubled rope held in the hands during descent. *(ABS-eye-l)*

absinthe [Fr.] Strong green liquor made from wine and wormwood. (Pronounced as spelt, or *absaṅt*)

absit omen [Lat.] May the omen (foreboding) come to nothing. *(ab-sit OH-men)*

ab urbe condita [Lat.] Dating from the foundation of the city (of Rome in 753 B.C.). *(ab oorbi KON-dita)* Sometimes abbreviated to **A.U.C.**

A.C. See **appellation d'origine contrôlée.**

a cappella [It.] (Of choral music) without instrumental accompaniment. (In early music) with instruments playing as an optional addition to or substitution for a voice part. *(a kap-EL-a)*

accablé [Fr.] Overwhelmed. *(akab-lay)*

accelerando [It.] (Of music) gradually becoming faster. *(at-shel-ay-RAN-doh* or *ak-sel-er-AN-doh)*

accouchement [Fr.] Confinement; lying-in for childbirth. *(ak-oosh-mahṅ)*

accoucheuse [Fr.] Midwife. *(ak-oosh-urz)* Also masculine **accoucheur**. *(ak-oosh-ur)*

acharnement [Fr.] Ferocity. *(ash-AH-nuh-mahṅ)*

à cheval [Fr.] On both sides. *(a shv-AL)* Usually applied to gambling stake placed equally on two chances.

acushla [Ir.] Darling. *(ak-OOSH-la)*

A.D. Abbreviation of **Anno Domini.**

adagio [It.] (In printed music) to be played slowly. *(ad-AH-zhoh)* Also, the slow movement of a symphony.

A.D.C. Abbreviation of **aide-de-camp.**

ad captandum (vulgus) [Lat.] (Intended) to appeal to popular emotion or prejudice. *(ad kap-TAN-dum vul-gus)*

addendum [Lat.] Something added. To be added (e.g. late addition to contents of a book). *(ad-END-um)* Plural **addenda.**

Adeste, fideles [Lat.] Come, you faithful ones. *(ad-ES-teh fee-DAY-lees)* First words of ancient hymn, popularly translated 'O come, all ye faithful'.

ad eundem (gradum) [Lat.] To the same university degree. *(ad ay-UND-em GRAH-dum)*

à deux [Fr.] For two. Between two. *(a DUR)*

ad fin. Abbreviation of **ad finem.**

ad finem [Lat.] At or towards the end. *(ad FEE-nem)*

ad hoc [Lat.] For a special purpose. Improvised in haste. *(ad HOK)*

ad hominem [Lat.] Intended to appeal to emotions or prejudices rather than to the mind. Personal abuse of an opponent, instead of reasoned argument. *(ad HOM-in-em)*

adieu [Fr.] Goodbye. Farewell. *(a-DEW* or *a-DYUR)* Plural **adieux.**

ad infinitum [Lat.] For ever. *(ad in-fin-EYE-tum)*

ad interim [Lat.] For the time being. *(ad INT-er-im)*

adiós [Sp.] Goodbye. *(ad-YOHS)*

ad lib (abbreviation of **ad libitum**) [Lat.] As much as one pleases. Unprepared remark. Speak without preparation. (In theatre) improvise lines. (In music) as one wishes. Freely. *(ad LIB)*

ad libitum [Lat.] To any desired extent. *(ad LIB-it-um)*

ad majorem Dei gloriam [Lat.] To the greater glory of God. *(ad ma-YOH-rem DAY-ee GLOR-i-am)*

ad nauseam [Lat.] To a nauseating degree. *(ad NORZ-ay-am)*

ad personam [Lat.] Same as **ad hominem.** *(ad per-SOH-nam)*

ad rem [Lat.] To the point (at issue). *(ad REM)*

adsum [Lat.] I am present. *(AD-sum)*

ad valorem [Lat.] (Of tax) in proportion to the value (of goods taxed). *(ad val-OR-em)*

ad verbum [Lat.] Verbatim. Word for word. *(ad VER-* or *WER-bum)*

advocatus diaboli [Lat.] Devil's advocate; one who draws attention to faults, not to state his personal opinion but to ensure thorough discussion. *(ad-vok-AH-tus dee-AB-olee)*

aegrotat [Lat.] Certificate that student is too ill to attend examination. Examination pass awarded in these circumstances. *(EYE-gro* or *groh-tat)*

aequo animo [Lat.] With equanimity. *(eye-kwoh AN-im-oh)*

aetatis [Lat.] At the age of. *(eye-TAH-tis)* Also **aetatis suae.** *(SOO-eye)* Abbreviated (often on grave-stones) to **aet.** or **aetat.**

affaire [Fr.] Affair. Scandal. Sensational event. *(af-AIR)*

affaire (de cœur) [Fr.] Love affair. *(af-AIR duh-KUR)*
affairé [Fr.] Busy. *(af-AIR-ay)*
affaire d'honneur [Fr.] Matter of honour. *(af-AIR don-UR)*
affiche [Fr.] Notice. Poster. *(a-FEESH)*
aficionado [Sp.] Enthusiast for particular pursuit, especially bull-fighting. *(af-ees-yon-AH-doh)*
à fond [Fr.] Thoroughly. Deep down. *(a FORṄ)*
a fortiori [Lat.] All the more. *(ay-forti-OR-i)*
agape [Gk.] Christian love. *(AG-apee)*
agent provocateur [Fr.] Secret agent employed to provoke others to action (e.g. crime) so as to secure their detection. *(AH-zhahṅ provokat-UR)*
aggiornamento [It.] Modernisation, especially of Roman Catholic Church. *(a-jor-nah-MEN-toh)*
agitato [It.] (Of music) played in an agitated fashion. *(ad-jee-TAH-toh)*
Agnus Dei [Lat.] Lamb of God. Part of the Mass beginning with these words. *(AG-nus* or *AN-yus* or *AN-yoos DAY-ee)*
à gogo [Fr.] In abundance. *(a-GOH-goh)*
agonistes [Gk.] Struggling with a powerful opponent. *(agon-ISS-teez)*
agora [Gk.] Place of public assembly. Market-place. *(AG-oh-ra)* Hence **agoraphobia.** Dread of public places.
agrégation [Fr.] Competitive examination for teaching posts in France. *(ag-ray-GAS-yoṁ)*
agrégé [Fr.] (In France) qualified to teach after passing competitive exam. *(ag-ray-zhay)* Feminine **agrégée.**
agréments [Fr.] The agreeable qualities of social life; refinements. *(ag-ray-mahṅ)*
aguardiente [Sp.] Rough liquor. *(ag-wah-DYEN-teh)*
ahimsa [Sanskrit] Doctrine of non-violence and the sacredness of life. *(a-HIM-sa)*
à huis clos [Fr.] In private; in secret; behind closed doors. *(a wee kloh)*
aide [Fr.] Assistant. *(ayd)*
aide-de-camp [Fr.] Officer who is confidential assistant to a senior officer. *(ayd* or *ed-duh-kahṅ)* Plural **aides-de-camp** (same pronunciation).
aide-mémoire [Fr.] Aid to the memory (e.g. set of notes). Diplomatic message setting out what has been agreed, discussed, etc. *(ayd-mem-wah)*
aiguille [Fr.] Sharp peak of rock; sharply pointed mountain-peak. *(ayg-WEEY)*
aiguillette [Fr.] Dangling point of shoulder braid on military uniform. *(ayg-wee-YET)*

aîné [Fr.] (The) elder. *(ay-nay)*

aïoli [Fr.] Garlic sauce, made with eggs, olive oil, garlic and lemon, and served with a wide variety of dishes, especially fish and vegetables. *(ay-ee-oh-lee)*

akvavit Same as **aquavit.**

à la [Fr.] In the manner of. As prepared by or for. *(a la)*

à la carte [Fr.] (From) that part of a menu where items are separately priced. *(a la KAHT)* See **prix fixe, table d'hôte.**

à la mode [Fr.] In the fashion. (Of beef) braised in wine. (In U.S.A.) with ice cream. *(a la MOD)*

à la page [Fr.] Up to date; in the latest fashion. *(a la PAHZH)*

à la russe [Fr.] In the Russian manner. *(a la ROO-s)*

à la rigueur [Fr.] If absolutely necessary. *(a la reeg-UR)*

albino [Sp., Port.] Person with deficiency of colouring pigment in skin, hair and eyes, so that the former are white and the latter pink. *(al-BEE-noh)* Also applied to animals, and to plants lacking normal colouring.

al dente [It.] Cooked so as to be still firm when eaten, not too soft through over-cooking. *(al-DEN-teh)* Usually applied to **pasta.**

alea jacta est [Lat.] The die is cast. *(a-LAY-a YAK-ta est)*

al fine [It.] Continue to the end. *(al FEE-neh)* Instruction in printed music. See also **da capo al fine.**

al fresco or **alfresco** [It.] In the open air. *(al-FRES-koh)*

alla breve [It.] (In music) with two minims (occasionally four) to the bar. *(a la BRAY-vay)*

alla marcia [It.] In march style. *(a la MAH-see-a)*

alla prima [It.] (Of painting) completed in one sitting. *(a la PREE-ma)*

allargando [It.] (Of music) becoming slower and fuller in tone. *(al-ah-GAN-doh)*

allegretto [It.] (Of music) in a fairly fast and lively style, but not as fast as **allegro.** *(a-lay-GRET-oh)*

allegro [It.] (Of music) merry, quick, lively. A movement or piece in this style. *(a-LAY-groh)*

allemande [Fr.] Short musical composition (often first movement of a suite) of moderately serious nature, and in moderate tempo, in two halves, each beginning with a repeated note. *(al-mahńd)* Probably originating in a German dance. The word is also applied to a fast country dance in waltz tempo, found in parts of Germany.

alluvium [Lat.] Deposit of sand, earth, etc. left by flood, especially in valley or delta. *(al-OO-vi-um)*

Alma Mater [Lat.] Name given to university, college or school by (usually past) pupils. *(al-ma MAY-ter* or *MAH-ter)*

à l'outrance [Fr.] To the bitter end. *(a loo-TRAHṄS)*

alpenhorn [Ger.] Long wooden horn played by Swiss herdsmen. *(ALP-en-horn)*

alpenstock [Ger.] Long staff, with iron tip or point, used in mountain-climbing. *(ALP-en-stok)*

alpha [Gk.] First letter of Greek alphabet, usually used to denote excellence, e.g. in an examination performance. *(AL-fa)*

Alpha and Omega [Gk.] The beginning and the end. *(AL-fa and OH-meg-a)*

al segno [It.] (In music) go (on) to the place marked with the sign. *(al-SAYN-yoh)* See **segno, dal segno, da capo al segno.**

alter ego [Lat.] Intimate friend. *(al-ter EE-goh* or *EG-oh)* Literally, one's 'other self' or double.

alto [It.] Highest adult male voice (sometimes called counter-tenor) corresponding to the range of a low female voice. *(AL-toh)* The low female voice is called **contralto**, often abbreviated to **alto**. Also applied to instrument of second highest pitch in a group (e.g. alto saxophone).

alto(-)relievo or **rilievo** [It.] Sculpture consisting of carved panel in which objects and figures project by more than half of their true proportions. *(al-toh* or *ol-toh rel-YAY-voh)* See also **bas-relief.**

alumnus [Lat.] Member or former member (e.g. student, pupil, graduate) of any learned establishment. Feminine **alumna**. Plurals **alumni** and **alumnae** respectively. *(al-UM-nus, -na, -nee, -neye)*

a.m. Abbreviation of **ante meridiem.** [Lat.] Before noon.

amah [Port.] Native wet-nurse or female servant. *(AH-ma)*

amanuensis [Lat.] Person who writes from dictation or copies a manuscript. *(amanu-EN-sis)*

ambience [Fr.] Pervading atmosphere; distinctive surroundings. *(ahṁ-byahṅ-s)*

ambrosia [Gk.] Food of the gods. Something delightful to taste (or smell). *(am-BROH-zya* or *-zhya)*

A.M.D.G. Abbreviation of **ad majorem dei gloriam.**

âme [Fr.] Soul *(ahm)*

âme damné [Fr.] Someone whose fortunes are inextricably bound up with those of another. Someone blindly devoted to another's wishes. Scapegoat. *(ahm dam-nay)* Literally, a 'damned (or lost) soul'.

amende honorable [Fr.] (Public) apology. Reparation. *(a-mahṅd on-or-AH-bl)*

à merveille [Fr.] Wonderfully. *(a mair-vay)*

ami [Fr.] Friend. *(a-mee)* Female **amie** (same pronunciation).

amicus curiae [Lat.] Disinterested adviser (to court of law). *(ami-kus KOO-ree-ee* or *KOO-ree-ay)*

amie [Fr.] Mistress. Lady friend. *(a-mee)*

Amontillado [Sp.] Medium dry sherry. *(a-mon-til-AH-doh)*

amoretto [It.] (In painting, sculpture, etc.) Cupid. *(am-or-ET-oh)* See **cupid.**

amoroso [Sp.] (Of sherry) sweet, rich, full. (Of music) tenderly. *(am-or-OH-soh)*

amor patriae [Lat.] Love of one's own country. Patriotism. *(am-or PAT-ree-eye* or *PAT-ree-ay)*

amour [Fr.] Love. Loved one. Love-affair, usually secret. *(am-oor)*

amourette [Fr.] Trivial love-affair. *(am-oor-et)*

amour propre [Fr.] Self-esteem; self-love; vanity. *(am-oor PROP-r)*

amphora [Lat.] Greek or Roman vessel with two handles, used for holding oil, wine, etc. *(AM-for-a)*

ampoule [Fr.] Sealed glass container containing drugs prior to their injection. *(am-pool)*

ampulla [Lat.] Small Roman globular flask or bottle with two handles. Vessel for holding consecrated oil, etc. (In physiology, biology or zoology) dilated end of a vessel, canal or duct. *(am-PUL-a)*

anabasis [Gk.] Military expedition. *(ana-BAY-sis)*

anacoluthon [Lat.] Lack of grammatical sequence in sentence or construction. *(an-akol-YOO-thon)*

anacrusis [Gk.] (In poetry) unstressed syllable(s) at beginning of a line of poetry. (In music) unstressed note(s) before first full bar. *(an-a-KROO-sis)*

ancien régime [Fr.] System of government or state of affairs in France before the Revolution. Any **régime** that has been replaced. *(ahṅ-syaṅ ray-ZHEEM)*

andante [It.] (Of music) moving along in moderately slow time (i.e. slower than **allegretto**). Piece of music written in such **tempo.** *(an-DANT-eh)*

andantino [It.] (Of music) a little faster or slower than **andante** (the performer must decide for himself). *(and-ant-EE-noh)*

angelus [Lat.] Sequence of prayers to be said at dawn, noon and sunset. The bell rung to signal these. *(AN-jel-us* or *-oos)*

angina (pectoris) [Lat.] Dangerous disease, marked by severe chest-pain. *(anj-EYE-na PEKT-oris)*

anglais [Fr.] English. *(AHṄ-glay).* Feminine **anglaise** *(ahṅ-GLEHZ)*

anglice [Lat.] In English. *(ANG-lik-eh)*

Angst [Ger.] Anxiety, often acute, usually without clear cause (e.g. feeling of physical or philosophical loneliness or isolation in a world which is unsympathetic or hostile). *(ahnkst)*

anima [Lat.] Soul. (In psychology) inner personality; feminine part of a man's personality. *(AN-ee-ma)*. See **animus.**

anima mundi [Lat.] Power governing the physical universe. *(an-ee-ma MUN-dee)* Literally, 'the soul of the world'.

animato [It.] (In printed music) to be played in an animated way. *(an-ee-MAH-toh)*

animus [Lat.] Mind. Animosity. (In psychology) masculine part of a woman's personality. *(AN-ee-mus)* See **anima.**

Anjou [Fr.] Pink wine from Loire region of France. *(ahṅ-zhoo)*

anna [Hind.] Former coin, worth one-sixteenth of a **rupee**, in India and Pakistan. *(AN-a)*

anno aetatis suae [Lat.] At the age of. *(AN-oh eye-TAH-tis SOO-eye)*

Anno Domini [Lat.] In the year of our Lord; of the Christian era. (Colloquially) the effects of old age. *(an-oh DOM-in-i* or *-eye)* Normally abbreviated to **A.D.**

anno regni [Lat.] In the year of the reign. *(an-oh REG-nee* or *REN-yee)*

annulus [Lat.] Ring. *(AN-(y)oo-lus)*

annus mirabilis [Lat.] Remarkable year. *(an-us mi-RAH-bi-lis)*

anorak [Eskimo] Waterproof hooded jacket, sometimes padded, for outdoor wear. *(AN-orak)*

anschluss [Ger.] Union. Annexation, especially of Austria by Germany, 1938. *(AN-shloos)*

ante [Lat.] Before; preceding. Previously mentioned. *(AN-teh)*

ante bellum [Lat.] Before a (stated) war, especially the American Civil War. *(an-teh BEL-um)*

ante meridiem [Lat.] Before noon. *(an-teh mer-ID-i-em)* Abbreviation **A.M.**

antipasto [It.] Dish of appetizing food eaten as first course of a meal. *(anti-PAS-toh)* Same as **hors d'œuvre.**

A.O.C. See **appellation d'origine contrôlée.**

à outrance [Fr.] To the bitter end. *(a-oo-TRAHṄS)*

apache [Fr. or Sp.] (Member of) warlike tribe of American Indians. (a-PATCH-i) Violent street ruffian, originally in Paris. *(a-PASH-uh)*

apartheid [Afrikaans] Strict segregation of racial groups, originally in South Africa. Any policy of separation of groups of people. *(a-PAHT-ayt)*

aperçu [Fr.] Insight; intuitive understanding. Summary; outline; survey. *(a-pehr-soo)*

aperitif or **apéritif** [Fr.] Alcoholic drink taken as appetizer before a meal. *(ap-ehr-it-eef)*

apfelstrudel [Ger.] Confectionery of apples, baked and spiced, with flaky pastry. *(AP-fel-stroodl)*

apologia [Gk.] Written statement defending one's own (or someone's) conduct or opinions. *(apol-OH-ja)*

a posteriori [Lat.] (Reasoning) from effect back to cause, i.e. inductively, from facts, experience, etc. *(ay* or *ah post-ay-ri-OH-ri)* See **a priori.**

apparat [Russ.] Communist party bureaucracy in U.S.S.R. and elsewhere. Any repressive or threatening bureaucracy. *(ap-ar-AH)*

apparatchik [Russ.] Member of **apparat**. Communist agent. *(ap-ar-AH-chik)*

apparatus (criticus) [Lat.] Materials for critical study of a text. *(ap-ar-AT-us KRIT-ik-us)*

appartement [Fr.] Flat. *(ap-aht-uh-mahn̈)*

appassionata, appassionato [It.] (Of music) played in a passionate manner. *(ap-as-yon-AH-ta, -toh)*

appellation d'origine contrôlée or **appellation contrôlée** [Fr.] (On labels of bottles of best quality French wine as) guarantee that wine has been grown at stated place and in prescribed way. *(ap-el-ah-syon̈ do-ri-zheen kon̈-trohl-ay)* Abbreviations **A.O.C., A.C.** See **vin delimité de qualité supérieure.**

appliqué [Fr.] (In needlework) decoration made by stitching pieces of material to surface of another material. *(ap-LEE-kay)*

appoggiatura [It.] Form of musical ornamentation, belonging to that kind called grace-notes, and comprising a note which takes the emphasis and part of the time-value from the following note on which it leans. *(ap-poj-yah-TOO-ra)*

après moi le déluge [Fr.] After me, the deluge. When I am dead, the world will end (*or* there will be disaster *or* life will not be worth living, etc.) *(ap-ray mwah luh day-loozh)* Correctly, **après nous** (us) **le déluge** (Madame de Pompadour, having premonition of French Revolution).

après-ski [Fr.] Relaxation or recreation after day's skiing. Worn or done on such occasions. Take part in such occupation. *(ap-ray skee)*

a priori [Lat.] (Reasoning) from cause to effect, i.e. deductively, without material evidence or experience. *(ay* or *ah pree-OR-i* or *-eye)* See **a posteriori.**

à propos or **apropos** [Fr.] With regard to. To the purpose or point. Appropriate(ly), opportune(ly), relevant(ly). *(a-prop-OH)*

aqua [Lat.] Water. *(A-kwa)*

aqua fortis [Lat.] Nitric acid. *(akwa FOR-tis)*

aqua regia [Lat.] Mixture of nitric and hydrochloric acids. *(akwa REJ-ee-a)*

aquarelle [Fr.] (Method of) painting using ink and thin, often transparent, water-colours. *(akwa-REL)*

aquavit [Scandinavian] Alcoholic spirit made from potatoes, etc. *(akwa-VIT)*

aqua(-)vitae [Lat.] Alcoholic spirit, especially brandy and whisky. *(akwa-VEET-eye)*

aquila [Lat.] Eagle. Church lectern in shape of eagle. *(ak-WIL-a)*

arabesque [Fr.] (In art) fanciful and intricate decoration of spirals, scrolls etc. intertwining. (In music) elaborate composition suggesting this style. (In ballet) posture with one leg stretched horizontally backwards, one arm extended forwards or upwards, the other backwards. *(ara-BESK)*

arak [Arabian] Alcoholic spirit made from rice, palm-tree sap, molasses, etc. *(a-RAK)*

arbiter elegantiarum [Lat.] Judge of style, good taste, etiquette, aesthetics. *(AH-bit-er el-eg-anti-AH-rum)*

arcana [Lat.] Secrets. Mysteries. *(ahk-AY-na)* Singular **arcanum.**

arcus senilis [Lat.] Narrow opaque band often encircling cornea of eye in old age. *(AHK-us sen-IL-is)*

arête [Fr.] Sharp mountain-ridge with steep sides formed by erosion. *(a-RET)*

argot [Fr.] Jargon or slang of a class, group, profession, trade, etc. (especially criminals). *(AH-goh)*

argumentum e (or **a** or **ex**) **silentio** [Lat.] Argument based on person's silence or on lack of evidence. Verdict so based. *(ahgu-MENT-um ay* or *ah* or *ex si-LENT-ee-oh* or *-LENSH-ee-oh)*

aria [It.] Accompanied solo vocal piece, often in three sections, of which the second offers development and variety, and the third repeats the first, in opera and oratorio. *(AH-ree-a)*

arioso [It.] Type of singing which shares the qualities of both **aria** and **recitativo**, i.e. aria-like melodious recitative. Short air in opera or oratorio. *(ah-ri-OH-soh)*

aristo [Fr.] (Playful or dismissive abbreviation of) aristocrat. *(ar-ee-stoh)*

a rivederci or **arrivederci** [It.] Goodbye. *(ah-ree-veh-DEHR-chi)*

armagnac [Fr.] Type of brandy distilled in south-western France. *(ahm-an-yak)*

arme blanche [Fr.] Cavalry sword or lance. Cavalry. *(ahm blahnsh)*

armoire [Fr.] Free-standing cupboard or wardrobe. *(ahm-WAHR)*

arpeggio [It.] Playing notes of a chord in succession (usually quickly and from the lowest upward) instead of simultaneously. *(ah-PEJ-(i)-oh)*

arrack Same as **arak.**

arrière-ban [Fr.] (Summoning of) vassals for military service. *(ari-air-barñ)*

arrière-goût [Fr.] After-taste. *(ari-air-goo)*

arrière-pensée [Fr.] Ulterior motive. *(ari-air-pahñ-say)*

arrière-plan [Fr.] (In paintings) background. *(ari-air-plahñ)*

arrivé [Fr.] (Person) newly famous, successful, established. *(ar-ee-vay)*

arrivederci. See **a rivederci.**

arrivisme [Fr.] Behaviour of **arriviste.** *(ar-eev-eesm)*

arriviste [Fr.] (Person who is) ambitious, self-seeking, on the make, determined to establish himself. *(ar-eev-eest)*

arrondissement [Fr.] District of Paris. Subdivision of French **département.** *(ar-orñ-DEES-mahñ)*

arroyo [Sp.] Gully, gulch. Creek, stream. Dried-up river-bed. (U.S.A.) *(ar-OH-yoh)*

ars amandi [Lat.] The art of loving. *(ahz am-AN-dee)*

ars amatoria [Lat.] The amatory art. *(ahz amat-OH-ree-a)*

ars est celare artem [Lat.] Art is to conceal art. (True art appears effortless.) *(ahz est kel-AH-ri AH-tem)*

ars gratia artis [Lat.] Art for art's sake. *(ahz GRAH-tee-a AH-tis)*

ars longa, vita brevis [Lat.] Art is long; life is short. *(ahz LONG-a VEE-ta BREV-is)*

ars poetica [Lat.] The art of poetry. *(ahz poh-ET-ika)*

art nouveau [Fr.] Style of art, architecture and decoration of late nineteenth century. *(ah noo-voh)*

a secco [It.] (Painting) on dry plaster. *(a SEK-oh)*

assai [It.] (In printed music) fairly. *(as-EYE)*

assemblage [Fr.] (Sculpture) constructed of miscellaneous objects. *(as-omb-LAHZH)*

assiette anglaise [Fr.] Dish of assorted cold meats. *(as-yet ahñ-glayz)*

assoluta Short for **prima ballerina assoluta.**

ataman [Russ.] Cossack chief. *(uh-tuh-MAN)*

atelier [Fr.] Workshop, studio of artist, craftsman or **couturier.** *(at-uhl-yay)*

a tempo [It.] (Of music) at the previous speed (e.g. to signify resumption of original **tempo** at end of a quicker or slower passage). *(ah-TEM-poh)*

atrium [Lat.] Centrally placed court or hall of Roman house. *(AT-ree-um)*

à trois [Fr.] For, of, among or with three (usually persons) only. *(a TRWAH)*

attaché [Fr.] Member of ambassador's staff. *(a-TASH-ay)*

attentat [Fr.] Attempted assassination. *(a-tahṅ-tah)*

aubade [Fr.] Song (sometimes poem) or piece of music appropriate to dawn. *(oh-bahd)*

auberge [Fr.] Inn. (In France) good quality restaurant. *(oh-bairzh)*

A.U.C. Abbreviation of **ab urbe condita.**

au contraire [Fr.] On the contrary. *(oh koṅt-rair)*

au courant [Fr.] Well-informed. Up-to-date. *(oh koo-roṅ)*

audi alteram partem [Lat.] Listen to the other side of the case. *(OW-dee ALT-eram PAH-tem)*

au fait [Fr.] Well-informed, conversant, expert. *(oh FAY)*

Auflage [Ger.] Edition. *(OWF-lah-guh)*

au fond [Fr.] Basically. *(oh FORṄ)*

auf Wiedersehen [Ger.] Goodbye. *(owf VEE-dair-zayn)*

au grand sérieux [Fr.] Very seriously. *(oh grahṅ say-ree-UR)*

au gratin [Fr.] Cooked with a covering of crisp breadcrumbs or grated cheese. *(oh grat-aṅ)*

auld lang syne [Scottish] (The) old times. *(orld lang seye-n)* Literally, old long-since.

au naturel [Fr.] In the natural state. Nude. (Of cooking) plainly and simply cooked. Uncooked. *(oh nat-yoor-EL)*

au pair [Fr.] Without wages. (Young girl, usually foreign) receiving board and lodging in exchange for doing housework, etc., for pocket money *(oh PAIR)*

au pied Abbreviation of **au pied de la lettre.**

au pied de la lettre [Fr.] Literally. *(oh pyay duh la lettr)*

au poivre [Fr.] (In cookery) with a strong flavouring of (crushed) peppercorns. *(oh pwah-vruh)*

aurea mediocritas [Lat.] The golden mean. *(oh* or *ow-ray-ah medi-OK-rit-as)*

au revoir [Fr.] Goodbye. *(oh ruh-VWAHR)*

Aurora [Lat.] Roman goddess of dawn. *(or-OH-ra)*

aurora australis [Lat.] Southern Lights (atmospheric phenomenon, probably electrical, consisting of bright glow and rays, near the southern magnetic pole, visible at night). *(or-OH-ra ows-TRAH-lis)*

aurora borealis [Lat.] Northern Lights (as above, but at northern magnetic pole). *(or-OH-ra boh-ree-AY* or *AH-lis)*

au sérieux [Fr.] Seriously. *(oh say-ree-UR)*

Ausländer [Ger.] Foreigner. Outsider. *(OWS-lender)*

aut Caesar aut nullus (or **nihil**) [Lat.] Either Caesar or nothing. Nothing but the best. *(owt KEYE-zar owt NUL-us* or *NI-hil)*

auteur [Fr.] Author. *(oh-tur)* Found in such expressions as 'auteur cinema', i.e. film-making in which the director is also composer of the script.

autobahn [Ger.] German motorway. *(OW-toh-bahn)* Plural **autobahnen** *(OW-toh-bahn-uhn)*

auto-da-fé [Port.] Sentence, or execution of sentence, of the Inquisition, especially burning of heretic. Death for a religious cause. *(ow-toh-dah-FAY)*

autopista [Sp.] Spanish motorway. *(OR-toh-pees-ta)*

autoroute [Fr.] French motorway. *(OH-toh-root)*

autostrada [It.] Italian motorway. *(ow-toh-STRAH-da)*

autre chose [Fr.] Something else. Something different. *(oh-truh shohz)*

autres temps, autres mœurs [Fr.] Other times, other customs. Customs, manners, etc. change with the times. *(oh-truh tahṅ oh-truh-mur-s)*

au vif [Fr.] (In painting) from life. *(oh VEEF)*

avant-courier or **courrier** or **coureur** [Fr.] Forerunner. *(avahṅ-koor-ee-ay* or *KOOR-ee-uh* or *koor-ur)*

avant-garde [Fr.] (Of art form) innovatory, experimental. Pioneers in any art form. *(avahṅ-GARD)*

avanti [It.] Move forward! *(a-VAN-ti)*

avatar [Sanskrit] Incarnation of deity. Manifestation. *(AV-at-ar)*

ave [Lat.] Hail! Welcome! *(AH-vay)*

ave atque vale [Lat.] Hail and farewell. *(AH-vay at-kwi VAH-lay)*

Ave Maria [Lat.] Hail, Mary! Prayer beginning thus. *(AH-vay ma-REE-a)*

avoirdupois [Fr.] British system of weights, based on the sixteen-ounce pound. (Colloquially) excess bodily weight. *(avwah-doo-PWAH)*

ayah [Port.] Native maidservant or nursemaid, usually of Europeans in India. *(EYE-a)*

B

baas [Dut.] (In Africa, especially South Africa) master, boss, employer. *(bahs)*

baasskap [Afrikaans] Domination, especially of non-whites by whites, in South Africa. *(BAHS-kahp)*

baba or **baba au rhum** or **Rum baba** [Fr.] Rich sponge-cake, plum-cake or pudding soaked in rum sauce. *(bahbah, -oh rerm)*

baboo See **babu**

babu or **baboo** [Hindi] (In India) native Hindoo gentleman; title of respect for such. Native clerk who writes English; native who speaks English (derogatory). Type of flowery and rather unidiomatic English *(BAH-boo)*

babushka [Russ.] Grandmother. Head-scarf tied under chin and worn by peasant women. *(bah-BOOSH-ka)*

baccalauréat [Fr.] (In France) examination concluding pre-university studies. *(ba-kal-oh-ray-ah)*

baccara(t) [Fr.] Game of cards played for money between banker and punters. *(BAK-a-rah)*

Bacchanal(e) [Lat.] Noisy, usually drunken, revel or reveller. Riotously drunken. *(BAK-an-ahl)*

Bacchanalia [Lat.] Drunken revelry. *(bak-an-AY-lee-a)*

Bacchantes [Lat.] Drunken women. *(bak-AN-tees)*

bachot [Fr.] (In colloquial French) abbreviation for **baccalauréat** *(bah-shoh)*

badinage [Fr.] Light-hearted banter. *(bah-deen-ahzh)*

Baedeker [from name of Karl Baedeker, German publisher] Guide-book. *(BAY-duh-kuh)*

bagarre [Fr.] Brawl. Scuffle. *(ba-GAH)*

bagel [Yiddish] Hard, doughnut-shaped bread roll. *(BAY-gl)*

bagatelle [Fr.] Trifling matter. (In music) short, unpretentious instrumental composition. Table game with balls, cue and numbered holes. *(bag-a-TEL)*

bagnio [It.] Brothel. Oriental prison. *(BAH-nyoh)*

baguette [Fr.] Long, narrow French loaf. Baton. Gem cut in narrow rectangular shape. (In architecture) moulding in semi-cylindrical shape. *(bag-ET)*

baignoire [Fr.] (In theatre) box on level of stalls. *(bayn-wahr)*

bain-marie [Fr.] (In cookery) vessel of hot water in which pans, etc. are slowly heated or kept hot. *(bań-ma-REE)*

baklava [Turk.] Pastry with honey and nuts. *(BAK-la-va)*

baksheesh, bakshish [Pers.] Tip. Gratuity. *(BAK-sheesh)*

baldacchino [It.] Canopy above altar, throne, priest, etc. *(bal-da-KEE-noh)* Anglicised as **baldachin** or **baldaquin.**

ballade [Fr.] Poem with three (or more than one group of three) seven- or eight-line stanzas, and a final four-line stanza (called 'Envoy'), all stanzas ending with the same line, as a refrain. *(bal-AD)*

Ballet Russe [Fr.] Russian Ballet. *(bal-ay roos)*

ballon d'essai [Fr.] Trial project to test public opinion. *(bal-orń des-AY)*

bal masqué [Fr.] Masked ball. *(bal mas-kay)*

bambino [It.] Young child. (In art) infant Jesus. *(bam-BEE-noh)* Feminine **bambina.**

banco [It.] Bank. (In some card games) stake matching that of banker. *(BAN-koh)*

bandeau [Fr.] Narrow band or ribbon for the hair. *(BAND-* or *BAHN-doh)*

banderilla [Sp.] Dart, usually decorated with streamers, thrust into neck or shoulders of bull in bull-fighting. *(ban-der-EEL-yah)*

banderillero [Sp.] Bull-fighter using **banderilla.** *(ban-der-eel-YEH-roh)*

banlieue [Fr.] Suburbs. *(bahń-lyur)*

banquette [Fr.] Long upholstered seat (as in public house, etc.) *(bahń-KET)*

banshee [Ir.] Spirit, usually female, whose wail outside house presages death. *(BAN-shee)*

banzai [Jap.] (In Japan) battle-cry; greeting to Emperor. *(banz-EYE)*

barcarolle [Fr.] Gondolier's song, or instrumental piece in same style. *(bah-ka-ROL)*

barège [Fr.] Silky gauze made from wool. *(bar-ehzh)*

bar mitzvah [Heb.] Religious ceremony of initiation of Jewish boys at age of 13. *(bah MITS-va)*

baroque [Fr.] Style of art, especially architecture and music, characterised by extravagant decoration, in the seventeenth and eighteenth century. *(bar-OK)*

barre [Fr.] Waist-high hand-rail in ballet practice-room for use in exercise. *(bah)*

Barsac [Fr.] Sweet white wine from Bordeaux region of France. *(BAH-sak)*

bas bleu [Fr.] Bluestocking: woman who has or affects literary or cultural tastes. *(bah blur)*

bas-relief [Fr.] Sculpture consisting of carved panel in which objects and figures project by less than half of their true proportions. *(bah-rel-EEF)* See **alto-relievo.**

basso [It.] (Of male singer) bass. *(BAS-oh)*

basso continuo [It.] (In music) figured bass, i.e. an instrumental accompaniment, usually by organ or harpsichord, originally constructed by accompanist from the composer's shorthand indications (with room for accompanist's own invention), but now normally written out in full. *(bas-oh kon-TIN-oo-oh* or *-TIN-yoo-oh)*

basso ostinato [It.] (In music) ground bass, i.e. short piece of bass repeated over and over again while melody and other upper parts vary. *(bas-oh os-tin-AH-toh)*

basso profundo or **profondo** [It.] Male singer with very deep bass voice. *(bas-oh proh-FUN-* or *-FON-doh)*

basso-relievo or **rilievo** [It.] Same as **bas-relief.** *(bas-oh ruh-LYEV-oh* or *ri-LYEV-oh)*

bateau [Fr.] (In Canada) small flat-bottomed boat. *(bah-toh)*

bateau-mouche [Fr.] Small passenger-boat on river Seine at Paris. *(bah-toh-moosh)* Plural **bateaux-mouches** (same pronunciation).

batik [Javanese] Method of decorating textiles by waxing parts not to be dyed, the wax being subsequently removed leaving a pattern. Fabric dyed in this way. *(ba-TEEK)*

batiste [Fr.] Fine, light fabric of cotton or linen. *(bat-EEST)*

batterie de cuisine [Fr.] Complete set of cooking utensils. *(batter-ee duh kwee-zeen)*

battue [Fr.] Driving of game by beaters towards shooting-party. *(bat-oo)*

Bauhaus [Ger.] German school of design (1919–1933), especially of architecture, relating technology to art. *(BOW-hows)*

bayadère [Fr.] Hindu dancing-girl. *(ba-ya-DAIR)*

Béarnaise [Fr.] (In cookery) sauce made of wine vinegar, egg yolks, butter and various herbs, including tarragon, served with steak, shellfish and richer kinds of grilled fish. *(bay-ahr-nayz)*

beatae memoriae [Lat.] Of blessed memory. *(bay-AHT-i* or *-eye mem-OR-ee-i* or *-eye)*

beau [Fr.] Fop. Admirer. *(boh)* Plural **beaux** (same pronunciation).

beau geste [Fr.] Magnanimous gesture. *(boh zhest)*

beau idéal [Fr.] Ideal model or type of beauty or excellence. *(boh ee-day-AHL)*

Beaujolais [Fr.] Red wine from area south of Mâcon in France. *(boh-zhol-ay)*

beau monde [Fr.] Fashionable society. *(boh MORND)*

beau sabreur [Fr.] Swashbuckling cavalryman. *(boh sab-RUR)*

Beaune [Fr.] Wine, mainly red, from region of Beaune, in Burgundy, France. *(bohn)*

beaux arts [Fr.] Fine arts *(boh-ZAH)*

beaux esprits [Fr.] Men of wit or genius. *(bohz es-pree)* Singular **bel esprit.**

beaux yeux [Fr.] Good looks, especially as a means of attracting those seeking to find favour. *(boh ZYUR)*

béchamel [Fr.] (In cookery) white sauce used in several dishes, and as base for several other sauces, made from milk, butter, flour, vegetables and spices. *(BAY-sham-el)*

bêche-de-mer [Fr.] Sea-slug eaten as delicacy in China. *(besh-duh-MAIR)*

béguine [Fr.] Member of religious lay sisterhood in Netherlands, not bound by strict vows. Dance of West Indian origin. Rhythm of such dance. *(bay-GEEN)*

bel canto [It.] (Of classical music, especially opera) lyrical singing with beauty of tone and accomplished technique, in the Italian tradition. *(bel KAN-toh)*

bel esprit [Fr.] Person of wit or genius. *(bel es-PREE)* Plural **beaux esprits.**

belle [Fr.] Beautiful woman. *(bel)* Usually applied to the most beautiful woman of a group.

belle époque [Fr.] Period of twenty years or so before First World War, thought to be culmination of delightful and settled way of life destroyed by that war. *(bel ay-POK)*

belle laide [Fr.] Woman whose ugliness is attractive. *(bel layd)*

belles-lettres [Fr.] Writings, especially essays, criticism or philosophic speculation, of a purely literary, aesthetic kind (as distinct from fiction, poetry and drama). *(bel-letr)*

Benedicite [Lat.] Invocation of blessing, especially at grace before meal. Name of canticle (beginning 'O all ye works of the Lord') in Book of Common Prayer, for Morning Prayer. *(ben-ed-EYE-si-ti)*

Benedictus [Lat.] Part of the Mass beginning 'Benedictus qui venit' (Blessed is he that cometh in the name of the Lord). *(ben-ed-IK-tus)*

bene esse [Lat.] Well-being. *(ben-eh ES-eh)*

ben trovato [It.] (Invention, discovery that is) ingenious, well done. *(ben troh-VAH-toh)*

berceuse [Fr.] Cradle-song; lullaby. *(bair-surz)*

bergère [Fr.] Shepherdess. Deep arm-chair. *(bair-ZHAIR)*

bergschrund [Ger.] (In mountaineering or geography) crevasse or gap between glacier and mountain side. *(BEHRK-shroont)*

bersagliere [It.] (In Italy) well-trained infantryman, especially rifleman. *(behr-sahl-YEH-reh)* Plural **bersaglieri.** *(-ree)*

bête noire [Fr.] Person (or thing) specially disliked. *(bet NWAHR)*

bêtise [Fr.] Foolish or inadvertent act or remark. *(bet-EEZ)*

bévue [Fr.] Accidental error or oversight. *(bay-voo)*

bey [Turk.] Governor of town or province. Title conferred by Sultan. *(bay)* Also a courtesy title.

bhang [Urdu] Indian hemp, chewed, smoked, eaten or drunk as narcotic or intoxicant. *(bang)*

bianco [It.] White. *(BYAN-koh)* Normally applied to wine.

bibelot [Fr.] Small curio or trinket with artistic merit. *(BEEB-loh)*

bidonville [Fr.] Shanty-town, especially one built of oil-drums. *(bee-doñ-veel)*

Biedermeier [Ger., from fictitious name] Conventional (as term of abuse). *(BEE-derm-eye-er)*

bien entendu [Fr.] Well understood. Of course. *(byan ahṅ-tahṅ-doo)*

biennale [It.] (Festival, exhibition, etc.) held every two years. *(byen-AH-leh)*

bien(-)pensant [Fr.] Right-thinking. Orthodox thinker. (In France) conformist, politically conservative, middle-class, materialistic. (In England) enlightened, progressive, intellectual (as terms of abuse). *(byaṅ pahṅ-sahṅ)*

bien trouvé [Fr.] Same as **ben trovato.** *(byaṅ troo-vay)*

bijou [Fr.] Jewel, trinket. (Of building, work of art) small and beautiful. *(bee-zhoo)* Plural **bijoux** (same pronunciation).

bijouterie [Fr.] Jewellery. Small articles of artistic value. *(bee-ZHOO-tuh-ree)*

Bildungsroman [Ger.] Novel tracing person's early life, especially emotional development. *(BIL-doongs-roh-mahn)*

billabong [Australian Aboriginal] Branch of river forming back-water or stagnant pool. *(BIL-ab-ong)*

billet(-)doux [Fr.] Love-letter. *(bil-ay* or *bee-yay doo)* Plural **billets(-)doux** (same pronunciation).

biltong [Afrikaans] Strips of meat dried in sun. *(BIL-tong)*

bis dat qui cito dat [Lat.] He who gives quickly gives twice (as much). *(BEE-s dat kwee KEE-toh dat)*

bise [Fr.] (In Switzerland and S.E. France) keen, dry, cold north or north-east wind. *(beez)*

bisque [Fr.] Soup made from shellfish. *(beesk)*

bistre [Fr.] (In painting) paint of brownish-yellow colour made from soot. Colour of this kind. Monochrome painting in this hue. *(BEE-ster)*

bistro [Fr.] Small bar, restaurant or wine-shop. *(BEE-stroh)*

bizarrerie [Fr.] Grotesqueness. *(beez-AH-rer-ee)*

blague [Fr.] Humbug. *(blahg)*

blagueur [Fr.] Pretentious talker. Boaster. Joker. *(blahg-UR)*

blanc de blancs [Fr.] Fairly rare champagne, fine and delicate, made from white grapes only. *(blahṅ duh blahṅ)*

blanquette [Fr.] Dish of white meat, often veal, with white sauce. *(blahṅ-ket)*

blasé [Fr.] Having had too much pleasure and therefore tired of it, or exhausted by it. Unimpressed, unconcerned. *(blah-zay)*

blitz [Ger.] German air-raids, especially on London, in Second World War. Rapid, intensive assault. *(blits)* Hence, colloquially, any intense activity to get something done.

blitzkrieg [Ger.] Sudden, violent attack or war. *(BLITS-kreeg)*

bloc [Fr.] Group of nations, individuals, parties, etc. combining for a common purpose. *(blok)*

blouson [Fr.] Waist-length jacket fitting tightly at waist. *(bloo-zorñ)*

Blut und Boden [Ger.] Blood and soil. *(bloot oont BOHdn)* Nazi slogan asserting importance of national bloodstock and territory.

Blut und Eisen [Ger.] Blood and iron. Courage (including the willingness to die) and military power. *(bloot oont EYE-zn)* Spoken by Bismarck, 1886.

Blutwurst [Ger.] Black pudding *(BLOOT-voorst)*

bocage [Fr.] (In pottery) decoration of trees and flowers. *(bok-ahzh)*

bodega [Sp.] Wine-shop. Wine-cellar. *(boh-DEG-a)*

Boer [Dut.] South African of Dutch descent, usually farmer. *(BOH-er)*

Bofors [Swedish, after name of town] Type of light anti-aircraft gun. *(BOH-fuhz)*

bois [Fr.] Wood. *(bwah)*

boiserie [Fr.] Woodwork. *(bwah-zuh-ree)*

boîte [Fr.] Disreputable club. *(bwaht)*

boîte de nuit [Fr.] Night-club. *(bwaht duh nwee)*

bolas [Sp.] Device consisting of heavy balls linked by cords, used to capture animals by being thrown so as to entangle their legs. *(BOH-las)*

bolero [Sp.] Lively Spanish dance. Music for this. Short open jacket, usually without sleeves. *(bol-AY-roh)*

bolus [Lat.] Large pill. *(BOH-lus)*

bombe [Fr.] Cone-shaped, piled-up or moulded confection, often of ice-cream, meringue, cream, etc. *(BOM-buh)* See **bombe surprise.**

bombé [Fr.] (Of furniture) of bulging shape. *(bom-bay)*

bombe surprise [Fr.] A **bombe** of which the ingredients are unspecified. *(bom soor-PREEZ)*

bonae memoriae [Lat.] Of happy memory. *(bon-eye* or *-ay mem-OR-ee-eye* or *-ay)*

bona fide [Lat.] Authentic. Sincere. Genuine. *(boh-nah FEYE-deh)*

bona fides [Lat.] Genuineness. Sincerity of intention. *(boh-nah FEYE-deez)*

bon appétit [Fr.] Eat well! Enjoy your meal! *(borñ nap-ay-tee)* Expression frequently used in France to someone about to begin a meal.

bona roba [It.] Prostitute. *(boh-na ROH-ba)*

bona vacantia [Lat.] Goods with no apparent owner. *(boh-na vak-AN-tee-a)*

bon-bon or **bonbon** [Fr.] Sweet. *(bonbon* or *borñ-borñ)*

bonbonnière [Fr.] Small fancy dish or box for sweets. *(boṅ-boṅ NYAIR)*

bon camarade [Fr.] Good friend; loyal, close companion. *(boṅ ka-ma-RAHD)*

bon copain [Fr.] More modern version of **bon camarade.** *(boṅ koh-pahṅ)*

bon goût [Fr.] Good taste. *(boṅ goo)*

bonhomie [Fr.] Geniality. *(bon-om-ee)*

bon marché [Fr.] Cheap. *(boṅ mahr-shay)*

bon mot [Fr.] Clever remark. Witty saying. *(boṅ moh* or *bon MOH)* Plural **bons mots** (same pronunciation).

bonne [Fr.] Maid. Nursemaid. *(bon)*

bonne amie [Fr.] Woman friend. Sweetheart. Mistress. *(bon-am-EE)*

bonne à tout faire [Fr.] Maid-of-all-work. *(bon-a-too-FAIR)*

bonne bouche [Fr.] Titbit. *(bon boosh)* Plural **bonnes bouches** (same pronunciation).

bonne chance [Fr.] Good luck. *(bon shahṅ-s)*

bonsai [Jap.] Dwarf plant, shrub or tree. Method of cultivating these, or art of creating gardens of them. *(BON-si)*

bonsens or **bon sens** [Fr.] Good sense. *(boṅ sahṅs)*

bon ton [Fr.] Good breeding. Fashionable society. *(boṅ toṅ)*

bon vivant [Fr.] Person who enjoys life, especially eating, drinking. *(boṅ vee-vahṅ)* Plural **bons vivants** (same pronunciation).

bon viveur [Fr.] Same as **bon vivant**, perhaps with emphasis on luxury rather than food. *(boṅ veev-UR)*

bon voyage [Fr.] Have a good journey! *(boṅ* or *bon vwa-YAHZH)*

Bordeaux [Fr.] Wine, especially claret, from region of Bordeaux, on south-west coast of France. *(bor-doh)*

bordel, bordello [It.] Brothel. *(bor-DEL(-oh))*

bordereau [Fr.] Memorandum. *(border-OH)*

borné [Fr.] Narrow-minded. *(BOR-nay)*

borsch, borscht or **bortsch** [Russ.] Beetroot soup, sometimes including cabbage, often highly spiced, served hot or cold, usually with sour cream. *(borsh, borsht, bortch)* The first spelling and pronunciation are preferred.

bossa nova [Port.] Brazilian dance resembling samba. *(bossa NOH-va)*

bottega [It.] Café. *(boh-TEH-ga)*

bouchée [Fr.] Small pastry, usually savoury. *(BOO-shay)*

bouche fermée [Fr.] (In music) singing with the mouth closed, i.e. humming. *(boosh fehr-may)*

bouclé [Fr.] Yarn, or fabric made of yarn, which is looped, so that it looks shaggy. *(BOO-klay)*

boudoir [Fr.] Small room for private use of woman. *(boo-* or *BOO-dwahr)*

bouffant [Fr.] (Of dress or hair-style) puffed out. *(BOO-fahṅ)*

bougie [Fr.] Candle. Thin, flexible surgical instrument suitable for passages of the body. *(BOO-zhee)*

bouillabaisse [Fr.] Thick (soup or) stew of several different fresh fish, with herbs, sometimes vegetables, cooked in water, oil and often wine, originating from Provence. *(boo-ee-yah-BES)*

bouilli [Fr.] Stewed or boiled meat. *(boo-ee-yee)*

bouillon [Fr.] Thin soup flavoured with beef or chicken. *(boo-ee-yorṅ)*

boule, boules [Fr.] Bowls played with heavy metal balls on uneven, gravelly terrain. *(bool)*

boulevard [Fr.] Street, usually wide and lined with trees, suitable for strolling, gossiping, sitting, etc. *(boo-luh-vah)*

boulevardier [Fr.] Pleasure-seeker who haunts boulevards where clubs, cafés, theatres, etc. are to be found. *(bool-vah-dyay)*

bouleversé [Fr.] Overwhelmed with emotion. Very upset. *(bool-vair-say)*

bouleversement [Fr.] Condition of being **bouleversé.** *(bool-vairs-mahṅ)*

bouquet [Fr.] Bunch of flowers. Perfume given off by wine. *(boo-kay* or *-KAY)*

bouquet garni [Fr.] (In cookery) bunch of herbs used for flavouring. *(boo-kay gah-nee)*

bourgeois [Fr.] Middle class. Conventional, humdrum, philistine, selfishly materialistic; uncultivated, unimaginative, smug. Person, etc. exhibiting such characteristics. *(BOOR-zhwah)* Originally, the class between gentlemen and peasants, e.g. merchants, manufacturers, shop-keepers.

bourgeoisie [Fr.] Class of people with **bourgeois** characteristics. *(boor-zhwah-ZEE)*

Bourgogne [Fr.] Burgundy. *(boor-gon-yuh)*

bourrée [Fr.] Lively dance, of French origin, very like the gavotte. *(BOO-ray)*

Bourse [Fr.] Paris Stock Exchange. *(boors)*

boustrophedon [Gk.] (Written) from right to left, and left to right, in alternate lines. *(boo-strof-EE-dn)*

boutique [Fr.] Small shop, usually selling unusual, expensive or fashionable items, especially clothes or accessories. *(boo-TEEK)*

boutonnière [Fr.] Flower or spray of flowers worn on lapel of jacket. *(boot-on-yair)*

bouzouki [Gk.] Form of mandolin specially associated with Greek music. *(boo-ZOO-ki)*

boyar [Russ.] Aristocrat, often member of landed gentry, in pre-revolutionary Russia. *(boh-YAH)*

brandade [Fr.] (In cookery) poached white fish, mixed with spices and mayonnaise, and served cold with creamy consistency. *(brahṅ-dad)*

brandade de morue [Fr.] Creamed salt cod, prepared with garlic, oil and milk. *(brahṅ-dad duh moh-roo)*

brasserie [Fr.] Beer saloon. Restaurant serving beer. *(brass-ree)*

Bratwurst [Ger.] Type of sausage for frying, or served fried. *(BRAHT-voorst)*

bravissimo [It.] Excellent! *(brahv-ISS-im-oh)*

bravo [It.] Well done! *(BRAH-voh)*

bravura [It.] Display of brilliance; daring or ambitious performance. Piece of music or musical style requiring great virtuosity and spirit. *(brahv-YOAR-a)*

bric-à-brac [Fr.] Miscellaneous old ornaments, trinkets, pieces of furniture, etc. *(brik-a-brak)*

Brie [Fr.] Type of soft, rich, French cheese. *(bree)*

brio [It.] Vivacity. *(BREE-oh)*

brioche [Fr.] Small, sweet light cake made with yeast. *(bree-osh)*

briquet, briquette [Fr.] Small block of compressed coal dust used for fuel. *(bree-kay, bree-KET)*

brisé [Fr.] Ballet leap during which feet are moved rapidly backwards and forwards. *(BREE-zay)*

brisling [Nor., Dan.] Small herring or sprat. *(BRIS-* or *BRIZ-ling)*

brochette [Fr.] Skewer. *(broh-SHET)*

broderie anglaise [Fr.] Open embroidery on white linen or cambric. *(broh-der-ee ahṅ-GLEHZ)*

Broederbond [Afrikaans] Association of white people, mainly in South Africa, seeking to uphold **apartheid** on Christian grounds. *(BRUR-duh-bont)*

brouhaha [Fr.] Uproar, hubbub; sensation. *(BROO-hah-hah)*

Brücke [Ger.] Early twentieth-century German school of painting. *(BROO-kuh)*

bruit [Fr.] Rumour. *(brwee)*

brûlé, brûlée [Fr.] Cooked or flavoured with burnt sugar. *(broo-lay)*

brut [Fr.] (Of wine) unsweetened, rough. (Of champagne) very dry. *(broo)*

buenas noches [Sp.] Good night. *(BWEH-nas NOH-ches)*

buenos días [Sp.] Good day. *(BWEH-nos DEE-as)*

buffa, buffo [It.] Comic. *(BOO-fa, -foh)*

Bundesrat [Ger.] Upper house of West German parliament. *(BOON-duhs-raht)*

Bundesrepublik [Ger.] West Germany. *(BOON-duhs-re-poob-LEEK)*

Bundestag [Ger.] Lower house of West German parliament. *(BOON-duhs-tahk)*

Bundeswehr [Ger.] Armed forces of West Germany. *(BOON-duhs-vayr)*

bureau de change [Fr.] Office for exchange of currency. *(boo-roh-duh-shahńzh)*

Bürgermeister [Ger.] Mayor. *(BOOR-ger-meye-ster)*

burnous [Fr. from Arab.] Hooded cape or cloak worn by Arabs and Moors. *(burn-OOS)*

bushido [Jap.] Code of honour of the **samurai.** *(BOO-shee-doh)*

buvette [Fr.] Roadside refreshment bar. *(boo-vet)*

bwana [Swa.] Master. *(BWAH-na)*

C

c., ca. Abbreviation of **circa.**

caballero [Sp.] Spanish gentleman. Horseman, knight. *(kabal-YEH-roh)*

cabana [Sp.] Beach hut. *(kab-AH-na)*

cabala, cabbala [Lat. from Heb.] Jewish occult doctrine, lore or religious philosophy. *(kab-AH-la)*

cabochon [Fr.] Polished but uncut gem. *(kah-boh-shoń)*

cabotin [Fr.] Second-rate actor. *(kah-boh-tań)*

cabriole [Fr.] Kind of curved leg found in much eighteenth-century furniture. (In ballet) a kind of leap. *(KAB-ree-ohl)*

cabriolet [Fr.] Light two-wheeled hooded vehicle drawn by horse. Car with folding top. *(KAB-ree-oh-lay)*

cache [Fr.] Hiding-place, or that which is hidden there, usually arms, ammunition or treasure. *(kash)*

cachet [Fr.] Distinguishing mark. Prestige. *(kash-ay)*

cachou [Fr.] Fragrant lozenge to sweeten the breath. *(KASH-oo)*

cachucha [Sp.] Spanish folk dance. *(kah-CHOO-chah)*

cacique [Sp.] Native chief in West Indies, etc. Local political boss in Spain, Latin America, etc. *(kah-SEEK)*

cacodemon, cacodaemon [Gk.] Evil spirit. *(kah-koh-DEE-mon)*

cacoethes [Lat.] Irresistible urge to do something, usually inadvisable. Thus **cacoethes loquendi**, compulsive talking; **cacoethes scribendi**, itch for writing. *(kakoh-EETH-eez, lok-WEND-ee, skree-BEND-ee)*

cadeau [Fr.] Gift. *(kah-doh)*

cadenza [It.] (In music) elaborate solo passage for voice or instrument, sometimes improvised, usually introduced towards the end of a song or instrumental piece or movement. *(kad-ENZ-ah)*

cadet [Fr.] The younger. *(kah-day)*

cadre [Fr.] Permanent nucleus of organisation (e.g. military) which can be expanded when necessary. Small, closely-knit group at centre of larger organisation (e.g. political). *(kah-druh)*

caduceus [Lat.] Ancient Greek or Roman herald's wand of office, especially that of Hermes or Mercury, the messenger of the gods. *(kad-OO-syus)*

caesura [Lat.] Slight pause or break in a line of verse, usually near middle. *(sez-YOAR-a)*

caeteris paribus [Lat.] Other things being equal. *(KEYE-ter-is PA-ri-bus)*

café [Fr.] Coffee. *(kaf-ay)*

café au lait [Fr.] Coffee with milk. *(kaf-ay oh lay)*

café crême [Fr.] Coffee with cream. *(kaf-ay krehm)*

café filtre [Fr.] Coffee made by slowly filtering hot water through ground coffee. *(kaf-ay feeltr)*

café noir [Fr.] Black coffee. *(kaf-ay nwah)*

caftan [Turk.] Long tunic, of Oriental origin, with or (more usually) without girdle at the waist, worn by women and sometimes men. *(KAF-tan)*

cagoule [Fr.] Long (usually knee-length) waterproof outer garment with hood, worn by mountain-walkers, etc. *(KAG-ool)*

cahier [Fr.] Notebook. *(ka-yay)*

caique [Fr.] Light rowing-boat. Single-masted Levantine sailing-ship. *(kah-EEK)*

Ça ira [Fr.] It (that) will happen. *(sa ee-ra)* Refrain, and name, of French revolutionary song.

calando [It.] (Of music) growing softer and slower. *(kal-AND-oh)*

Calvados [Fr.] Famous apple-brandy made in Northern France. *(KAL-vad-oss)*

camarade [Fr.] Comrade. *(kam-ar-ahd)*

camaraderie [Fr.] Comradeship. Close fellowship, trust and sociability among groups of friends. *(kam-ar-AHD-er-ee)*

camarón [Sp.] Shrimp. *(kam-ar-ON)*

Camembert [Fr.] Soft, rich French cheese. *(kam-ahṁ-bair)*

camera obscura [Lat.] Box with small hole for projecting image on to screen in darkened room. *(kam-er-a ob-SKYOO-ra)*

camino real [Sp.] Royal road or main highway. Best means to an end. *(kam-EE-noh ray-AHL)*

campanile [It.] Bell-tower, usually detached, often found in Italy. *(kam-pan-EE-leh)*

canaille [Fr.] The rabble, mob, populace. *(kan-EYE)*

canapé [Fr.] Small piece of bread, toast, etc. with savoury titbit on top. *(KAN-a-pay)*

canard [Fr.] False report. Hoax. False belief or rumour. *(KAN-ah(d))*

can(-)can [Fr.] Lively dance by woman or troupe of women, with much display of petticoats, legs, etc. *(kan-kan)*

cannelloni [It.] Large fat tubes of pasta, or small pancakes, filled with savoury mixture of meat or cheese, etc. *(kan-el-OH-ni)*

cantabile [It.] (Of music) in smooth, flowing style. *(kan-TAH-bil-ay)*

cantaloup(e) [Fr.] Small ribbed melon with orange interior. *(KANT-al-oop)*

cantata [It.] Short sacred or secular musical work with solos, chorus and orchestra, intended for concert (not staged) performance. *(kan-TAH-ta)*

Cantate (Domino) [Lat.] Sung version of Psalm 98, 'Sing to the Lord'. *(kan-TAH-teh)*

cantatrice [It. and Fr.] Professional woman singer. *(KAN-ta-tree-s)*

cante hondo [Sp.] Kind of Spanish song, usually mournful. *(kan-ti HON-doh)*

cantilena [It.] Simple, smooth, melodious, slow song. *(kan-til-AY-na)*

canto [It.] Division of long poem. *(KAN-toh)*

canton [Fr.] Subdivision of a country. One of the States of the Swiss confederation. *(KAN-ton* or *kahn̊-tom̊)*

canzona, canzone [It.] Short instrumental piece with a marked melody. *(kan-ZOH-* or *-TSOH-na, -nay)*

canzonet, canzonetta [It.] Short, light song or madrigal. *(kan-zohn-ET, kan-zohn-ET-a)*

cap-à-pie, -pied or **-pié** [Fr.] (Of armour) from head to foot. *(kap-a-pay* or *-pyay)*

capias [Lat.] Writ authorising arrest. *(KAP-ee-ass)*

caporal [Fr.] Type of French tobacco. *(kap-or-al)*

cappuccino [It.] Coffee, usually **espresso**, with hot (usually frothed) milk. *(kap-oo-CHEE-noh)*

capriccio [It.] Lively musical composition, usually short, in free style. *(kap-REE-chee-oh)*

capriccioso [It.] (Music) in lively, free, whimsical style. *(kap-ree-chee-OH-zoh)*

caput mortuum [Lat.] Worthless residue. *(kap-ut MOR-too-um)*

carabiniere [It.] Armed Italian policeman. *(kara-bin-YAIR-i)* Plural **-ieri** *(-YAIR-ee)*

caramba [Sp.] Exclamation of surprise, annoyance, pleasure, etc. *(kar-AMB-a)*

carbonnade [Fr.] Rich stew of beef, onions, beer and seasoning. *(kah-bon-ahd)*

caritas [Lat.] Love of God and one's neighbour. *(KAR-it-as)*

carnet [Fr.] Permit in form of small booklet. *(kah-nay)*

carnet vert [Fr.] Green card: international insurance certificate required for touring by car in Europe. *(kah-nay vair)*

carpe diem [Lat.] Make the most of the present. *(kah-peh DEE-em)* From Horace, *Odes*.

carte [Fr.] Menu. Map. *(kaht)*

carte blanche [Fr.] Complete freedom of action. Absolute discretionary power. *(kaht blahṅ-sh)*

carte d'identité [Fr.] Identity card. *(kaht dee-dahṅ-tee-tay)*

cartel [Fr.] Agreement among manufacturers or other self-interested groups to control prices, policies, etc. to their advantage. *(kaht-EL)*

cartouche [Fr.] Architectural ornament in form of a scroll; any such ornament or drawing bearing an inscription, e.g. in heraldry. (In archeology) oval frame containing names of Egyptian Pharaohs. *(kaht-OOSH)*

casbah [Arab.] Native or Arab quarter of North African town, especially Algiers. *(KAZ-bah)* Also applied to citadel in such town, and to district around it.

cassata [It.] Neapolitan ice cream with fruit and nuts. *(kas-AH-ta)*

casse-croûte [Fr.] Snack. *(kas-kroot)*

casse-noisette [Fr.] Nutcracker. *(kas-nwa-zet)*

cassis [Fr.] Blackcurrant syrup used in drinks. *(kas-ees)* Also **Cassis**, a white wine from the south coast of France, east of Marseille.

cassoulet [Fr.] Dish consisting of white haricot beans, various meats and spices, cooked at length. *(kas-oo-lay)*

castrato [It.] Adult male singer castrated when young to preserve soprano voice. *(kass-TRAH-toh)*

casus belli [Lat.] Occurrence or circumstance justifying or giving rise to war. *(kas-us BEL-i* or *-eye)*

catachresis [Lat. from Gk.] Wrong use of word or words. *(ka-ta-KREE-sis)*

cathedra [Lat. from Gk.] Papal or bishop's throne. *(kath-AY-dra)*

caudillo [Sp.] Leader (in Spanish-speaking countries). *(kow-DEEL-yoh)*

cause célèbre [Fr.] Matter, especially disagreement, controversy or lawsuit, that becomes widely known and discussed. *(kohz sel-EHB-ruh)*

causerie [Fr.] Chat. Informal or light-hearted essay (usually on literary topic). *(kohz-er-ee)*

ça va(?) [Fr.] Common French expression, often used as greeting, meaning 'everything all right(?)' *(sa va)*

ça va sans dire [Fr.] That goes without saying. *(sa va sahn̉ dee-r)*

cavatina [It.] Short, simple song. Piece of instrumental music, usually slow and short. *(kava-TEEN-a)*

cave [Fr.] Wine-cellar. Establishment dealing with storage of wine. *(kahv)*

cave [Lat.] Look out. *(KAY-vi)* (School slang)

caveat [Lat.] Warning. Proviso. *(KAV-ay-at)*

caveat emptor [Lat.] The buyer (not the seller) is responsible for the quality of what is bought. *(KAV-ay-at EMP-tor)* Literally, 'Let the buyer beware'.

cavo rilievo [It.] Form of sculpture consisting of panel in which only the outlines of figures, etc. are incised. *(KAH-voh ril-YAY-voh)*

C.D. Abbreviation of **corps diplomatique.**

ceilidh(e) [Ir. and Gael.] Social gathering with dancing, singing, music and story-telling. *(KAY-li)*

cerebellum [Lat.] Smaller part of brain. *(seri-BEL-um)*

cerebrum [Lat.] Principal part of brain. *(SERI-brum)*

C'est magnifique, mais ce n'est pas la guerre [Fr.] It is magnificent, but it is not war. *(say man-yee-feek meh suh nay pah la gair)* Said by Maréchal Bosquet of the Charge of the Light Brigade, 1854. Applied to anything that is impressive but not according to rule.

c'est à dire [Fr.] That is to say. *(set-a-dee-r)*

c'est la guerre [Fr.] That's (the sort of thing that happens in) war. *(say-la-gair)*

c'est la vie [Fr.] That's life. *(say-la-vee)*

ceteris paribus Same as **caeteris paribus.**

cha See **char.**

Chablis [Fr.] Good quality greenish-white dry wine from town of Chablis, south-east of Paris. *(shab-lee)*

chaconne [Fr.] (Dance to) piece of music based on recurrent bass tune with changing upper parts. *(shak-on)*

chacun à son gout [Fr.] Everyone to his own taste. *(shak-ern̉-na-sorn̉-goo)*

chacun à son métier [Fr.] Everyone to his own trade. *(shak-ern̉-na-sorn̉-may-tyay)*

chacun pour soi [Fr.] Everyone for himself. *(shak-ern̉-poor-swah)*

chagrin d'amour [Fr.] Unhappiness resulting from being in love. *(shag-ran̉ dam-oor)*

chaise [Fr.] Light open carriage for one or two people. *(shayz)*

chaise longue [Fr.] Kind of sofa with only one arm. *(shayz lorng)*

chambré [Fr.] Brought to room temperature. *(shahṁ-bray)* Normally applied to wine.

chanson [Fr.] Song. *(shahṅ-soṅ)*

chanson de geste [Fr.] One of a group of medieval French epic poems (e.g. the Chanson de Roland). *(shahṅ-soṅ-duh-zhest)*

chansonnier [Fr.] Composer-performer of popular songs (usually French, and solo). *(shahṅson-yay)*

chanteuse [Fr.] Female singer of popular songs. *(shahṅ-TURZ)*

Chantilly [Fr.] Kind of lace. Type of cream, sweetened and whipped. *(shahṅ-tee-yee)*

chaparral [Sp.] Dense growth of brushwood in parts of America, especially Mexico. *(shap-ar-AL)*

chapat(t)i [Hind.] Small, flat, thin cake made with unleavened bread. *(cha-PAT-i)*

chapelle ardente [Fr.] Room or chapel for lying-in-state of important person and illuminated by candles, etc. *(shap-el ard-ahṅt)*

chaptalisation [Fr.] Addition of sugar to wine before its fermentation to increase alcoholic strength. *(shap-tal-ee-zas-yoṅ)*

char [from Chin.] Tea. *(char)* Slang.

char-à-banc, charabanc [Fr.] Vehicle, often open-topped, with seats for large number of people, formerly horse-drawn, now mechanically propelled and usually called a coach. *(shara-bahṅk* or *-bang)*

charcuterie [Fr.] Cold cooked meat. Shop selling this. *(shah-KOOT-ree)*

chargé d'affaires [Fr.] Diplomatic representative at court or government of a country which does not merit an ambassador. Deputy to ambassador or to someone of higher diplomatic rank. *(shah-zhay daf-AIR)*

charivari [Fr.] Raucous or cacophonous music or sounds, made in derision or rowdy celebration of someone. *(sha-ri-VAH-ri)*

charlotte russe [Fr.] Sponge cake with custard enclosed. *(shah-lot roos)*

chartreuse [Fr.] Liqueur, of green or yellow colour, made of brandy, herbs, etc. *(shaht-RURZ)*

charpoy [Urdu] Light bed. Camp bed. *(CHAH-poy)*

chasse [Fr.] Liqueur, brandy, etc. taken after coffee. *(shas)*

chassé [Fr.] Gliding step in dancing. *(shas-ay)*

chassé-croisé [Fr.] Dance movement involving partners changing place. *(shas-ay-krwaz-ay)*

chasseur alpin [Fr.] French infantryman trained to operate in mountainous conditions (e.g. on skis). *(shas-ur alp-aṅ)*

château [Fr.] (In France) castle, palace, large country house, estate, especially one giving its name to wine grown nearby. *(shah-toh or SHAT-oh)*

châteaubriand [Fr.] Large thick steak cut from the centre of the fillet, usually big enough for two. *(shah-toh-bree-ahṅ)*

château en Espagne [Fr.] Castle in Spain; castle in the air; imagined good fortune. *(shah-toh on ess-pan-yuh)* Plural **châteaux en Espagne** (same pronunciation).

châtelaine, chatelaine [Fr.] Mistress of a **château.** Short chains or clasps, attached to woman's belt, for carrying keys, etc. *(shaht-len, shat-uh-layn)*

chaud-froid [Fr.] Dish of cold cooked meat, usually chicken (or fish) in jelly or sauce. *(shoh-frwah)*

chee-chee See **chichi.**

chef de mission [Fr.] Organiser, leader or manager of team, especially sports team on tour. *(shef-duh-MEE-syoṅ)*

chef d'équipe [Fr.] Team manager. *(shef-day-KEEP)*

chef d'œuvre [Fr.] Masterpiece. *(shay DUR-vruh)* Plural **chefs d'œuvre** (same pronunciation).

chemin de fer [Fr.] Form of **baccarat.** *(shmaṅ-duh-fur)*

chemise [Fr.] Loose-fitting undergarment worn by women. Loose-fitting dress hanging straight from shoulders. *(shmeez)*

cherchez la femme [Fr.] Look for the woman. *(shair-shay-la-fam)* Used to indicate that a mystery, etc. will be understood when the involvement of a woman is established.

chère amie [Fr.] Mistress. *(shair am-ee)*

chéri [Fr.] Darling. Dear. (Form of address) *(shay-REE)* Feminine **chérie** (same pronunciation).

che sarà sarà [It.] What will be, will be. *(kay-sa-RAH-sa-RAH)* Sometimes spelt **serà.**

chevaux de frise [Fr.] Iron spikes on wall or fence for security. Formerly piece of military equipment, consisting of iron spikes on timber, to repel cavalry. *(sh-voh-duh-freez)*

chez [Fr.] At the house of. *(shay)*

chez moi [Fr.] At my house *(shay mwah)*

chez nous [Fr.] At our house *(shay noo)*

chianti [It.] Popular wine from region between Florence and Siena, Italy. *(kee-AN-ti)*

chic [Fr.] Elegant, stylish. Elegance, style. *(sheek)*

chicane [Fr.] (In motor-racing) a barrier lining the course, or that part of a course (usually narrow and in the form of an S-bend) so lined. *(shik-AYN)*

chichi [Fr.] Pretentious, affected (in a fussy, over-elaborate way). *(shee-shee)*

chignon [Fr.] Coil of hair on pad at back of head. *(SHEE-nyoṅ)*

chil(l)i con carne [Sp.] Mexican stew of minced beef, beans and flavouring of chilli (type of red pepper). *(chill-i-kon-KAH-nay)*

chin-chin [Chin.] Expression used as informal greeting, farewell or (most usually) toast. *(chin-chin)*

chinoiserie [Fr.] (Use of) Chinese style in decoration, furniture, etc. Object or objects in such style. *(sheen-WAH-zer-ee)*

chipolata [Fr.] Small spicy sausage. *(chip-oh-LAH-ta)*

chorale [Ger.] Hymn-tune. Hymn sung in unison or parts. Choir. *(kor-AHL)*

chose jugée [Fr.] Something already settled (so that there is no point in discussing it). *(shohz zhoo-zhay)*

chou(x) [Fr.] Kind of light pastry, fried and usually served with sweet filling (as in **éclair**). *(shoo)*

choucroute [Fr.] Type of pickled cabbage. *(shoo-kroot)* Same as **sauerkraut.**

chow See **ciao.**

chow mein [Chin.] Chinese dish of fried noodles, meat and vegetables. *(chow-MAYN)*

Christe eleison [Lat. and Gk.] Christ have mercy. *(KRIS-teh el-AY-ees-on)*

chronique scandaleuse [Fr.] Scandalous story, news, history, gossip. *(kron-eek skahn̄-da-lurz)*

chupatti Same as **chapat(t)i.**

chutzpah [Yid.] Audacity, cheek, nerve. *(HU-tspa* or *KU-tspa)*

chypre [Fr.] Perfume made from sandalwood. *(sheepruh)*

ciao [It.] Goodbye. Hello. *(chow)* Colloquial.

ciborium [Lat.] Receptacle for the reservation of the Eucharist, usually chalice with lid. *(sib-OH-ree-um)*

cicada [Lat.] Tree-cricket found in warm climates and best known for its continuous chirrupping. *(sik-AH-da)*

cicerone [It.] Person available to act as guide to visitors to antiquities. *(si-ser-OH-ni)*

cicisbeo [It.] Married woman's known lover. *(chi-chiz-BAY-oh)*

ci-devant [Fr.] Former. Formerly. *(see-duh-vahn̄)*

cigar(r)illo [Sp.] Small cigar. *(si-gar-IL-oh)*

ci-gît [Fr.] Here lies. *(see-zhee)* Found in epitaphs on French grave-stones.

cinéast(e) [Fr.] Devotee of cinema. Film producer, director or technical assistant. *(sin-ay-AST)*

cinéma(-)vérité [Fr.] Technique or style of film-making that aims at realism, often achieved by using hand-held cameras, improvised dialogue, documentary material, etc. *(sin-em-* or *AYM-a vay-ree-tay)*

cinquecento [It.] The sixteenth century (i.e. the fifteen hundreds) with particular reference to Italian art and architecture in that period. *(ching-kwich-ENT-oh)*

circa [Lat.] Approximately. *(SER-ka* or *KER-ka)* Always followed by date; thus 'circa (or c.) 1500' means 'about 1500'.

circiter Same as **circa** (but less common). *(SER-kit-a)*

ciré [Fr.] (Of fabric) with smooth shiny surface, sometimes obtained by waxing or heating. *(see-ray)*

cire perdue [Fr.] (In sculpture) a technique of bronze-casting: a clay model or other core is coated with wax and placed in a mould; molten metal is poured into the mould, melting the wax outline and replacing it with bronze. *(seer pair-doo)*

cirque [Fr.] (In geology) deep round hollow at head of valley or in mountain-side, formed by erosion. *(seerk)*

civis Romanus sum [Lat.] I am a Roman citizen. *(KIV-* or *KIW-is roh-MAH-nus SUM)* Formula used to prevent arbitrary condemnation or beating.

claque [Fr.] Group of people hired to applaud in theatre. Organised vociferous group at public meeting, etc. in support of a speaker, to impress others present. *(klak)*

claqueur [Fr.] Member of **claque.** *(klak-ur)*

classico [It.] (Of wine) best of the region. *(KLAS-ee-koh)*

clepsydra [Lat.] Water-clock. *(KLEP-sid-ra)*

cloche [Fr.] Bell-shaped and closely fitting hat for women. Glass cover for outdoor plants, especially seedlings. *(klosh)*

cloisonné [Fr.] Enamel work in which thin strips of metal are attached in the desired pattern to a metal surface; differently coloured enamels are then applied, being kept apart by the metal strips. *(KLWAH-zon-ay)*

cloqué [Fr.] (Fabric with pattern that is) raised. *(klok-ay)*

clos [Fr.] Vineyard. *(kloh)*

clou [Fr.] Main point of interest. *(kloo)*

cocotte [Fr.] Small oven-proof dish for cooking and serving individual portion (e.g. baked egg). Prostitute. *(kok-OT)*

codex [Lat.] Volume of manuscripts. *(KOH-dex)*

cogito, ergo sum [Lat.] I think, therefore I am. *(KOG-i-toh UR-goh SUM)* Axiom of Descartes, formulated as starting-point of his system of philosophy.

cognac [Fr.] French brandy distilled in and around town of Cognac, north of Bordeaux. *(KON-yak)*

cognomen [Lat.] Nickname. Surname. *(kog-NOH-men)*

cognoscenti [It.] People who have expert knowledge or understanding (usually of artistic matters). *(kon-yo-SHEN-ti)*

coiffeur [Fr.] Hairdresser. *(kwahf-UR)* Feminine **coiffeuse** *(kwahf-URZ)*

coiffure [Fr.] Hair-style. *(kwahf-OOR)*

cointreau [Fr.] Colourless liqueur of orange flavour. *(KWAHN-troh)*

coitus interruptus [Lat.] Sexual intercourse ended before climax. *(coy-tus in-ter-UP-tus)*

col [Fr.] Ridge or pass between two higher parts of mountain range. *(kol)*

collage [Fr.] Art form in which objects and pieces of materials are stuck to a surface. *(KOL-ahzh)*

colla voce [It.] (In printed music) to be played in a way appropriate to the singing voice (i.e. the accompanist(s) should follow the singer). *(kol-a VOH-cheh)*

collectanea [Lat.] Miscellany of collected passages, quotations, notes, etc. *(kol-ekt-AYN-ee-a)*

colleen [Ir.] Girl. *(kol-EEN)*

coloratura [It.] Florid passages or embellishment in vocal music. A **coloratura soprano** has a voice which is light and flexible, suitable for the singing of music with such decoration. *(kol-or-a-TOO-rah)*

colporteur [Fr.] Travelling book-seller, especially seller or distributor of bibles. *(kol-port-ur)*

columbarium [Lat.] Building with niches for urns containing ashes of the dead. *(kol-um-BAH-ree-um)*

Comédie Française [Fr.] State-aided theatre in Paris, and home of French classical drama. *(kom-ay-dee frahñ-sehz)*

comédie humaine [Fr.] Comedy of life; human life seen as a comedy or drama. *(kom-ay-dee oo-mehn)*

comédie noire [Fr.] Black (i.e. bitter) comedy. *(kom-ay-dee nwahr)*

comme ci, comme ça [Fr.] So-so; neither good nor bad. *(kom-see kom-sah)*

commedia dell'arte [It.] Italian popular and often knockabout comedy, especially of sixteenth to eighteenth centuries, improvised and with stock characters (often masked) moving in exaggerated or stylised way. Any play with these characteristics. *(kom-ay-dyah del-aht-ay)*

comme il faut [Fr.] As it should be (especially of manners, behaviour, etc.). *(kom-eel-foh)*

commère [Fr.] Lady **compère.** *(KOM-air)*

commis [Fr.] (Of waiter or chef) junior, assistant. *(kom-i)*

commissar [Russ.] Head of government department in U.S.S.R. *(kom-iss-AH)*

commune [Fr.] Smallest local government unit in France *(kom-oon)* Group of people living collectively, sharing home, property, food, etc. *(KOM-yoon)*

communiqué [Fr.] Official communication, usually announcement at end of meeting of political leaders. *(kom-YOO-ni-kay)*

compère [Fr.] Person who acts as announcer at dance, party, variety entertainment, contest, etc. *(KOM-pair)* See **commère.**

compos mentis [Lat.] In one's right mind; sane. *(kom-pos MEN-tis)* Opposite **non compos mentis.**

compote [Fr.] Fruit preserved or stewed in syrup. *(kom-pot)*

compte rendu [Fr.] Report. Review. *(koṁt roṅ-doo)*

comte [Fr.] Count. *(koṁt)*

comtesse [Fr.] Countess. *(koṁt-ess)*

con Abbreviation of **contra.**

con amore [It.] Tenderly, lovingly. *(kon am-OH-reh)*

con brio [It.] With spirit. *(kon BREE-oh)*

concertante [It.] Orchestral piece with group of individual instruments playing together, sometimes in alternation with the rest of the orchestra, sometimes combining with it. *(kon-cher-TANT-eh)*

concertino [It.] Short and light type of **concerto.** *(kon-cher-TEEN-oh)*

concerto [It.] Musical composition for orchestra and one solo instrument (sometimes two). *(kon-CHER-toh)*

concerto grosso [It.] Musical composition for group of solo instruments alternating with rest of orchestra (or with strings of orchestra) and playing with whole orchestra from time to time. *(kon-CHER-toh GROS-oh)*

concierge [Fr.] (In France, etc.) door-keeper, usually woman, of block of flats, etc. *(koṁ-see-erzh)*

concordia discors [Lat.] Harmony in discord. *(kon-KOR-dee-a DIS-korz)*

concours [Fr.] Contest. Competition. *(koṁ-koor)*

concours d'élégance [Fr.] Parade of cars, usually old ones, with prizes for best-looking. *(koṁ-koor day-lay-gahṅ-s)*

confrère [Fr.] Fellow-member of profession. *(koṁ-frair)*

con fuoco [It.] (Of music) fierily. *(kon FWOH-koh)*

congé [Fr.] Leave-taking. Permission to leave. Dismissal. *(koṁ-zhay)*

con moto [It.] (Of music) with spirited movement. *(kon MOH-toh)*

conquistador [Sp.] Conqueror, especially Spanish conqueror of Mexico and Peru in sixteenth century. *(kon-KWIST-ad-or)*

conservatoire [Fr.] Academy of music (or other arts). *(kon-SERV-at-wah* or *koṅ-SAIRV-at-wahr)*

consommé [Fr.] Clear meat soup. *(kon* or *koṁ-SOM-ay)*

con sordino [It.] (Of music) with the use of a mute on the instrument. *(kon sord-EE-noh)*

con spirito [It.] (Of music) with spirit. *(kon-SPIR-it-oh)*

consummatum est [Lat.] It is finished. *(kon-sum-AH-tum est)* Christ's last words on the Cross.

contadino, contadina [It.] (In Italy) peasant man, woman. *(kon-tad-EE-noh, -na)* Plurals **contadini, contadine.**

conte [Fr.] Short story. *(korńt)*

contessa [It.] (In Italy) countess. *(kon-TES-a)*

continuo [It.] Same as **basso continuo.** The instrument, usually harpsichord or organ, which supplies unbroken background or accompaniment, usually in some orchestral or vocal music. *(kon-TIN-yoo-* or *-oo-oh)*

contra [Lat.] Against. *(KON-tra)*

contralto See **alto.**

contra mundum [Lat.] Against the world. *(kon-tra MUN-dum)* Applied to an innovator or innovation defying received opinion, practice, etc.

contrat social [Fr.] Social contract; doctrine that the individual must subordinate himself to the common will. *(korń-trah soh-syal)*

contretemps [Fr.] Mishap. Unexpected, embarrassing or irritating occurrence. *(KORŃ-truh-tahń)*

conversazione [It.] Social gathering of learned society, with part of the proceedings usually devoted to display or performance of its work, interests, etc. *(kon-ver-sat-zi-OH-ni)*

copain [Fr.] Pal. *(koh-pahń)*

copeck [Russ.] Russian coin, worth one hundredth of a rouble. *(KOH-pek)*

coq au vin [Fr.] Chicken cooked in wine. *(kok oh vań)*

coquette [Fr.] Flirtatious woman. *(kok-ET)*

coquetterie [Fr.] Flirtatious behaviour *(kok-ET-er-ee)*

coquillage [Fr.] Decoration, usually of furniture, in form of shell or shellfish. *(kok-ee-yahzh)*

coquilles St Jacques [Fr.] Type of shellfish. *(kok-ee sahń zhak)*

coram populo [Lat.] In public. *(KOH-ram POP-yoo* or *-oo-loh)*

cor anglais [Fr.] Musical instrument resembling oboe but lower in pitch. *(kor AHŃ-glay* or *ORŃ-glay)*

cordon bleu [Fr.] First class. *(kor-dorń blur)* Usually applied to cookery or cook.

cordon sanitaire [Fr.] Quarantine zone or line encircling or marking off infected area. Political, military or police encirclement or demarcation of area (e.g. country) thought to be dangerous. *(kor-dorń san-it-air)*

corniche [Fr.] Road cut into side of hill or cliff, especially coastal road cut into cliffs overlooking Mediterranean in Southern France. *(kor-NEESH)*

corps de ballet [Fr.] (In ballet) group who dance together (i.e. not soloists). *(kor duh BAL-ay)*

corps d'élite [Fr.] Select group. *(kor day-LEET)*

corps diplomatique [Fr.] Body of official representatives of foreign governments in any country. *(kor dip-loh-mat-EEK)*

corpus [Lat.] Body. Collection (e.g. of pieces of knowledge related to a certain subject). *(KOR-pus)*

Corpus Christi [Lat.] Feast of the Body of Christ (or Blessed Sacrament or Holy Eucharist) celebrated on the Thursday after Trinity Sunday. *(KOR-pus KRIS-ti)*

corpus delicti [Lat.] Everything that constitutes a particular breach of the law. (Colloquially) the evidence, especially a corpse, in a crime. *(KOR-pus del-IK-ti)*

corpus juris [Lat.] Body of law. *(KOR-pus JOO-* or *YOO-ris)*

corrida (de toros) [Sp.] Bull-fight. Bull-fighting. *(kor-EE-da)*

corrigendum [Lat.] Thing to be corrected (especially printing error in book). *(ko-ri-JEN-dum)* Plural **corrigenda.**

cortège [Fr.] Procession (usually funeral procession). *(kor-tayzh)*

Cortes [Sp.] Spanish legislative assembly. *(KOR-tes* or *-tez)*

Cosa Nostra [It.] American branch of **mafia.** *(KOH-za NOS-tra)*

côte [Fr.] Hillside. Coast. *(koht)* Found on labels of French wine-bottles to indicate area where contents have been grown.

coteau [Fr.] Hillside. Slope. *(kot-oh)* Plural **coteaux** (same pronunciation). Found on French wine-labels to indicate origin of wine.

Côte d'Azur [Fr.] French Riviera, the sea-side region in the south east of France, including Nice, Cannes, etc. *(koht daz-OOR)*

Côte de Beaune [Fr.] Southern stretch of **Côte d'Or**, including Beaune but mainly lying south-west of it. *(koht duh bohn)*

Côte de Nuits [Fr.] Northern stretch of **Côte d'Or** where some of the best Burgundy is grown. *(koht duh nwee)*

Côte d'Or [Fr.] Narrow strip of territory (about 40 miles long) stretching south-west from Dijon through Beaune, where Burgundy is grown in Southern France. *(koht dor)*

côtelette [Fr.] Cutlet; chop. *(koht-let)*

coterie [Fr.] Small, select group of people sharing same interests (e.g. social, intellectual). *(koht-er-ee)*

cotta [Lat.] Short surplice. *(KOT-a)*

couchette [Fr.] Sleeping-berth, usually in form of reclining seat, on train or boat. *(koo-SHET)*

coulée [Fr.] Deep ravine. Lava flow. *(koo-lay)*

coulisse [Fr.] Wings of stage in theatre. *(koo-LEE-s)*

couloir [Fr.] Deep gorge or gully on steep mountain-side. *(kool-wahr)*

coup [Fr.] Successful stroke or move. Skilful, often unexpected, execution of plan. *(koo)*

coup de foudre [Fr.] Sudden and surprising happening. Love at first sight. *(koo duh foodr)*

coup de grâce [Fr.] Death-dealing blow. Act, stroke, etc. that ends something. *(koo duh grahs)*

coup de main [Fr.] Sudden attack. *(koo duh maṅ)*

coup d'essai [Fr.] First attempt. *(koo des-ay)*

coup d'état [Fr.] Take-over of government by violent (often sudden) or illegal means. *(koo day-tah)*

coup de théâtre [Fr.] Achievement of dramatic effect. Sudden or sensational action. *(koo duh tay-ar-truh)*

coup d'œil [Fr.] Glance giving general view. *(koo duh-y)*

coupe [Fr.] Dessert, usually served in glass dish. *(koop)*

coupé [Fr.] Car, usually sports-car, with two seats. *(koo-pay)*

courgette [Fr.] Small variety of vegetable marrow. *(koor-ZHET)*

court bouillon [Fr.] (In cookery) vegetable stock in which fish is poached. *(koor bwee-yoṙṅ)*

couscous [Fr. from Arab.] North African dish made by steaming (paste of) flour over broth, often with meat, vegetables or fruit added. *(koos-koos)*

coûte que coûte [Fr.] At all costs. *(koot kuh koot)*

couture [Fr.] Dressmaking. *(koot-oor)*

couturier [Fr.] Dressmaker. Fashion designer. *(koot-OOR-ee-ay)*

couvert [Fr.] A place-setting at table (i.e. cutlery, napkin, glass, etc.) for which a separate charge is made at some French restaurants. *(koo-vair)*

craquelure [Fr.] Fine cracks in painting or its varnish, or (deliberately) in pottery glaze. *(KRAK-loor)*

crèche [Fr.] Place where very young children can be left (while parents are at work, etc.). *(kresh* or *kraysh)*

credo [Lat.] Creed. Set of beliefs. The Apostles' or Nicene Creed (which begins in Latin with the word *Credo*, 'I believe'). Musical setting of Nicene Creed. *(KRAY-doh)*

crème [Fr.] Cream. *(krehm)*

crème brulée [Fr.] Cream custard cooked, then sprinkled with sugar which is then caramelised. *(krehm broo-lay)*

crème caramel [Fr.] Dessert of egg custard with syrup. *(krehm ka-ra-mel)*

crème de la crème [Fr.] The very best (people, etc.). *(krehm duh la krehm)*

crème de menthe [Fr.] Peppermint liqueur. *(krehm duh moṅt)*

Créole, Creole [Fr.] (In West Indies, sometimes in parts of Central and South America) person born and naturalised in the country, but of European or African Negro descent. *(KRAY-ohl)* See below.

créole, creole [Fr.] Born or grown in W. Indies, but not indigenous. *(KRAY-ohl)* See above. Also applied to music, language, etc.

crêpe [Fr.] Thin fabric with wrinkled surface. Pancake. *(krayp)*

crêpe de Chine [Fr.] Fine **crêpe** made of raw silk. *(krayp duh sheen)*

crêpe Suzette [Fr.] Dessert pancake flavoured with liqueur. *(krayp soo-ZET)*

crescendo [It.] Gradual increase in loudness. *(kresh-EN-doh)*

cri de cœur [Fr.] Heartfelt appeal or protest. *(kree duh kur)*

crime passionnel [Fr.] Crime, usually murder, motivated by sexual passion. *(kreem pas-yon-EL)*

crise de conscience [Fr.] Severe pressure from one's conscientious scruples. *(kreez duh korṅ-syahṅ-s)*

crise de nerfs [Fr.] Attack of hysteria. Brief nervous breakdown or loss of will-power. *(kreez duh nair)*

critique [Fr.] Critical analysis, usually long and thorough. *(krit-EEK)*

Croesus Immensely wealthy king of Lydia in sixth century B.C. *(KREE-sus)*

croissant [Fr.] Crescent-shaped bread-roll of light, flaky pastry, usually eaten as part of French breakfast. *(krwah-sahṅ)*

croix de guerre [Fr.] French military decoration. *(krwah duh gair)*

croquette [Fr.] Fried ball of potato, meat or fish, usually covered with breadcrumbs. *(kro-KET)*

croûte [Fr.] Piece of crisply fried bread used as base for savouries, eggs, etc. *(kroot)*

croûtons [Fr.] Small cubes of bread, fried and served as garnish, usually with soups. *(kroot-orṅ)*

cru [Fr.] Grade of French wine. French vineyard or wine-producing region. *(kroo)* See below, and also **grand cru, premier cru.**

cru classé [Fr.] (Of wine) growth of the first five official classes of quality of claret. *(kroo klas-ay)*

cru exceptionnel [Fr.] (Of wine) of the second rank of clarets (after **cru classé**). *(kroo ek-sep-syon-el)*

crudités [Fr.] Sliced or shredded raw vegetables (usually tomatoes, beetroot, cucumber, radishes, celery, beans, peppers, carrots, celeriac, shallots) seasoned and dressed, served as first course to a meal, often with a little pâté, cooked meat, fish or egg. *(kroo-deet-ay)*

csárdás [Hung.] Hungarian national dance, part slow and melancholy, part quick and fiery. *(CHAR-dahsh)*

crux ansata [Lat.] T-shaped cross surmounted by circle. *(krux ans-AH-ta)*

cui bono? [Lat.] Who is the beneficiary (and therefore responsible)? *(kwee BON-oh)*

cuisine [Fr.] (Style of) cookery. *(kwee-zeen)*

cuisson [Fr.] Juices left in pan after meat, fish, poultry, etc. have been cooked. *(kwee-sorn̍)*

cul-de-sac [Fr.] Road, etc. closed at one end. Dead end. *(kool-duh-sak)*

culotte [Fr.] Women's trousers made to look like skirt. *(kool-OT)* Usually **culottes** (same pronunciation).

cum [Lat.] With. *(kum)*

cum grano salis [Lat.] With a grain of salt. With caution. *(kum GRAH-noh SAH-lis)*

cum laude [Lat.] With distinction. *(kum LOW-deh)*

curé [Fr.] Parish priest in France, etc. *(koo-ray)*

Curia [Lat.] Court of the Pope. Government departments of the Vatican. *(KOO-ree-a)*

curriculum vitae [Lat.] Brief autobiography in note form, normally used when applying for a post. *(kur-RIK-yoo-lum VEET-eye)*

cuvée [Fr.] Quantity of wine, of good quality, reserved for special purpose or customer. Blend of wines. *(koo-vay)*

cwm [Welsh] Same as **cirque.** *(koom)*

czar [Russ.] Emperor of Russia. *(zahr)*

czardas More usual spelling of **csárdás.**

czarevitch [Russ.] Son, especially eldest son, of **czar.** *(ZAHR-eh-vitch)*

czarina [Russ.] Empress of Russia. Wife of **czar.** *(zahr-EE-na)*

D

da capo [It.] (In music) repeat from the beginning. *(da KAH-poh)*

da capo al fine [It.] (In music) repeat from beginning to end. *(da KAH-poh al FEE-neh)*

da capo al segno [It.] (In music) repeat from the beginning and continue to the point marked with a sign. *(da KAH-poh al SAYN-yoh)* See **segno.**

dacha [Russ.] Country house or villa in Russia. *(DA-sha)*

dada [Fr.] Literary and artistic movement of early twentieth century, advocating the unconventional and absurd, and intending to shock. *(dah-dah)* Hence **dadaism, dadaist.**

dahabeeyah, dahabiah, dahabiyeh [Arab.] Sailing-boat for passengers on Nile. *(da-hab-EE-yah* or *-ah* or *-yeh)*

Dáil [Ir.] Lower house of parliament in Irish Republic. *(doyl)*

daimio [Jap.] Japanese feudal nobleman, vassal of the Emperor. *(DEYE-myoh)*

Dalai Lama [Tibetan] (Former) chief priest (or priest-king) of Tibet. *(DAL-eye LAH-ma)*

dak [Hindi] Relay of men or horses. Goods or mail transported thus. Travel by this system. *(dork* or *duk)*

dal segno [It.] (In music) go back to the point marked with a sign. *(dal SAYN-yoh)* See **segno.**

dame d'honneur [Fr.] Lady-in-waiting. *(dam don-UR)*

damnosa hereditas or **haereditas** [Lat.] Inheritance that bestows more hardship or debt than benefit. *(dam-NOH-sa her-ED-it-ass)*

danke [Ger.] Thank you. *(DAHN-kuh)*

danse du ventre [Fr.] Belly-dance. *(dahṅs doo vahṅtr)*

danse macabre [Fr.] Dance of death (especially medieval representation of personified Death leading mankind in a dance to the grave). *(dahṅs mak-AH-br)* Now applied to any bizarre ritual.

danseur [Fr.] Male dancer, usually in ballet. *(dahṅ-SUR)*

danseuse [Fr.] Female dancer, usually in ballet. *(dahṅ-SURZ)*

darshan [Hindi] Seeing an important or holy person. *(DAR-shahn)*

data Plural of **datum.** *(DAY-ta)*

datum [Lat.] Something known or assumed as fact, and used as the basis for a calculation, piece of reasoning, case, argument, etc. *(DAY-tm)*

daube [Fr.] Braised meat. Meat for braising. *(dohb)*

dauphin [Fr.] Eldest son of King of France. *(DOH-faṅ)*

dawk Same as **dak.**

D.C. Abbreviation of **da capo.**

débâcle [Fr.] Sudden collapse or downfall; confused or humiliating disaster. *(day-BAH-kluh)*

de bene esse [Lat.] Provisionally. On certain conditions. *(duh ben-eh ES-eh)*

débris, debris [Fr.] Fragments of anything destroyed, wrecked or ruined. *(DAY-bree, DEB-ri)*

début, debut [Fr.] First appearance as a performer. *(DAY-boo* or *DEB-yoo)*

débutante, debutante [Fr.] Young woman making first formal social appearances. *(DAY-* or *DEB-yoo-tahnt)*

déclassé [Fr.] Having lost social status. *(day-clas-ay)* Feminine **déclassée.**

décolletage [Fr.] Low-cut neck of dress. State of being **décolleté.** *(day-KOL-tahzh)*

décolleté, décolletée [Fr.] Wearing a low-cut dress. Having a low-cut neck. *(day-KOL-tay)*

décor [Fr.] Decoration and furnishing of stage, room, etc. *(DAY-kor)*

decrescendo [It.] Decreasing in loudness. *(dee-* or *day-kresh-END-oh)*

découpage [Fr.] Decoration of surfaces with paper cut-outs. *(day-koop-ahzh)*

de facto [Lat.] (Existing) in fact, whether legal or not. *(day-FAKT-oh)* See **de jure.**

défense d'entrer [Fr.] No admission. *(day-fahn̈s dahn̈-tray)*

défense de fumer [Fr.] No smoking. *(day-fahn̈s duh foo-may)*

dégagé [Fr.] Unconstrained. Not **engagé.** *(day-gah-zhay)*

dégringolade [Fr.] Rapid deterioration. *(day-gran̈g-oh-LAHD)*

de gustibus (non est disputandum) [Lat.] There is no point in arguing about taste. There is no accounting for tastes. *(day-GUST-i-bus non est dis-poo-TAN-dum)*

de haut en bas [Fr.] In a condescending or patronising manner. *(duh-oh-ahn̈-bah)*

Dei gratia [Lat.] By the grace of God. *(day-ee GRAH-ti-a* or *-shi-a)* Found on British coins, sometimes abbreviated to **D.G.**

déjà vu [Fr.] Trite, unoriginal, boringly familiar. Psychologically, the illusion of having previously experienced a present situation. *(day-zhah-voo)*

de jure [Lat.] By right, by law. *(day* or *dee JOOR-i* or *YOOR-eh)*

dekko [Hind.] A look. *(DEK-oh)* (Slang)

del credere [It.] Business arrangement guaranteeing a buyer's solvency. *(del KRAY-deh-reh)*

delenda est Carthago [Lat.] Carthage must be destroyed. *(del-END-da est kar-THAH-goh)* Words used by Cato the Elder, now having proverbial force: whatever obstructs us must be destroyed, removed, etc.

delirium tremens [Lat.] Delirious state of mind, with hallucinations and trembling, due to prolonged and excessive consumption of alcohol. *(del-IR-i-um TREE-mens)* Abbreviation **D.T.'s**.

de luxe [Fr.] Luxurious; of a sumptuous kind. *(di LUKS* or *LOOKS)*

démarche [Fr.] Political or diplomatic proceeding, usually initiating new policy or action. *(day-mahsh)*

démenti [Fr.]. Official denial (of rumour, statement, etc.). *(day-mahn̈-tee)*

dementia [Lat.] Insanity consisting of loss of mental powers because of brain damage. *(di-MENSH-a)*

demi-mondaine [Fr.] Woman of low repute. *(dem-i-mon̈-DAYN)*

demi-monde [Fr.] Low society. Women of low repute. *(dem-i morṅd)*

demi-pension [Fr.] Accommodation at hotel, boarding-house, etc. with breakfast and only one main meal. *(dem-i PAHN-syorṅ)*

demi-tasse [Fr.] Small cup of coffee. Small coffee-cup. *(dem-i-TAS)*

demi-vierge [Fr.] Licentious virgin. *(dem-i vee-AIRZH)*

démodé [Fr.] Out of fashion. *(day-moh-day)*

de mortuis (nil nisi bonum) [Lat.] (Say) nothing but good about those who are dead. Do not speak ill of the dead. *(day MOR-too-ees nil nee-see BON-um* or *BOH-num)*

denier [Fr.] Unit of weight to measure fineness of yarn. *(DEN-yer)*

de nos jours [Fr.] Of our time. *(duh noh zhoor)* Always used after a noun.

dénouement [Fr.] Final unravelling, resolution, solution of mystery, complications, events, plot of play, story, etc. *(day-NOO-mahṅ)*

de nouveau [Fr.] Afresh, again. *(duh noo-voh)*

de novo [Lat.] Afresh, again. *(day* or *dee NOH-voh)*

deoch(-)an(-)doris or **doruis** [Gael.] Parting drink. *(dok* or *dokh-an-DO-ris)*

Deo gratias [Lat.] Thanks be to God. *(DAY-oh GRAH-ti-ahs* or *GRAH-shyuhs)*

Deo Optimo Maximo [Lat.] To God the best and greatest. *(DAY-oh OP-tee-moh MAK-see-moh)* Motto of the Benedictine order.

Deo volente [Lat.] God willing. Unless anything prevents it. *(DAY-oh vol-EN-teh)* Abbreviation **D.V.**

département [Fr.] (In France) largest local government unit. *(day-pah-tuh-mahṅ)*

depot, dépôt [Fr.] Headquarters; warehouse; store-house; garage for buses; (in U.S.A.) bus or railway station; base where stores or supplies are kept or deposited. *(DEP-oh)*

de profundis [Lat.] (Cry) from the depths (of despair, sorrow). *(day prof-UND-ees* or *-iss)* Opening words of Psalm 130.

député [Fr.] Member of lower house of parliament in France. *(day-poo-tay)*

déraciné [Fr.] (Person) uprooted from his natural environment. *(day-rass-ee-nay)*

de règle [Fr.] Customary. *(duh REH-gl)*

de rigueur [Fr.] Required (by etiquette, custom, etc.) *(duh ree-GUR)*

dernier cri [Fr.] Very latest fashion. *(der-nyay kree)*

dernier luxe [Fr.] Highest degree of luxury. *(der-nyay looks)*

derrière [Fr.] Buttocks. *(deh-ri-AIR)*

déshabillé [Fr.] (State of) being carelessly or informally dressed, or being undressed. Dressing-gown. *(dayz-ab-ee-yay)*

desiderratum [Lat.] Thing needed or desired. *(des-id-er-AH-tum)* Plural **desiderata.**
désolé [Fr.] Extremely sorry. *(day-zol-ay)*
détente [Fr.] Relaxation of tension, especially between countries. *(day-TAHṄT)*
détenu [Fr.] Person detained in custody. *(day-tuhn-oo)*
détour, detour [Fr.] Deviation (in travelling). Make a deviation. *(DAY- or DEE-toor)*
détraqué [Fr.] Deranged. Deranged person. *(day-trak-ay)*
de trop [Fr.] Not wanted. In the way. Excessive. *(duh TROH)*
deus [Lat.] God. *(DAY-oos)*
deus ex machina [Lat.] Person who intervenes opportunely to solve problem, especially in play, novel, etc. *(DAY-oos ex MAK-ee-na)*
Deus misereatur [Lat.] God be merciful. *(DAY-oos miz-e-ri-AH-toor)* Opening words of Psalm 67.
Deus vobiscum [Lat.] God be with you. *(DAY-oos voh-* or *woh-BIS-kum)*
dévot [Fr.] Devotee. *(day-voh)* Feminine **dévote** *(day-vot)*
D.G. Abbreviation of **Dei gratia.** (Found on some British coins.)
dhobi [Hindi] Indian washerman (or washerwoman). *(DOH-bi)*
dhoti [Hindi] Loin-cloth worn by male Hindu. *(DOH-ti)*
dhow [Not known] Arabian sailing ship. *(dow)*
diablerie [Fr.] Devilry, (evil) mischief, sorcery. *(DYAH-bler-ee)*
dialogue des sourds [Fr.] Conversation between the deaf, i.e. between people who do not listen to each other. *(dee-a-log day soor)*
diamanté [Fr.] (Material) given sparkling appearance with powdered crystal or artificial brilliants. *(dee-a-MAṄ-tay* or *deye-a-MAN-ti)*
Diaspora [Gk.] Dispersion of the Jews into non-Jewish lands. *(di-ASP-or-a)*
dictum [Lat.] Formal pronouncement, usually by person with authority. Current saying. *(DIK-tum)* Plural **dicta.**
Dies irae [Lat.] Day of Wrath, Day of Judgement. Latin hymn sung at Requiem Mass. *(DEE-ayz* or *-es EE-ray* or *-reye* or *-ree)*
dies non [Lat.] Day on which no legal business is transacted. *(DEE-ayz NOHN)*
Dieu et mon droit [Fr.] God and my right(s). *(DYUR ay moṅ DRWAH)* Motto of English Sovereign.
diktat [Ger.] Imposition of will by victor, or by person in authority, in form of severe terms. Categorical statement. *(DIK-tat)*
dilettante [It.] Person who trifles with a subject of study, especially the arts. Dabbler. *(dil-et-ANT-i)*

diminuendo [It.] (Of music) gradually diminishing in volume. *(dim-in-oo* or *-yoo-END-oh)*

dîner [Fr.] Dinner. To dine. *(dee-nay)*

Ding an sich [Ger.] (In philosophy) thing in itself; reality behind appearance. *(ding an zikh)*

Directoire [Fr.] (Of art, fashion, décor) in the style of the period of French history known as the Directory, 1795–9, characterised by extravagant imitation of classical forms. *(dee-rekt-WAHR)* Often found in **directoire knickers**, which are straight and knee-length.

dirigisme [Fr.] Policy of state planning and direction in national economy and social matters. *(dee-ree-ZHEE-zm)*

dirigiste [Fr.] Characteristic of or exponent of **dirigisme.** *(dee-ree-ZHEEST)*

dirndl [Ger.] Woman's dress in style of traditional Alpine peasant costume of Switzerland, Austria and Bavaria, consisting of bodice, blouse with short puffed sleeves, and full skirt with tight waist-band. *(DURN-dl)* Usually found in **dirndl skirt**, a skirt in the above style.

dis aliter visum [Lat.] The gods deemed otherwise. *(DIS AL-iter VEE-zum)* From Vergil, *Aeneid*

discothèque [Fr.] Dance, or club for dancing, to recorded music. *(DIS-koh-tek)* Often abbreviated to **disco.**

diseur [Fr.] Male entertainer who uses monologue. *(dee-ZUR)*

diseuse [Fr.] Female entertainer who uses monologue. *(dee-ZURZ)*

disjecta membra [Lat.] Scattered remains, fragments, usually of literary works. *(dis-YEK-ta MEM-bra)*

distingué [Fr.] Of distinguished bearing, air, features, manners, etc. *(dees-TAṄ-gay)*

distrait [Fr.] Inattentive; absent-minded; preoccupied; distracted. *(dees-tray)*

diva [It.] Distinguished female singer, usually in opera. *(DEE-va)* Same as **prima donna.**

divertimento [It.] Suite of instrumental music, usually for small forces, and in a number of movements, of a light and entertaining style. *(diverti-MEN-toh)*

divertissement [Fr.] Short dance, usually performed between acts of ballet, or between longer dances in ballet. Short piece of music in light style. *(dee-vert-EES-mahṅ)*

divorcé(e) [Fr.] Divorced man (woman). *(div-or-say)*

djellaba [Arab.] Variation of **jellaba**.

djibba(h) [Arab.] Variation of **jibba(h)**.

djinn [Arab.] Variation of **jinn.**

dolce [It.] (In music) sweetly; sweet. (Of Italian wine) very sweet. *(DOL-cheh)*

dolce far niente [It.] Pleasant idleness. *(dol-cheh far ni-EN-teh)*

dolce vita [It.] Life of luxury. *(dol-cheh VEE-ta)*

D.O.M. Abbreviation of **Deo Optimo Maximo**, and found on the labels of bottles of Benedictine.

Dominus vobiscum [Lat.] The Lord be with you. *(DOM-inus vohb-EES-kum)*

donna [It.] Title of respect given to lady *(DON-a)*

donné(e) [Fr.] Subject or theme of story, etc. *(don-nay)*

doppelgänger [Ger.] Supernatural apparition identical to a person who is living. *(DOP-el-geng-er)*

doré [Fr.] Golden. Gilded. *(doh-ray)*

dot [Fr.] Dowry. *(dot)*

douane [Fr.] Customs-office. *(doo-AHN)*

douanier [Fr.] Customs-officer. *(doo-ahn-yay)*

double entendre [Fr.] Double meaning. Word or phrase with two meanings (one of them usually indecorous). *(doo-blahṅ-TAHṄ-dr)*

double entente [Fr.] Same as **double entendre**. *(doo-blahṅ-TAHṄT)*

doublure [Fr.] Ornamental lining, usually leather, on inside of book-cover. *(doo-BLOOR)*

doucement [Fr.] Gently. *(doo-smahṅ)*

douceur [Fr.] Bribe. Gratuity. *(doo-sur)*

douceur de vivre [Fr.] Enjoyment of living well. *(doo-sur duh vee-vr)*

douche [Fr.] Jet of water applied to body for medicinal purposes or for bathing. Device for producing such a jet. Shower-bath. *(doosh)*

doux [Fr.] Sweet. *(doo)*

doyen [Fr.] Senior member of a body of colleagues, especially diplomatic corps. *(dwah-YAṄ)* Feminine **doyenne** *(dwah-YEN)*

dragée [Fr.] Tiny silvered ball for cake-decoration. Chocolate-coated sweet. *(DRAH-zhay)*

dramatis personae [Lat.] Characters in a play. *(dram-AT-is per-SOHN-eye* or *-ee)*

Drang nach Osten [Ger.] Expansionism in the East (by Germany) *(drang nahkh OH-sten)*

dressage [Fr.] Training or exhibiting (usually in competition) of horse in obedience and skill, especially that of small, intricate movements. *(DRES-ahzh)*

droit de(du) seigneur [Fr.] (Supposed) right of feudal lord to have sexual intercourse with vassal's bride on her wedding-night. *(drwah duh(doo) say-NYUR)*

drôle [Fr.] Droll. *(drohl)*

D.T., D.T's Abbreviation of **delirium tremens.**

duc [Fr.] Duke. *(dook)*

duce [It.] Leader. *(DOO-cheh)* Especially associated with Mussolini, Italian leader.

duchesse [Fr.] Duchess. Kind of satin, soft and heavy. Kind of lace. Set of decorative mats for dressing-table. *(doo-SHESS)* Most frequently found in **duchesse potatoes**, mashed potatoes, mixed with egg and seasoning, baked or fried, and served as patties.

dueña, duenna [Sp.] Chaperone. *(doo-EN-ya, doo-EN-a)*

dulce et decorum est pro patria mori [Lat.] It is sweet and proper to die for one's country. *(DOOL-cheh* or *-keh et dek-OR-um est proh PAT-ri-ah mor-EE)*

dum spiro, spero [Lat.] While I breathe, I hope. While there's life, there's hope. *(dum SPEE-* or *SPEYE-roh SPAY-* or *SPER-oh)*

duo [It.] Pair (e.g. of performers). (In music) piece for two voices or instruments. *(DYOO-oh* or *DOO-oh)*

duomo [It.] (In Italy) cathedral. *(DWOH-moh)*

durbar [Urdu] Ceremonial public audience or reception by Indian prince or by British viceroy or governor in India. Hall where such ceremony takes place. *(DUR-bar)*

duvet [Fr.] Single bed-cover, filled with down, etc. used instead of bed-clothes. *(DOO-vay)*

D.V. Abbreviation of **Deo volente.**

dybbuk [Heb.] (In Jewish folk-lore) evil spirit, often possessing human-being. *(DIB-uk)*

E

eau de Cologne [Fr.] Mild perfume, originally made at Cologne, Germany. *(oh duh kol-OHN)*

eau de Javelle [Fr.] Solution of sodium hypochlorite, used as bleach, disinfectant, etc. *(oh duh zhav-EL)*

eau de Nil [Fr.] Pale green colour. *(oh duh NIL)*

eau de toilette [Fr.] Lightly perfumed liquid, applied to body after washing. *(oh duh twal-ET)*

eau de vie [Fr.] Brandy (often of rough quality). *(oh duh VEE)*

eau sucrée [Fr.] Mixture of water and sugar. *(oh SOO-kray)*

ébauche [Fr.] Quick sketch; rough outline of piece of art or literature. *(ay-bohsh)*

Ecce Homo [Lat.] Name given to painting (or other representation) of Christ wearing crown of thorns. *(ek-eh HOH-moh)* Literally, 'Behold the man', words spoken by Pilate when presenting Christ to the people.

ecce signum [Lat.] Behold the sign. *(ek-eh SIG-num)* Used when producing proof or evidence.

echelon, échelon [Fr.] Military formation of troops in parallel groups clear of those in front and behind. Groups of people of equal rank in any organisation. *(ESH-el-on)*

echt [Ger.] Genuine. *(ekht)*

éclair [Fr.] Small finger-shaped cake made with **chou(x)** pastry filled with cream and topped with icing, usually of chocolate. *(ay-KLAIR)*

éclaircissement [Fr.] Explanation. *(ay-klair-SEE-smahṅ)*

éclat [Fr.] Brilliant success or display. Dazzling effect. Great applause. *(ay-KLAH)*

école [Fr.] School. *(ay-KOL)*

écossaise [Fr.] Dance, probably of Scottish origin, but having no resemblance to authentic Scottish country dances, in fast march tempo. *(ay-kos-ayz)* Most frequently found as title to nineteenth-century piano pieces, most of them having no Scottish idiom, however.

écritoire [Fr.] Writing-desk. *(ay-kreet-WAHR)*

écru [Fr.] Colour of unbleached linen. *(ay-kroo)*

écurie [Fr.] Stable. Motor-racing team. *(ay-koo-REE)*

Edda [Icelandic] Collection of Icelandic epic poetry (c.1200) and of miscellaneous prose works on Icelandic poetry (c.1230). *(ED-a)*

edelweiss [Ger.] Alpine plant with white flowers. *(AYDL-veye-s)*

édition de luxe [Fr.] Book published in expensive form (e.g. with good quality paper, fine binding etc.). *(ay-dee-syoṅ duh looks)*

editio princeps [Lat.] First printed edition of a book. *(ed-IT-ee-oh* or *ed-ISH-ee-oh PRIN-keps* or *-seps)*

effendi [Turk.] (In Turkey, and some Eastern Mediterranean and Arabic countries) person of consequence. *(ef-END-di)* Also title of respect.

e.g. Abbreviation of **exempli gratia.**

egaré [Fr.] Straying or strayed (from the truth). *(ay-ga-ray)*

ego [Lat.] That part of the mind that is aware of the individuality of the self. Self-esteem. *(E-goh, EE-goh)*

eheu fugaces [Lat.] Alas, the transitory (years are slipping by). *(eh-HEH-oo foo-GAH-kays* or *-says)* First two words of a line from Horace's *Odes*.

Eisen und Blut [Ger.] Iron and blood (i.e. military strength and human self-sacrifice). *(EYE-zn unt BLOOT)* Slogan of Bismarck, German Chancellor.

eisteddfod [Welsh] Congress of Welsh bards. National competition of song, poetry, etc. *(is-TETH-vod, eye-STED-fod)*

élan [Fr.] Vivacious impetuosity. *(ay-LAHṄ)*

élan vital [Fr.] Life-force. *(ay-LAHṄ vee-TAHL)* Phrase popularised by Bergson, philosopher.

eldorado, El Dorado [Sp.] Fictitious country, rich in gold. *(el-dor-AH-doh)*

élite [Fr.] Very best (of a group, society, etc.). Select few. *(ay-LEET)*

éloge [Fr.] Oration in honour of dead. *(ay-LOZH)*

Elysium [Lat.] (In Greek mythology) abode of the blessed after death. Paradise. *(el-IZ-ee-um)*

embarras de choix [Fr.] A large number of options, making choice difficult. *(ahṅ-bah-rah duh SHWAH)*

embarras de richesse(s) [Fr.] Embarrassment of riches. Abundance which is difficult to appreciate, choose from, etc. *(ahṅ-bah-rah duh ree-SHESS)* Correctly, **embarras des richesses.**

embonpoint [Fr.] (Of people, especially men) plumpness, especially of stomach. *(ahṅ-boṅ-pwaṅ)*

embouchure [Fr.] Way of applying mouth to brass or woodwind instrument in order to play it. Part of such instrument to which mouth is applied. *(ahṅ-boo-shoor)*

embusqué [Fr.] Person who avoids military service by being in essential non-military employment. *(ahṅ-boo-skay)*

emeritus [Lat.] Honorary title given to person who has retired from paid employment, usually in learned profession. *(em-EHR-it-us)* Normally applied to professor. Plural **emeriti.**

émeute [Fr.] Popular revolt. *(ay-MURT, i-MYOOT)*

émigré [Fr.] Emigrant. *(AY-mee-gray)*

éminence grise [Fr.] One who exercises considerable influence or power (e.g. as confidential adviser, private secretary, etc. to important person) appropriate to higher office than he in fact occupies. Power behind the throne. *(ay-mee-nahṅs GREEZ)* Sometimes incorrectly applied to person who is eminent and aged.

emir [Arab.] Title of Muslim ruler. *(ay-MEER)*

employé [Fr.] Employee. *(ahṅ-PLWAH-yay)* Feminine **employée** (same pronunciation).

empressement [Fr.] Eager cordiality. *(ahṅ-PRES-mahṅ)*

en attendant [Fr.] While waiting. *(ahṅ at-ahṅ-dahṅ)*

en avant [Fr.] Ahead. Move forward! *(ahṅ av-AHṄ)*

en bloc [Fr.] Wholesale; all together; as a single entity. *(ahṅ BLOK)*

en brochette [Fr.] (In cookery) on a skewer. *(ahṅ brosh-ET)*

en brosse [Fr.] (Of hair) cut very short and bristly, like a brush. In a crew-cut. *(ahṅ BROS)*

en cabochon [Fr.] (Of precious stone) polished and set, but not cut. *(ahṅ kab-oh-shoṅ)*

en casserole [Fr.] Cooked in a single earthenware dish. *(ahṅ KAS-er-ohl)*

enceinte [Fr.] Pregnant. (In military parlance) fortified enclosure. *(ahṅ-SAṄT)*

enchanté [Fr.] Enchanted, delighted. *(ahṅ-shahṅ-tay)* Used in French greeting.

en clair [Fr.] Not in code or cipher, but in ordinary language. *(ahṅ KLAIR)*

encomium [Lat.] Formal oration, literary composition, etc., in praise. *(en-KOH-mi-um)*

en coquille [Fr.] (Of fish) served in the shell. *(ahṅ kok-EE-y)*

encore [Fr.] Repetition of (usually part of) song, etc. at public performance in response to audience's applause. Additional item performed in response to such applause or demand. Call used by audience to request either of these, or to express pleasure. (As a verb) make such a request; be subject to such a request. *(AHṄ-kor* or *ON-kohr)*

en daube [Fr.] Braised. *(ahṅ dohb)*

en déshabillé [Fr.] In a state of undress. Dressed informally. *(ahṅ days-ab-ee-yay)*

en face [Fr.] Facing forwards. On facing page of book. *(ahṅ FAS)*

en famille [Fr.] With the family (i.e. without formality); as one of the family; at home. *(ahṅ fam-EE-y)*

enfant gâté [Fr.] Spoiled child. Adult who behaves petulantly, or like a spoiled child, needing or given excessive indulgence. *(ahṅ-fahṅ gah-tay)* Plural **enfants gâtés** (same pronunciation).

enfant terrible [Fr.] Over-precocious, awkward or unruly child. Unruly adult who causes embarrassment or consternation, especially by unconventional attitudes or behaviour, ostentatiously expressed. *(ahṅ-fahṅ ter-EEBL)* Plural **enfants terribles** (same pronunciation).

en fête [Fr.] In carnival mood. (Of town, etc.) engaged in some special celebratory or recreational event(s), with appropriate jollification. *(ahṅ FEHT* or *FAYT)*

engagé [Fr.] (Of writer, thinker, politician, etc.) dedicated to a particular moral, social or political philosophy, and committed to its spread. *(ahṅ-gahzh-ay)*

engagement [Fr.] The state of being **engagé.** *(ahṅ-gahzh-uh-mahṅ)*

en garçon [Fr.] As a bachelor. *(ahṅ gar-soṅ)*

en grande tenue [Fr.] In full dress, especially formal evening wear, military or academic dress, etc. *(ahṅ grahṅd tuhn-oo)*

enjambement [Fr.] (In poetry) running on a sentence from one line or stanza to the next, without punctuation, thus over-riding the pause which metre would normally impose. *(ahṅ-JAHṀ-buh-mahṅ)*

en masse [Fr.] All together. In a mass. *(ahṅ MAS)*

ennui [Fr.] Boredom. World-weariness. Sense of mental dissatisfaction deriving from lack of occupation. *(on-WEE, ahṅ-WEE)*

ennuyé [Fr.] Suffering from **ennui.** *(ahṅ-wee-ay)* Feminine **ennuyée** (same pronunciation).

en pantoufles [Fr.] In an informal manner and relaxed atmosphere. *(ahṅ pahṅ-TOOFL)*

en passant [Fr.] In passing. By the way. *(ahṅ PAS-ahṅ)*

en pension [Fr.] Living as a boarder. Staying at a hotel and paying fixed rate for meals and accommodation. *(ahṅ PAHṄ-syoṅ)* See **demi-pension, pension.**

en plein [Fr.] (Of bet in gambling) placed entirely on one number, card, etc., not spread over several. *(ahṅ PLAṄ)*

en plein air [Fr.] In the open air. *(ahṅ plaṅ air)*

en poste [Fr.] (Of diplomat) appointed to an official post. *(ahṅ PO-st)*

en prise [Fr.] (Of chess piece) in such a position that it can be taken. *(ahṅ PREEZ)*

en rapport [Fr.] In harmony, in sympathy. *(ahṅ rap-or)*

en règle [Fr.] In order. *(ahṅ REH-gl)*

en revanche [Fr.] In retaliation. *(ahṅ rev-ahṅsh)*

en route [Fr.] On the way. *(ahṅ ROOT)*

en secondes noces [Fr.] By or in a second marriage. *(ahṅ zeg-oṅd nohs)*

ensemble [Fr.] General effect. (In music, etc.) group of players, performers, etc. Concerted performance by group. *(ahṅ-SAHṄ-bl)*

en suite [Fr.] Immediately adjacent, or as part of a single unit. *(ahṅ SWEET)*

entente [Fr.] Friendly relationship, usually between countries. Group of states enjoying such friendliness. *(ahṅ-TAHṄT)*

entente cordiale [Fr.] Same as **entente**, but particularly applied to Britain, France and Russia during first decade of the twentieth century. *(ahṅ-TAHṄT kor-DYAHL)*

entourage [Fr.] Attendants, advisers, friends, disciples, of someone wealthy or important. *(AHṄ- or ON-too-rahzh)*

en-tout-cas [Fr.] Umbrella serving also as sunshade. *(ahṅ-too-kah)*

entr'acte [Fr.] Interval between acts of opera, ballet, play, etc. Music or other performance during such interval. *(ON- or AHṄ-trakt)*

entrain [Fr.] Animation, liveliness, briskness, enthusiasm, spirit. *(ahṅ-tran)*

entrechat [Fr.] (In ballet) leap with (one or) several crossings and uncrossings of legs in quick succession. *(ON-* or *AHṄ- truh-shah)*

entrecôte [Fr.] Sirloin steak. *(ahṅ-truh-koht)*

entrée [Fr.] Admission by right or privilege, usually into circle of important people. Main course of meal. *(ON-* or *AHṄ-tray)*

entremets [Fr.] Small course, usually savoury, served between main courses of meal. Sweet dish. Side dish of food supplementary to main course. *(ahṅ-truh-may)*

entre nous [Fr.] Between ourselves (i.e. confidentially). *(ahṅ-truh NOO)*

entrepôt [Fr.] Warehouse. Commercial centre for collection and distribution of goods. *(ON-* or *AHṄ-truh-pot)*

entrepreneur [Fr.] Person of enterprise, beginning or running a business (or acting as intermediary) with chance of profit or loss. *(ahṅ-truh-pruhn-UR)*

entresol [Fr.] Low storey between ground and first floors *(AHṄ-truh-sol)*

épatant [Fr.] Astonishing, stunning (especially in an unconventional way). *(ay-pat-ahṅ)*

épater les bourgeois [Fr.] Shock those of conventional tastes, beliefs, etc. *(ay-pat-ay lay BOOR-zhwah)* See **bourgeois.**

epée [Fr.] (In fencing) foil with covered point. *(ay-pay)*

épergne, epergne [Fr.] Ornamental centre-piece for table, usually holding flowers or fruit in a number of separate dishes. *(ay-PAIRN)*

ephemera [Gk.] Thing or things of short-lived interest, value, use, etc. *(ef-EM-er-a)*

E pluribus unum [Lat.] Out of many, one. *(ay PLOO-ri-bus OO-num)* Motto of U.S.A.

épopée, epopee [Fr.] Epic poem; epic poetry. *(ay-pop-ay, EP-op-ee)*

epos [Gk.] Epic poem. Unwritten epic poem or heroic happening(s) later recorded in written epic poetry. *(EP-os)*

épris [Fr.] In love. *(ay-pree)* Feminine **éprise** *(ay-preez)*

équipe [Fr.] Team, usually in motor-racing. *(ay-KEEP)*

ergo [Lat.] Therefore. *(UR-goh)*

Eros [Gk.] Sexual love. God of love. *(EAR-os)*

erratum [Lat.] Mistake in printed document. *(er-AH-tum)* Plural **errata** *(er-AH-ta)* Especially applied to list of mistakes, usually printing errors, attached to printed book.

ersatz [Ger.] Inferior substitute or imitation. Of inferior nature. *(AIR-zats)*

escalope [Fr.] Slice of meat, especially veal, without bone. *(ES-kal-op)*

escargot [Fr.] Edible snail *(es-kar-goh)*

escritoire [Fr.] Writing-desk. *(ES-kree-twah)*

espadrille [Fr.] Light casual shoe with canvas upper, the sole being made of rope, plaited fibre or synthetic rubber. *(es-pa-DREE-y, es-pa-DREEL)*

espressivo [It.] (Of music) to be played expressively, with feeling. *(es-pres-EE-voh)*

espresso [It.] (Coffee) made by action of steam pressure on grains. *(es-PRES-oh)*

esprit [Fr.] Wit. Liveliness. *(es-PREE)*

esprit de corps [Fr.] Spirit of loyalty among people belonging to same group (e.g. regiment, school, etc.). *(es-pree duh KOR)*

esprit de l'escalier [Fr.] Witty remark or retort that one thinks of after the opportunity to make it has passed. *(es-pree duh les-KAL-yay)*

esprit fort [Fr.] Free-thinker. *(es-pree FOR)*

estaminet [Fr.] (In France) small bar. *(es-ta-mee-nay)*

étagère [Fr.] Piece of furniture consisting of set of open shelves, either hanging on wall or standing on floor, to hold ornaments, etc. *(ay-tah-ZHAIR)*

et al. [Lat.] And others. *(et al)*. Abbreviation of **et alia, et alii.**

et alia [Lat.] And other things *(et AL-i-a)*

et alii [Lat.] And other people *(et AL-i-ee)*

étape [Fr.] Stage or stopping-place in a journey or race (especially cycle-race). *(ay-TAP)*

étatisme [Fr.] Authority, or increase in authority, of state over individual. *(ay-tat-eezm)*

etc. Abbreviation of **et cetera.**

et cetera [Lat.] And the rest. And so on. *(et SET-ra)* The spelling **et caetera** is archaic. Also found as one word **etceteras**, sundries, extras, accessories.

Et in Arcadia ego [Lat.] And I too was in Arcadia (i.e. the earthly paradise). Even I, Death, am in Arcadia. *(et in ahk-AY-* or *-AH-dee-a EG-oh)* Inscription on tomb. The latter translation is preferable.

étoile [Fr.] Star. Something star-shaped. *(ay-TWAHL)*

étrier [Fr.] (In mountaineering) short rope ladder. *(AY-tree-ay)*

et seq. Abbreviation of **et sequentia.**

et sequentia [Lat.] And the following. *(et sek-WENT-ee-a)* Usually found, abbreviated to **et seq.**, in footnotes or index in book to refer to following pages, chapters, etc.

et sequentes [Lat.] Same as **et sequentia**, but less frequently found. *(et sek-WENT-ays)*

et tu, Brute! [Lat.] And you (too), Brutus. *(et TOO, BROO-teh)* Said to have been uttered by Julius Caesar when he found his friend Brutus among his assassins, and thus used by Shakespeare in *Julius Caesar*. Now used as mock reproach to a friend who lets one down.

étude [Fr.] (In musical composition) piece designed to demonstrate a particular technical difficulty. Study. *(ay-TOOD)*

étui [Fr.] Small case for needles, etc. *(ay-TWEE)*

eureka [Gk.] I have found it. *(yoo-REE-ka)* Archimedes' cry of triumph at discovering the principle of specific gravity. Thus, any exclamation of delight at having made a discovery.

ewigkeit [Ger.] Thin air. The unknown. *(AY-vig-keye-t)* Usually found in the phrase *into the ewigkeit*.

ex [Lat.] Supplied directly from. *(ex)*

ex- [Lat.] Former. *(ex)*

exalté [Fr.] Elated: in a state of exaltation. *(egs-AHL-tay)*

ex cathedra [Lat.] With great authority; pontifically. *(ex kath-AY-* or *-EE-dra)* Use of the term often implies that pronouncements so made do not brook any argument or contradiction.

excelsior [Lat.] Higher. Aim higher. *(ex-EL-see-or)*

exceptis excipiendis [Lat.] With exceptions as appropriate. *(ex-sep-tis ex-si-pi-END-is)*

excursus [Lat.] Detailed discussion of a point by way of digression or in appendix of book. *(ex-KUR-sus)*

ex div. [Lat.] Not including next dividend. *(ex DIV)* Used of stocks, shares, etc.

ex dono [Lat.] From, by or as the gift of. *(ex DOH-noh* or *DON-oh)* Normally found on book-plate indicating name of donor to library, collection etc. See **ex libris.**

exeat [Lat.] Permission, written or spoken, for temporary absence (from school, etc.). *(EGS-ay-at)*

exempli gratia [Lat.] For example. *(eg-ZEM-pli GRAH-sha* or *GRAH-tee-a)* Commonly abbreviated to **e.g.**

exeunt [Lat.] (In stage direction in play script) they go out; they leave the stage. *(EGS-ay-unt)*

exeunt omnes [Lat.] (In stage direction in play script) they all go out; they all leave the stage. *(EGS-ay-unt OM-nays)*

ex gratia [Lat.] (Of payment) as a favour, not by right. *(ex GRAY-sha)*

ex hypothesi [Lat.] In consequence of the hypothesis made. *(ex hip-OTH-i-si)*

exit [Lat.] (In stage direction in play script) he goes out; he leaves the stage. *(EGS-it)* In its more common uses (e.g. to signify a door, etc.) the word is now to be regarded as English rather than foreign.

ex libris [Lat.] From the library of. *(ex LIB-ris)* Normally followed by the name of the owner or donor, and found on book-plate affixed to front of book in library. See below.

ex(-)libris [Lat.] Book-plate (label with name, coat of arms, etc. of owner) affixed to front of book. *(ex-LIB-ris)*

ex nihilo [Lat.] Out of nothing. *(ex NI-hil-oh)*

ex officio [Lat.] By virtue of one's office. *(ex of-ISH-i-oh* or *of-IS-i-oh)*

ex parte [Lat.] (In law) by, or in the interests of, one party only. (Of legal injunction) granted temporarily to one party in the absence of the defendants. *(ex PAH-ti)*

experto crede [Lat.] Believe one who knows from experience. *(ex-PER-toh KRAY-deh)* Usually applied to oneself. From Vergil, *Aeneid.*

explication de texte [Fr.] Detailed analysis of style, etc. of piece of literature in accordance with strict rules. *(ex-plee-KAS-yoṅ duh TEXT)*

exposé [Fr.] Exposure, uncovering, of something discreditable. Orderly, reasoned explanation of facts, ideas, etc. *(ex-POH-zay)*

ex post facto [Lat.] Retrospective. *(ex pohst FAK-toh)* Usually applied to change in law which makes legal or illegal something which happened before the law was changed.

expresso. Same as **espresso.**

ex silentio [Lat.] In consequence of the absence of evidence to the contrary. *(ex sil-ENSH-i-oh* or *sil-ENT-i-oh)*

extraordinaire [Fr.] Extraordinary. Above average. Noted. *(ex-tra-or-din-AIR)* Usually found in patter of **compère** introducing artist. The word is placed after the noun (**illusionist extraordinaire**).

ex voto [Lat.] As a result of a vow. *(ex VOH-toh)* Applied to the making of prayers, offerings, etc.

F

f. Abbreviation of **forte** (in musical sense).

fabliau [Fr.] Short versified story in Old French, usually ribald, satirical, humorous or obscene. *(FAB-li-oh)* Plural **fabliaux** (same pronunciation).

façade [Fr.] Front of building. Outward appearance, especially one that is deceptive. *(fas-AHD* or *-AD)*

facia [Lat.] Long wooden board as facing on exterior of building (e.g. as decoration, or over shop-front to carry owner's name). Instrument or control panel, especially dash-board of car. *(FAY-sha)*

facile princeps [Lat.] Acknowledged leader. By far the best. *(fas-il-i PRIN-seps; fak-il-i PRIN-keps)*

façon de parler [Fr.] Manner of speaking. Something said as mere words, without meaning or sincerity. *(FAS-oṁ duh PAH-lay)*

factotum [Lat.] Person, especially servant, able to do many kinds of work. *(fak-TOH-tum)*

fado [Port.] Popular Portuguese ballad or folk-song, usually in melancholy style, and sung to guitar. *(FAH-doo)*

faeces, fæces [Lat.] Excrement. *(FEE-seez)*

faience, faïence [Fr.] Decorated and glazed earthenware or porcelain. *(FAH-yahṅs)*

fainéant [Fr.] (Person who is) idle, inactive. *(FAY-nay-ahṅ)*

fainéantise, fainéantism(e) [Fr.] Indolence; inactivity; apathy. *(fay-nay-ahṅ-TEEZ, -TEEZM)*

faisandé [Fr.] (Of story, play, joke, etc.) spicy, indelicate, slightly indecent. *(fay-zahṅ-day)*

fait accompli [Fr.] Accomplished fact: something done which cannot be readily undone. *(fet ak-oṁ-plee* or *ak-OM-pli)*

faites vos jeux [Fr.] Place your bets. *(fet voh ZHUR)*

fakir [Arab.] Muslim or Hindu holy man, living abstemiously, often by begging. *(FA-keer* or *fa-KEER)*

Falange [Sp.] Fascist party in Spain. *(fal-ANJ)*

falsetto [It.] High-pitched artificial singing or speaking voice (head-voice), usually used by men. *(fol-* or *forl-SET-oh)* See **alto.**

famille jaune/noire/rose/verte [Fr.] Chinese porcelain predominately coloured yellow/black/pink/green. *(fam-ee-y zhohn/nwahr/rohz/vairt)*

fandango [Sp.] Lively Spanish dance for a single couple. *(fan-DAN-goh)*

fanfaron(n)ade [Fr.] Boastful, arrogant talk or action. *(fahṅ-fah-ron-AHD* or *fan-fah-ron-ayd)*

fantaisie [Fr.] Fantasy. Exercise of fancy. Whimsical speculation. *(fahṅ-tez-ee)* Also found (in musical composition) as alternative to **fantasia.**

fantaisiste [Fr.] Person (especially artist) who indulges in **fantaisie.** *(fahṅ-tez-EEST)*

fantasia [It.] Musical composition in which musical form is less important than exercise of free-ranging imagination, fancy, etc.

(fan-TAY-zee-a) Also applied to composition consisting of, or based on, several well-known tunes.

fantoccini [It.] Mechanically operated puppets. Marionette show. *(fan-toh-CHEE-nee)*

farandole [Fr.] Lively dance from Provence. Music for such a dance, using pipe and tabor. *(fa-rand-ohl)*

farceur [Fr.] Joker. Writer of farce, or actor skilled in farce. *(fahs-UR)*

farci [Fr.] (In cookery) stuffed. *(fah-see)*

far niente [It.] Idleness. *(fah-ni-EN-teh)* See **dolce far niente**, the more usual phrase.

farouche [Fr.] Sullen. Lacking social graces; unaccustomed to polite society. *(fah-ROOSH)*

farrago [Lat.] Hotchpotch. *(fah-RAH-goh)*

fascia Same as **facia.**

fata morgana [It.] Kind of mirage or illusion. *(fah-ta mor-GAH-na)* Seen especially in Southern Italy, notably in Straits of Messina.

faubourg [Fr.] Suburb, especially of Paris. *(foh-boorg)*

fauna [Lat.] Animal characteristic of a given region. *(FOR-na)*

faute de mieux [Fr.] For lack of anything better. *(foht duh MYUH)*

fauteuil [Fr.] Armchair-shaped seat in theatre, bus, etc. *(foht-UR-y)*

faux bonhomme [Fr.] Person who seems good-natured but in reality is not. *(foh bon-OM)*

faux(-)naïf [Fr.] (Person) pretending to be ingenuous. *(foh neye-EEF)*

faux pas [Fr.] False step, mistake, indiscretion, usually in regard to social convention or human relationship. *(foh pah)*

favela [Port.] (In Brazil) shack; slum; shanty-town. *(fav-EL-a)*

F.D. Abbreviation of **fidei defensor.** Found on some British coins.

feces Same as **faeces.**

fecit [Lat.] Made (this). *(FAY-kit)* Found on work of art, preceded by artist's name, to identify him.

feis [Ir.] Irish (occasionally Scottish) festival or competition involving singing, dancing, etc. *(fesh* or *faysh)*

fellah [Arab.] (In Egypt) peasant. *(FEL-a)*

felo de se [Lat.] Suicide. Person who kills himself while performing illegal act. *(fel-oh duh SAY* or *SEE)*

felucca [It.] (In Mediterranean) small ship with oars or sails or both. *(fel-OO-ka)*

femme de chambre [Fr.] Chambermaid. *(fam duh SHAHṀBR)*

femme fatale [Fr.] Woman who brings misfortune to those who fall in love with her. *(fam fat-AHL)*

femme savante [Fr.] Bluestocking. *(fam sav-AHṄT)* Plural **femmes savantes** (same pronunciation).

ferae naturae [Lat.] (Of animals) not domesticated. *(FER-ee* or *-eye nat-YOOR-ee* or *-eye)*

festina lente [Lat.] Make haste slowly. More haste, less speed. *(fes-TEE-na LEN-teh)*

Festschrift [Ger.] Collection of essays presented to scholar, or published in his honour, to mark his birthday or some other important occasion. *(FEST-shrift)*

fête [Fr.] Festival. Large-scale entertainment, usually in open air. Entertain or celebrate (a person) lavishly. *(feht, fayt)*

fête champêtre [Fr.] Rural **fête.** Outdoor festival. *(feht shahṅ-PEH-truh)*

feu de joie [Fr.] Rifle-fire salute at public celebration or ceremony. *(fur duh ZHWAH)*

feuilleton [Fr.] Novel published serially. Part of newspaper devoted to regular literary column, reviews, light fiction, etc. *(FUR-yuh-torṅ)*

fiacre [Fr.] Small four-wheeled cab. *(fee-AHK-ruh)*

fiancé [Fr.] Man to whom one is betrothed. *(fee-AHṄ-say)* Feminine **fiancée** (same pronunciation).

fiasco [It.] Failure; ignominious result; breakdown. *(fee-ASK-oh)*

fiat [Lat.] Order, decree. Authorisation, especially one given by person holding great power. *(FEE-at)*

fiat lux [Lat.] Let there be light. *(fee-at LOOKS* or *LUKS)*

fichu [Fr.] Scarf or shawl, usually triangular, often of lace or muslin, worn over the head or shoulders. *(FEE-shoo)*

Fid. Def. Abbreviation of **fidei defensor**. Found on some British coins.

fidei defensor [Lat.] Defender of the Faith. *(fid-AY-ee def-EN-sor)* Normally abbreviated to **F.D.** or **Fid. Def.** and found on British coins.

fidus Achates [Lat.] Faithful friend, companion or follower. *(FEE-* or *FEYE-dus ak-AH-tez* or *-teez)*

fieri facias [Lat.] Writ authorising sheriff to execute judgement against debtor by seizing his goods. *(FEE-* or *FEYE-er-i FAK-* or *FASH-i-as)*

fiesta [Sp.] (In Spanish-speaking countries) festivity, holiday, religious festival, celebration, carnival. *(fee-EST-a)* Often in honour of saints, with bull-fight, etc.

figura [Lat.] Person (or thing) representing or symbolising something. *(fig-YOO-ra)*

figurant [Fr.] (In ballet) dancer who appears only in a group. Actor with very small part. *(fig-oo-rahṅ, FIG-yoo-rant)* Feminine

figurante *(fig-oo-rahn̍t, fig-yoo-RAN-ti)*

figurine [Fr.] Statuette. *(fig-yoo-reen)*

filet [Fr.] (Of meat, fish) fillet; boneless steak. Kind of lace or net with square mesh. *(fee-lay)*

filet mignon [Fr.] Tenderloin steak. *(fee-lay mee-nyoṅ)*

fille de joie [Fr.] Prostitute. *(FEE-y duh ZHWAH)*

fils [Fr.] The son. *(feess)* Always immediately preceded by a name, to indicate difference between son and father of same name. See **père.**

filtre Abbreviation of **café filtre.**

finale [It.] Last movement of musical composition, opera, variety performance, etc. *(fin-AH-leh)*

fin de siècle [Fr.] End of the nineteenth century. Decadent; characterised by relaxed morals, taste, customs, etc. *(faṅ duh SYEH-kl)*

fine [It.] (In music) end. *(FEE-neh)* *See* **al fine, da capo al fine.**

fine champagne [Fr.] Fine old liqueur brandy. *(feen shahṅ-PAN-y)*

fines herbes [Fr.] (In cookery) mixed herbs used for seasoning. *(feen ZEHRB)*

finis [Lat.] End; finish. *(FI-nis)*

fino [Sp.] Pale dry sherry. *(FEE-noh)*

fiord Same as **fjord.**

fjord [Norw.] Long narrow coastal inlet between high cliffs. *(fyord, FEE-ord)*

fl. Abbreviation of **floruit.**

flageolets [Fr.] White haricot beans. *(flazh-oh-lay)*

flagrante delicto See **in flagrante delicto.**

flak [Ger.] Anti-aircraft fire. Barrage of hostile criticism. *(flak)* Abbreviation of German word meaning anti-aircraft gun.

flambé [Fr.] (In cookery) covered with spirit, usually brandy, and set alight. *(flahṅ-bay)*

flambeau [Fr.] Flaming torch. *(flahṅ-boh, FLAM-boh)* Plural **flambeaux** (same pronunciation).

flamenco [Sp.] Spanish dance (sometimes with song) accompanied by guitar, characterised by rapid stamping of feet. *(flam-ENK-oh)*

flan [Fr.] (In French cookery) egg custard served as dessert. *(flahṅ)* Not to be confused with an English flan, which is pastry covered with cooked fruit, cheese, etc., or a sponge cake base covered with fruit, etc.

flânerie [Fr.] Idleness, especially that of man-about-town. *(flahn-ree)*

flâneur [Fr.] Idler, lounger, gossiper, especially man-about-town. *(flahn-UR)*

flèche [Fr.] Slender spire. *(flesh)*

fleur de coin [Fr.] Mint condition of coin. *(flur duh kwaṅ)*

fleur-de-lis [Fr.] Lily flower. *(flur duh LEES)* Royal arms of France.

fleur-de-lys Same as **fleur-de-lis.**

flic [Fr.] French policeman. *(fleek)* Slang.

flor. Abbreviation of **floruit.**

flora [Lat.] Plants characteristic of a particular area or period. Written description of these. *(FLOR-a)*

floreat [Lat.] May (it) flourish. *(FLO-ray-at)* Always followed by name of school, etc. on which good fortune is being wished.

florilegium [Lat.] Anthology. *(flo-ri-LEG-* or *-LEJ-i-um)*

floruit [Lat.] He or she flourished, produced his or her major work. *(FLO-roo-it)* Always followed by a date, to indicate when artist, etc. did most important work, usually when exact date of birth and death are not known.

foie gras Abbreviation of **pâté de foie gras.**

folie [Fr.] Madness. *(fol-ee)*

folie à deux [Fr.] Delusion shared by two people closely (often emotionally) involved with each other. *(fol-ee a duh)*

folie de grandeur [Fr.] Delusion of grandeur. Conviction that one is all-important. *(fol-ee duh grahṅ-DUR)*

fonctionnaire [Fr.] Minor official. *(foṁk-syoṁ-NAIR)*

fondue [Fr.] Dish of melted cheese, particularly popular in Switzerland. *(foṁ-doo)*

fons et origo [Lat.] Source and origin. *(fonz et OR-ig-oh)*

force de frappe [Fr.] Strike-force. *(fors duh FRAP)* Applied especially to nuclear strike-power.

force majeur [Fr.] Irresistible force. Compelling circumstance. *(fors mazh-UR)* Often used in insurance policies to describe unforseeable circumstances which the insurance does not cover.

forte [Fr.] Person's strong point. *(FOR-teh)* See below.

forte [It.] (In music) loudly. *(FOR-teh)* See above.

forte-piano [It.] (In music) loudly, then immediately softly. *(for-teh pee-AH-noh)* Usually applied to the way a single note is to be played by strings, wind or brass.

fortissimo [It.] (Of music) very loudly. *(fort-IS-im-oh)*

fouetté [Fr.] (In ballet) step in which dancer balances on toes of one foot; the other leg is crooked, and the foot rapidly rotated. *(fwet-ay)*

fourgon [Fr.] Luggage-van. *(foor-goṁ)*

foyer [Fr.] Entrance hall in theatre or hotel. Any large circulation-space for audience's use during interval, etc. in concert hall, theatre, etc. *(FWAH-yay)*

fp. Abbreviation of **forte-piano.**

fracas [Fr.] Uproar. Disturbance. Noisy quarrel. *(FRA-kah)*

fraise [Fr.] Strawberry. *(frehz)*

framboise [Fr.] Raspberry. *(frahn̈-bwahz)*

français [Fr.] French. *(frahn̈-say)* Feminine **française** *(frahn̈-sehz)*

franc-tireur [Fr.] Sharp-shooter. Guerrilla. *(frahn̈ tee-RUR)* Also applied to member of irregular infantry corps of snipers.

Franglais [Fr.] French with heavy use of English words or expressions. Use of English word or words in speaking French. *(FRAHṄ-glay)* The word is a **portmanteau** word formed by running together the French words **français** and **anglais.**

frankfurter [Ger.] Seasoned smoked sausage, normally served hot after immersion in boiling water. *(FRANK-fur-ter)*

frappé [Fr.] (Of drink) chilled. Iced. *(frap-ay)*

frate [It.] Friar. *(FRAH-teh)*

Frau [Ger.] (In Germany) title of married woman. German woman. *(frow)*

Fräulein [Ger.] (In Germany) title of unmarried woman. German spinster. *(FROYL-eye-n)*

frère [Fr.] Brother. *(frair)*

fresco [It.] (Method of) painting done in plaster (usually of wall or ceiling) while it is still wet. *(FRES-koh)* Plural **frescoes** or **frescos.**

fresco secco [It.] Painting on dry plaster. *(FRES-koh SEK-oh)*

fricandeau [Fr.] (In cookery) small pieces of meat, fried or stewed, and served in sauce. *(FREE-kan̈-doh)* Almost always applied to veal stew.

fricassée [Fr.] (In cookery) small pieces of meat or fowl, fried and/or stewed, and served in sauce. *(free-kas-ay* or *-ee)*

frijoles [Sp.] Kidney beans. *(free-HOH-les)*

frisson [Fr.] Thrill, shudder, shiver (of excitement, anticipation, etc.). *(FREE-som̈)*

fritto misto [It.] Mixed grill of fish, or meat, fowl or vegetables, cut small and fried in batter. *(FREE-toh MEE-stoh)*

froideur [Fr.] Coldness. Cooling-off of relationship. *(frwah-dur)*

fromage [Fr.] Cheese. *(from-ahzh)*

fronde [Fr.] Party of political rebels. *(from̈d)* Also **Fronde,** party that unsuccessfully revolted against Mazarin during Louis XIV's minority.

frondeur [Fr.] Rebel, usually political. *(from̈d-UR, frond-UR)*

frou-frou [Fr.] Rustling, especially of woman's silk dress. Elaborate, over-fussy decoration, especially of women's clothing. *(froo-froo)*

fruit de mer [Fr.] Sea-food. *(frwee duh MAIR)* Plural **fruits de mer** (same pronunciation).

fuehrer Same as **führer.**

führer [Ger.] Leader, especially dictator. *(FOO-ruh, FYOO-ruh)* With capital letter, normal title of Adolf Hitler.

Führerprinzip [Ger.] Principle that dictatorship is desirable. *(FOO-ruh-print-seep)*

furore [It.] Uproar. Fury. Enthusiastic admiration. *(fyoo-* or *foo-ROAR-i)*

fustanella [It.] (In Greece) stiff white kilt, especially worn by soldiers. *(fust-an-EL-a)*

G

gaffe [Fr.] Blunder. *(gaf)*

galantine [Fr.] (In cooking) white meat, especially veal or chicken, boned, boiled, pressed and served cold in jelly, aspic, etc. *(GAL-ahṅ-teen, GAL-ant-eye-n)*

galop [Fr.] Quick, lively dance in march time, characterised by change of step, or hop. Music for this. *(ga-LOP)*

gamin [Fr.] Street urchin. (Person) having the attractively pert, impudent or mischievous manner supposed to be typical of street urchin. *(ga-maṅ)* Feminine **gamine** *(ga-MEEN)*

gaminerie [Fr.] Manner which is **gamin.** *(gam-aṅ-ner-ee)*

garçon [Fr.] Waiter, especially French or in French restaurant. *(GAH-soṅ)*

garni [Fr.] (In cookery) garnished, with the appropriate accompaniment (e.g. vegetables). *(gah-nee)*

gasthaus, Gasthaus [Ger.] (In Germany) small inn or hotel. *(GAHST-hows)*

gasthof, Gasthof [Ger.] (In Germany) hotel. *(GAHST-hof)*

gastronome [Fr.] Judge of good food and drink. *(GAST-roh-nohm)*

gâteau [Fr.] Large, rich cake, often with liqueurs, cream, elaborate decoration, etc. *(GAH-* or *GA-toh)* Plural **gâteaux** (same pronunciation).

gauche [Fr.] Awkward, clumsy, graceless, especially in social matters. *(gohsh)*

gaucherie [Fr.] **gauche** act or manners. *(gohsh-er-ee)*

gaucho [Sp.] (In South America) cowboy or mounted herdsman. *(GOW-choh)*

gaudeamus igitur [Lat.] Let us therefore rejoice. *(gow-day-AH-mus IG-* or *IJ-it-oor* or *-ur)* Opening words of student song.

Gauleiter [Ger.] District leader in Nazi party. Any petty dictator. *(GOWL-eye-ter)*

Gauloise [Fr.] Brand of French cigarettes. *(GOHL-wahz)*

gavotte [Fr.] Stately dance resembling minuet, especially popular in eighteenth and nineteenth centuries. *(gav-OT)*

gazpacho [Sp.] Cold vegetable soup. *(gaz-PACH-oh)*

gefilte [Yiddish] (Of fish) minced, blended, seasoned, shaped, and cooked in vegetable broth. *(guh-FIL-ter)*

Gehenna [Lat.] Hell. *(guh-HEN-a)*

geisha [Jap.] Japanese professional hostess, entertaining men with song and dance. Japanese prostitute. *(GAY-sha)*

geist, Geist [Ger.] Soul. Spirit. Intelligence. *(geye-st)*

geld, Geld [Ger.] Money. *(gelt)* Slang.

Gemeinschaft [Ger.] Association, community. *(guh-MEYE-nsh-ahft)*

gemütlich [Ger.] Cosy, good-natured, genial, amiable, homely, kindly, comfortable. *(guh-MOOT-leekh)* Also **gemütlichkeit, Gemütlichkeit**, the quality of being **gemütlich** *(-keye-t)*.

gendarme [Fr.] (In France) policeman; soldier employed on police duty. *(zhoṅ-* or *zhon-dahm)*

gendarmerie [Fr.] (In France) force of **gendarmes**. Its headquarters. *(zhoṅ-DAHM-er-ee)*

generalissimo [It.] Supreme commander, especially of combined armed forces. *(jen-er-al-IS-im-oh)*

genie [Fr.] Sprite or goblin, especially in Arabian tales. *(JEE-ni)* Plural **genii** *(JEE-ni-ee)*

genius loci [Lat.] Particular character, influence, association of a place. Guardian deity of a place. *(JEE-ni-us LOHS-eye* or *GEH-ni-us LO(H)-kee)*

genre [Fr.] Kind, sort, style, especially of work of art. *(zhahṅr)*

genus [Lat.] Group or class (often of animals or plants) usually containing a number of species, having common characteristics. *(JEE-nus, GEH-nus)*

Gesellschaft [Ger.] Commercial company. *(guh-ZEL-shahft)*

gesso [It.] Plaster prepared for painting (or sculpture). *(JES-oh)*

Gestalt [Ger.] (In psychology) a perceived unity or whole that is more than the sum of its parts. *(gesh-TAHLT)*

Gestapo [Ger.] German secret police during Nazi regime. Any organisation with similarly brutal characteristics. *(gest-AH-poh)*

gesundheit, Gesundheit [Ger.] Good health! *(guh-ZOONT-heye-t)* Exclamation used as toast, or to person who sneezes.

ghat [Hindi] Flight of steps leading down to river. *(gort)*

ghetto [It.] Jewish quarter in town or city. Part of town or city, especially poor area, where minority-group lives. Isolated or segregated area for people of supposedly inferior class, race, religion, etc. *(GET-oh)*

giallo antico [It.] (In Italy) rich yellow marble found among Roman ruins. *(jah-loh an-TEEK-oh)*

gigolo [Fr.] Man paid to be escort or dancing partner. Man kept or paid by (usually older) woman for his companionship, sexual attentions, etc. *(ZHIG-oh-loh)*

gigot [Fr.] Leg of mutton. *(ZHEE-goh)* Also applied to style of sleeve of blouse (e.g. in Edwardian period), tight from wrist to below elbow, then very full to shoulder, thus similar in shape to leg of mutton.

gigue [Fr.] (In musical terminology) jig; music suggestive of lively dance. *(zheeg)*

Gioconda [It.] Looking (especially smiling) enigmatically. *(joh-KON-da)* Epithet of da Vinci's Mona Lisa.

giocoso [It.] (Of music) to be played cheerfully. *(joh-KOH-zoh)*

girandole [Fr.] Branched candle-stick. *(ZHEE-ran-dohl)*

glace [Fr.] Ice-cream. *(glas)*

glacé [Fr.] (Of fruit) iced; sugared; glazed. *(GLAS-ay)*

Gleichschaltung [Ger.] Standardisation of political and other institutions among authoritarian states. Elimination of political opposition. *(GLEYE-kh-shal-tung)*

glissade [Fr.] (In mountaineering) slide down slope, usually of snow or ice, usually on foot. *(glis-AYD)*

glissando [It.] (In music) playing a run of adjacent notes in quick succession as a single gliding sound (e.g. on piano, by drawing finger up or down part of keyboard instead of playing each note with different finger). *(glis-AND-oh)* Often abbreviated to **gliss.** Plural **glissandi.** *(-dee)*

glissée [Fr.] (In dancing) sliding step. *(GLEE-say)*

glockenspiel [Ger.] Musical instrument, normally consisting of metal plates (or bells or tubes), played with small hammers, producing light bell-like sound. *(GLOK-uhn-shpeel)*

gloire [Fr.] Glory. *(glwahr)* A word with peculiarly French overtones, in which intense patriotic, republican sense is prominent.

Gloria [Lat.] Part of Mass consisting of prayer beginning 'Glory be to God on high'. Music for this. *(GLOR-ee-a)* Abbreviation of **gloria in excelsis Deo.**

Gloria in excelsis Deo [Lat.] Glory be to God on high. *(GLOR-ee-a in ex-KEL-* or *-CHEL-sis DAY-oh)* See **gloria.**

Gloria Patri [Lat.] Glory be to the Father. *(GLOR-ee-a PAT-* or *PAHT-ri)*

gnocchi [It.] Small dumplings, of flour, potato or rice, usually served with cheese. *(NOK-* or *NYOK-i)*

gnomon [Gk.] Plate or rod which casts shadow on face of sun-dial, indicating time of day. *(NOH-mon)*

gnosis [Gk.] Knowledge of spiritual mysteries. *(NOH-sis)*

godet [Fr.] Triangular piece of material in garment to make flare. *(GOD-ay)*

gombeen [Ir.] Usury. *(gom-BEEN)* Thus **gombeen-man**, money-lender.

gondola [It.] Light boat with high pointed bow and stern, propelled by single oarsman at stern, used as passenger boat on canals of Venice. *(GON-doh-la)*

gopak [Russ.] Lively Russian dance. *(GOH-pak)*

Gorgonzola [It.] Type of Italian cheese, semi-soft, rich and blue-veined. *(gor-gon-ZOH-la)*

Gorsedd [Welsh] Meeting of Welsh bards and druids. *(GOR-seth)* The *th* is pronounced as in *than*.

Götterdämmerung [Ger.] Twilight of the Gods. Collapse and downfall of regime. *(ger-tuh-DEM-er-ung)*

gouache [Fr.] (In art) painting, or method of painting, in opaque water-colours. *(goo-ASH)*

goulash [Magyar] Stew of meat and vegetables, strongly seasoned. *(GOO-lash)*

gourmand [Fr.] Glutton. Gluttonous. *(goor-mahṅ)*

gourmandise [Fr.] Gluttony. *(goor-mahṅ-deez)*

gourmet [Fr.] Expert in good food. *(GOOR-may)*

goy [Heb.] (In Jewish parlance) non-Jew; gentile. *(goy)* Plural **goyim** *(GOY-im)*

gradatim [Lat.] Gradually; by degrees. *(grad-AH-tim)*

graffito [It.] Word, phrase, slogan, etc., often humorous or indecent, written or scratched on wall in public place. *(graf-EE-toh)* Plural **graffiti** *(graf-EE-ti)* is usually used as singular in preference to the above.

grand cru [Fr.] Famous vineyard or group of vineyards. Wine of the finest quality. *(grahṅ kroo)*

grande amoureuse [Fr.] Woman whose love-affairs are spectacular. *(grahṅd am-oor-urz)*

grande dame [Fr.] Great lady; lady of aristocratic dignity and bearing. *(grahṅd dam)*

grande école [Fr.] (In France) élite college of higher education, especially for public services. *(grahṅd ay-kol)*

grande passion [Fr.] Great passion; overwhelming love(-affair). *(grahṅd pas-yoṅ)*

grande tenue [Fr.] Full dress. *(grahṅd tuh-noo)*

Grand Guignol [Fr.] Short horror-play. Having macabre characteristics. *(grahṅ GEEN-yol)*

grandioso [It.] (Of music) in the grand style. *(gran-di-OH-soh)*

grand luxe [Fr.] The highest standard of luxury. *(grahṅ looks)*

grand mal [Fr.] Severe form of epilepsy. *(grahṅ mal)* See **petit mal.**

Grand Prix [Fr.] Major competition, usually international, in motor-racing, golf, etc. *(grahṅ pree)*

grand seigneur [Fr.] Great nobleman. Person who behaves as if he were such. *(grahṅ sehn-YUR)*

grand siècle [Fr.] (In France) the seventeenth century, especially the reign of Louis XIV. Any classical or golden age. *(grahṅ SYEK-luh)*

grand vin [Fr.] Great wine. *(grahṅ vaṅ)*

gran turismo [It.] High-performance car, speedy, spacious, luxurious, suitable for travelling in comfort over distances when touring. *(gran toor-IZ-moh)* Now used loosely by the motor trade to designate any mildly expensive or luxurious car.

grappa [It.] Italian brandy distilled from grape-skins after wine-making. *(gra-pa)*

gratin [Fr.] (In cookery) with crisp crust of breadcrumbs or grated cheese. *(grat-aṅ)* Usually found as **au gratin.**

gratiné [Fr.] (In cookery) covered with grated cheese or bread-crumbs. *(grat-ee-nay)* See above.

gratis [Lat.] Without charge. *(GRA-* or *GRAH-tis)*

gravamen [Lat.] Grievance. Most serious part of accusation. *(grav-AY-men)*

grave [It.] (In music) in grave, solemn style. *(GRAH-vay)*

Graves [Fr.] Wine, usually dry white, but sometimes red, from around Bordeaux or to the south east, along the bank of the Garonne. *(grahv)*

gravitas [Lat.] Solemn bearing. Serious-mindedness. *(GRAV-it-ahs)*

grazioso [It.] (In music) gracefully. *(grahts-YOH-soh)*

greffier [Fr.] Notary. *(GREF-yay)*

gringo [Sp.] (In Spanish America, especially Mexico) foreigner, especially American. *(GREEN-goh)*

grippe [Fr.] Influenza. *(greep)*

gros-grain [Fr.] Fabric made of corded silk. *(GROH-grahṅ* or *-grayṅ)*

gros point [Fr.] Cross-stitch. Embroidery executed in cross-stitches. *(groh pwaṅ)*

gruyère [Fr.] Mild, pale Swiss cheese, made from cow's milk and having numerous cavities. *(groo-yair)*

G.T. Abbreviation of **gran turismo.**

guano [Sp.] Bird-droppings, especially of sea-birds, used as manure. *(GWAH-noh)* Applied particularly to excrement accumulated over a very long period, especially in caves.

guéridon [Fr.] Small decorative table or ornamental stand. *(ger-ee-doṅ)*

guerrilla [Sp.] Person taking part in irregular warfare (e.g. revolutionary; terrorist; civilian engaged on sabotage of enemy invaders). *(gur-IL-a)* Often misspelt **guerilla.**

guichet [Fr.] Ticket-office window. Grille, grating, hatch through which business can be transacted. *(GEE-shay)*

guru [Hindi] Hindu spiritual teacher, or head of religious sect. Teacher or leader in matters of the spirit. *(GOO-roo)*

gutta-percha [Malay] Hard-wearing substance made from gum of Malayan trees. *(GUT-a PUR-cha)*

Gymnasium [Ger.] (In Germany) grammar school. *(gim-NAH-zyum)*

H

habanera [Sp.] Cuban dance in slow time, with rhythm similar to tango. Music for this. *(aban-AIR-a)*

habeas corpus [Lat.] Writ ordering prisoner or accused person to be brought before court. *(hab-ay-as KOR-pus)* Specially used when lawfulness of detention is to be established. Literally, 'you are to produce the body'.

habitué [Fr.] Habitual visitor, customer or frequenter of a place. *(ab-IT-too-* or *tyoo-ay)*

hacienda [Sp.] (In Spanish-speaking country) estate or plantation with house. Farm; ranch. *(has-* or *as-YEN-da)*

hadj [Arab.] Moslem pilgrimage to Mecca. *(haj)*

hadji [Arab.] Muslim who has made pilgrimage to Mecca. *(HAJ-i)*

haiku [Jap.] Highly concentrated Japanese verse form consisting of seventeen syllables arranged in three lines (5,7,5). *(HEYE-koo)*

hajj Same as **hadj.**

hajji Same as **hadji.**

haka [Maori] (In New Zealand) aboriginal dance. *(HAH-ka)* Best known from performances of rugby players before match.

hakenkreuz, Hakenkreuz [Ger.] Swastika. *(HAH-ken-kroyts)*

hakim [Arb.] Moslem physician. *(hah-KEEM)*

halitus [Lat.] Vapour. Emanation. *(HAL-it-us)*

halva(h) [Yiddish] Sweetmeat of ground sesame and honey. *(hahl-VAH)*

hamartia [Gk.] Tragic flaw, error or sin, especially character-defect, leading inevitably to downfall or death (especially in literature). *(ham-ar-TEE-a, ham-AR-tee-a)*

hara-kiri [Jap.] Suicide by disembowelment, as practiced ceremoniously by **samurai** in disgrace or facing death-sentence. *(ha-ra-KI-ri)* Loosely applied to any suicidal act, especially by soldier, etc. with high-minded (e.g. patriotic) intent.

harem [Arab.] Part of Muslim house where women live in seclusion. Women living thus. Any collection of concubines. *(HAH-reem, hah-REEM)*

haricot vert [Fr.] Green bean; string bean. *(ar-i-koh VAIR)*

hari-kari Incorrect version of **hara-kiri.**

hasta la vista [Sp.] Good-bye. *(AHS-ta la VEES-ta)*

hausfrau, Hausfrau [Ger.] (In Germany) housewife. *(HOWS-frow)* With implication of devotion and dullness.

haute bourgeoisie [Fr.] Upper-middle or professional class. *(oht boor-zhwah-ZEE)*

haute couture [Fr.] High-class dress-design and dress-making. *(oht koo-TOOR* or *koo-TYOHR)*

haute cuisine [Fr.] High-class cooking, especially French. *(oht kwee-ZEEN)*

haute école [Fr.] The most demanding feats of horsemanship. *(oht ay-kol)*

haute époque [Fr.] Art, especially architecture and furniture, of the reigns of Louis XIV, XV and XVI in France (i.e. mid-seventeenth century until French Revolution). *(oht ay-pok)*

hauteur [Fr.] Haughtiness. *(oht-UR)*

haute vulgarisation [Fr.] Popularisation of scholarly or obstruse matters. *(oht vool-gar-eez-AH-syorṅ)*

haut monde [Fr.] High society. *(oh MORṄD)*

hegira [Arab.] Muhammad's flight from Mecca (A.D.622). Any escape, flight, exodus or sudden departure. *(hej-EYE-ra, HEJ-i-ra)* Also applied to Muslim era dated from Muhammad's flight.

heil [Ger.] Hail! Long live . . .! *(heye-l)*

hejira Same as **hegira.**

Heldentenor [Ger.] (Singer with) tenor voice suited to powerful heroic rôles in opera. *(HEL-duhn-ten-or)*

helix [Gk.] Thing shaped like corkscrew or spring. *(HEE-lix)*

herbarium [Lat.] Collection of dried plants, catalogued, displayed or systematically arranged. Display of this. *(herb-AIR-i-um)*

Herr [Ger.] Mr. *(hair)* Plural **Herren** *(HAIR-uhn)*

Herrenvolk [Ger.] Master-race. *(HAIR-uhn-fol-k)* Applied by Nazis to German nation.

hic et ubique [Lat.] Here, (there) and everywhere. *(heek et OOB-ik-way)*

hic iacet Same as **hic jacet.**

hic jacet [Lat.] Here lies. *(heek YAK-et)* Followed by name of person. Found on tombstones, etc.

hidalgo [Sp.] (In Spain) nobleman; gentleman. *(ee-DAHL-goh, hid-AL-goh)*

hinterland [Ger.] District behind a coastal district, (sometimes with suggestion of remoteness, backwardness, poverty, etc.). Hence, any remote or fringe area. *(HIN-ter-land)*

hoi polloi [Gk.] The masses; the rabble. *(hoy-POL-oy)* Strictly speaking, it is incorrect to put 'the' before this expression, because that is what the first word means.

hokku Same as **haiku.**

hollandaise [Fr.] (In cookery) sauce of egg-yolks, butter and lemon-juice (often with white wine or wine vinegar). *(ol-ahn̊d-ez)* Usually served with fish.

hombre [Sp.] Man. *(OM-bray)*

homme d'affaires [Fr.] Businessman. *(om daf-AIR)*

homme du monde [Fr.] Man of the world. Mature or well-travelled man. *(om doo MORN̊D)*

homme moyen sensuel [Fr.] Average man; man in the street. *(om mweye-ahn̊ sahn̊-swel)*

homo erectus [Lat.] Species of early man, the first to stand habitually. *(HOM-oh* or *HOH-moh ir-EK-tus)*

homo sapiens [Lat.] Species of modern man; rational man as a species. *(HOM-oh* or *HOH-moh SAP-i-enz)*

homunculus [Lat.] Little man; manikin; pigmy. *(hom-UNK-oo-lus)*

Honi soit qui mal y pense [Fr.] Shame on him who thinks ill of it. *(on-ee SWA kee mal ee PAHN̊S)* Motto of the Order of the Garter.

honnête homme [Fr.] Honest, decent man. *(on-et OM)*

honoris causa [Lat.] As a mark of respect. In recognition of merit, esteem or distinction. *(on-OR-is KOW-zah)* Applied usually to honorary degree, i.e. awarded without examination.

hookah [Arab.] Oriental tobacco-pipe in which smoke passes through water in vase before being inhaled through long tube. *(HOO-ka)*

horribile dictu [Lat.] Horrible to relate. *(hor-EEB-il-eh DIK-too)*

hors concours [Fr.] (Exhibit) not competing for prize. Unrivalled; unequalled. *(or kom̊-koor)*

hors de combat [Fr.] Disabled. Out of action; out of the fighting. *(or duh kom̊-bah)*

hors d'œuvre [Fr.] Dish served as appetiser as first course of meal. *(or DUR-vruh* or *-DURV)*

hortus siccus [Lat.] Same as **herbarium.** *(HOR-tus SEE-kus)*

hôtel de ville [Fr.] (In France) town-hall. *(oh-tel duh veel)*

hôtelier [Fr.] Hotel-keeper. Hotel-owner. *(oh-tel-yay)* Now becoming anglicised as **hotelier** *(hoh-TELI-ay)*

houri [Pers.] Nymph in Muslim paradise. Any exceedingly attractive woman. *(HOO-ri)*

howdah [Urdu] Seat, usually with canopy, on elephant's back. *(HOW-dah)*

hubris [Gk.] Overweening pride, arrogance or presumption, especially (in Greek tragedy) towards the gods, thus bringing retribution. *(HYOO-bris)*

hula(-hula) [Hawaiian] (In Hawaii) graceful traditional dance performed by women with arm and hip movements representing story. *(HOO-lah)* Also applied to long grass skirt worn by such dancers.

hwyl [Welsh] (In Wales) emotional fervour characteristic of passionate preaching, rugby crowds, etc. *(HOO-il)*

hysteron proteron [Gk.] Inversion of natural order of logic, ideas, etc. *(his-ter-on PROT-er-on)*

I

iacta alea est [Lat.] The die is cast. *(YAK-ta AL-ay-a est)* Said to be spoken by Caesar on crossing the Rubicon.

ibid. Abbreviation of **ibidem.**

ibidem [Lat.] In the same place, book, chapter, etc. *(IB-id-em)* Most frequently found, in abbreviated form **ibid.**, in footnote in scholarly books, to refer to a book or chapter identified in the preceding footnote, so that repetition of full title, etc. is avoided.

ich dien [Ger.] I serve. *(ikh DEEN)* Motto of Prince of Wales.

id [Lat.] The unconscious, instinctive, inherited impulses of an individual. *(id)* Term used in psychology.

id. Abbreviation of **idem.**

idée fixe [Fr.] Fixed idea. Obsession. Idea that cannot be budged from the mind. *(ee-day FEEKS)* Plural **idées fixes** (same pronunciation).

idée reçue [Fr.] Idea, notion, opinion, doctrine that is generally accepted. *(ee-day ruh-SOO)* Plural **idées reçues** (same pronunciation).

idem [Lat.] The same. *(ID-em)* Used especially in footnote in scholarly books, to refer to author already named in previous footnote, so as to avoid repetition of his name. Often abbreviated to **id.**

id est [Lat.] That is. That is to say. *(id est)* Normally abbreviated to **i.e.**

i.e. Abbreviation of **id est.**

Iesus Hominum Salvator [Lat.] Jesus, the Saviour of Mankind. *(YEH-sus or ee-AY-sus HOM-in-um sal-VAH-tor)* Often abbreviated to **I.H.S.**

Iesus Nazarenus Rex Iudaeorum [Lat.] Jesus of Nazareth, King of the Jews. *(YEH-sus* or *ee-AY-sus Naz-ar-AY-nus rex yoo-day-OR-um)* See **I.N.R.I.**

ignis fatuus [Lat.] Will-o'-the-wisp. *(ig-nis FAT-oo-us* or *-yoo-us)* Name given to phosphorescent light hovering or flitting over marshy ground due to spontaneous combustion of gas from marsh. Hence, any deceptive or insubstantial guiding principle.

ignoratio elenchi [Lat.] (In logic) refuting an argument not advanced by opponent. *(ig-nor-AHT-ee-oh* or *ig-nor-AHSH-yoh el-ENG-ki)*

ignotum per ignotus [Lat.] Explanation that is more obscure than the thing being explained. Explanation of something obscure by reference to something even more obscure. *(ig-NOH-tum per ig-NOH-tus)*

I.H.S. Abbreviation of **Iesus Hominum Salvator**, or of **in hoc signo**, or of Greek word for Jesus.

illuminati [Lat., It.] People claiming special enlightenment. *(il-oo-min-AH-tee)* Also eighteenth-century Bavarian secret society holding deistic and republican views.

ils ne passeront pas [Fr.] They shall not pass. *(eel nuh pahs-uhr-oṅ pah)* Order issued to French at Battle of Verdun, 1916.

imago [Lat.] (In psychology) subconscious or mental picture of idealised person (self, parent, etc.). *(im-AH-goh)*

imam [Arab.] Moslem priest. Title of certain Moslem leaders. *(im-AHM)*

imbroglio [It.] Confused or complicated situation, misunderstanding, mix-up, etc. *(im-BROHL-yoh)*

Immortel [Fr.] Member of French Academy. *(im-or-tel)* Also **les Immortels**, the members of the French Academy. *(layz im-or-tel)*

impair [Fr.] (In roulette) odd number. *(aṁ-pair)* See **pair**.

impasse [Fr.] Deadlock. Situation from which there is no escape. *(aṁ-pas;* now increasingly anglicised to *IM-pas)*

impasto [It.] (In art) application of paint very thickly. This style of painting. *(im-PAS-toh)*

impedimenta [Lat.] Encumbrances, especially baggage, travelling-equipment, etc. *(im-ped-im-ENT-a)*

imperium [Lat.] Absolute power. Empire. *(im-PEH-ri-um)*

imperium in imperio [Lat.] Supreme authority within jurisdiction of another authority. *(im-PEH-ri-um in im-PEH-ri-oh)*

imprimatur [Lat.] Authority, official approval (especially to print or publish something). Sanction. *(im-prim-AH-toor* or *-AY-tuh)*

imprimatura [It.] (In painting) coloured wash or transparent glaze used as primer or after completion of preliminary drawing. *(im-pree-mat-OOR-ah)*

impromptu [Lat.] Without preparation. Musical composition with the character of an improvisation. *(im-PROMPT-yoo)*

in absentia [Lat.] In the absence (of a person). *(in ab-SENT-ee-a)*

in aeternum [Lat.] For ever. *(in eye-TERN-um)*

inamorato [It.] Lover. *(in-am-or-AH-toh)* Feminine **inamorata.** *(in-am-or-AH-tah)*

in camera [Lat.] In private or secret session, not in public. *(in KAM-era)* Often applied to legal proceedings.

incipit [Lat.] Here begins. *(in-KIP-* or *-SIP-it)* First words of book, manuscript, etc.

incognito [It.] Under an assumed name. In disguise; with one's identity kept secret. *(in-kog-NEE-toh)*

incommunicado [Sp.] Without means of communication with other people. In solitary confinement. *(in-kom-yoo-nik-AH-doh)*

incubus [Lat.] Evil spirit supposed to descend on people in their sleep, and specially to have sexual intercourse with women. *(IN-kyoo-bus)* Hence, any person who is a burden to another. See **succubus.**

incunabula [Lat.] Early books, printed before sixteenth century. *(in-kyoo-NAB-yoo-lah)* Singular **incunabulum.**

index librorum prohibitorum [Lat.] List of books prohibited by Roman Catholic Church, or to be read by Roman Catholics only in censored versions. *(in-dex lib-ROR-um proh-HIB-it-or-um)*

in esse [Lat.] In existence; in being; in real fact. *(in ES-eh)* As opposed to **in posse.**

in extenso [Lat.] In full; at full length. *(in ex-TEN-soh)*

in extremis [Lat.] At the point of death. *(in ex-TREE-* or *-TREH-mis)*

infanta [Sp., Port.] Daughter of King and Queen of Spain or Portugal. *(in-FAN-ta)* Usually eldest daughter who is not heir to throne.

inferno [It.] Hell. *(in-FER-noh)* Also applied to any place or scene of horror or misery, especially a conflagration.

in flagrante delicto [Lat.] In the very act of committing an offence. *(in flag-RAN-ti del-IK-toh)*

in forma pauperis [Lat.] Not liable for costs on account of poverty. *(in FOR-ma POR-* or *POW-per-is)*

infra [Lat.] Below, further on (in book). *(IN-fra)* Often found in footnote in book, to refer reader to subsequent page.

infra dig. Abbreviation of **infra dignitatem.**

infra dignitatem [Lat.] Beneath one's dignity. Not suitable to one's position. *(in-fra dig-nit-AH-tem)* Almost always abbreviated to **infra dig.**

ingénue [Fr.] Young woman of artless, ingenuous, innocent simplicity. *(AṄ-zhay-noo)* Specially applied to type of stage rôle, or to actress playing such a rôle in play.

in hoc signo [Lat.] In this sign (i.e. the sign of the Cross). *(in hok SIG-noh* or *SEE-nyoh)* Often as abbreviation of **in hoc signo vinces**, in this sign thou shalt conquer (motto of Constantine the Great). See also **I.H.S.**

in loco parentis [Lat.] In the place of a parent (i.e. with authority and responsibility proper to a parent). *(in LOK-oh par-EN-tis)* Especially applied to responsibility of school-teacher.

in medias res [Lat.] Into the middle of things, especially of a narrative. Without preamble or introduction. *(in MED-i-ahs RAYS)*

in memoriam [Lat.] In memory (of). *(in mem-OR-ee-am)* Also applied to any piece of writing, etc., in memory of dead person.

in nomine Patris et Filii et Spiritus Sancti [Lat.] In the name of the Father, and of the Son, and of the Holy Spirit. *(in nom-in-eh PAH-tris et FEEL-i-ee et SPI-ri-toos SANK-tee)*

in partibus [Lat.] In heathen or heretical areas. *(in PAHT-i-bus)* Applied to bishop, especially Roman Catholic, of non-Christian see.

in pectore [Lat.] In one's heart; secretly. *(in PEK-toh-reh)*

in perpetuum [Lat.] For ever. *(in per-PET-oo-um)*

in petto [It.] Same as **in pectore.** *(in PET-oh)* Applied particularly to Cardinals appointed but not named.

in posse [Lat.] Potentially. *(in POS-eh)* As opposed to **in esse.**

in propria persona [Lat.] In his or her own person. *(in PROH-* or *PRO-pree-a per-SOH-na)*

in puris naturalibus [Lat.] Stark naked. *(in PYOO-* or *POO-ris nat-yoo* or *-oo-RAHL-ib-us)*

in re [Lat.] Concerning; in the matter of. *(in ray)* See **re.**

I.N.R.I. Abbreviation of **Iesus Nazarenus Rex Iudaeorum.** In paintings of the Crucifixion, often inscribed on notice above head of Christ.

in saecula saeculorum [Lat.] For ever and ever. *(in SEYE-koo-la seye-koo-LOH-rum)*

in situ [Lat.] In its original place. On the spot. *(in SIT-yoo* or *-oo)*

insouciance [Fr.] Lack of concern. *(in-SOO-see-ans* or *aṅ-soo-syahṅs)*

insouciant [Fr.] Unconcerned. Carefree. *(in-SOO-see-ant* or *aṅ-soo-syahṅ)*

instanter [Lat.] Immediately. *(in-STAN-ter)*

in statu pupillari [Lat.] Having the status of pupils or a pupil. In junior status (at university, etc.) *(in STAT-oo* or *-yoo poo-* or *pyoo-pil-AH-ri)*

in statu quo [Lat.] In the same state as before. *(in STAT-oo* or *-yoo kwoh)*

intaglio [It.] Incised carving. Engraved design. Method of printing from engraved plates. *(in-TAL-* or *-TAHL-yoh)*

inter alia [Lat.] Amongst other things. *(in-ter AY-li-a* or *A-li-a* or *AH-li-a)* Should not be used of people.

intermezzo [It.] Short instrumental piece of music, especially between acts of opera or major divisions of choral work. *(in-ter-METS-oh)*

Internationale [Fr.] French revolutionary song, now adopted as socialist anthem. *(an̄-ter-nas-yon-AHL* or *in-ter-nash-on-AHL)*

interregnum [Lat.] Period between rulers. *(in-ter-REG-num)* Also applied to any period after departure of person in authority and before arrival of successor (e.g. period when parish is without priest).

inter se [Lat.] Between or among themselves. *(in-ter SAY)*

inter vivos [Lat.] Between living people. *(in-ter VEE-vohs)* Applied, in law, to gift made during life of benefactor.

in toto [Lat.] Completely. As a whole. *(in TOH-toh)*

intra muros [Lat.] Within the confines (of an establishment, policy, etc.). *(in-tra MOO-* or *-MYOO-rohs)*

intra vires [Lat.] Within the authority or power (of a body, person, etc.). *(in-tra VEE* or *VEYE-rays)*

in utero [Lat.] In the womb. *(in YOO-ter-oh)*

in vacuo [Lat.] In a vacuum. Without reference to related circumstances, arguments, etc. *(in VAK-yoo-oh)*

in vino veritas [Lat.] In wine there is the truth. A drunken man always speaks the truth. *(in VEE-noh VER-it-ahs)*

in vitro [Lat.] In the test-tube. In laboratory conditions. *(in VIT-* or *VEET-roh)* Compare **in vivo.**

in vivo [Lat.] In the living body. *(in VEE-voh)* Compare **in vitro.**

ipse dixit [Lat.] Dogmatic assertion by person in authority, on the basis of that authority alone. *(ip-si DIX-it)*

ipsissima verba [Lat.] The precise words. *(ip-SIS-im-a VER-ba)*

ipso facto [Lat.] By that very fact. *(ip-soh FAK-toh)*

J

jabot [Fr.] Ornamental ruffle or frill, often of lace, on front of woman's bodice or blouse, especially at throat. *(ZHAB-oh)*

jacquard, Jacquard [Fr.] Loom using perforated cards to form patterns on woven fabric. Fabric thus woven. *(ZHAK-ar)*

J

jacquerie [Fr.] Peasants' revolt. *(ZHAK-er-ee)*

jacta alea est or **est alea** [Lat.] Same as **iacta alea est.**

jaeger Same as **Jäger.**

Jäger [Ger.] (In German or Austrian army) rifleman. Hunter. *(YAY-ger)*

Jah, Jahveh, Jahweh [Heb.] Jehova. Name of God in Old Testament. *(yah, YAH-vay, YAH-way)*

jalousie [Fr.] Blind or shutter made of slats to exclude rain but admit sunlight. *(ZHAH-loo-zee)*

jambon [Fr.] Ham *(zhahm-bon̄)*

jardinière [Fr.] Decorative pot or stand for display of flowers. *(zhah-din-YAIR)*

jaspé [Fr.] Randomly coloured. Mottled. *(JAS-* or *ZHAS-pay)*

jellaba [Arab.] Loose cloak with hood, worn by male Arab. *(JEL-ab-a)*

je ne sais quoi [Fr.] An indefinable thing, feeling, etc. *(zhuh-nuh-say-kwah)*

jeté [Fr.] (In ballet) leap from one foot to the other, the free leg being extended or kicked. *(zhuh-tay)*

jeu [Fr.] Game. *(zhur)*

jeu de mots [Fr.] Play on words. Pun. *(zhur duh moh)*

jeu d'esprit [Fr.] Light-hearted or witty trifle. *(zhur des-pree)*

jeune fille [Fr.] Young girl. *(zhurn fee-y)*

jeune premier [Fr.] Actor playing main part of young hero or lover. *(zhurn pruhm-yay)*

jeunesse dorée [Fr.] Gilded youth. Young men and women of talent, wealth or fashion. *(zhurn-es doh-ray)*

jeux sont faits See **les jeux sont faits.**

jibba(h) [Arab.] Long coat worn by male Muslim. *(JIB-a)*

jinn, jinnee, jinni [Arab.] Spirit, with supernatural power, able to take human or animal form. *(jin, jin-EE)* Plural **jinn.**

jinricksha(w), jinrickisha [Jap.] Light, two-wheeled hooded cab pulled by one person (or two). *(jin-RIK-shor)*

jiu-jitsu [Jap.] Same as **ju-jitsu.**

joie de vivre [Fr.] Joy of being alive. Feeling of high-spirited enjoyment of life. *(zhwah duh vee-vruh)*

jolie-laide [Fr.] Woman whose ugliness is attractive. *(zhol-ee lehd)*

jongleur [Fr.] Wandering minstrel. *(zhon̄-glur)*

jour de fête [Fr.] Festival; feast-day; holiday. *(joor duh feht)*

Jubilate Deo [Lat.] O be joyful in the Lord. Canticle consisting of Psalm 100. *(joob-il-AH-teh DAY-oh)* First two words of Latin version of Psalm 100.

ju-jitsu [Jap.] Japanese system of wrestling, using opponent's own weight (or strength) to throw him. *(joo-JIT-soo)*

ju(-)ju [Fr.] West African fetish or charm, supposed to exercise supernatural power or to deserve veneration. *(joo-joo)*

julienne [Fr.] Soup of vegetables cooked in meat broth. *(zhoo-LYEN)* In cookery, the word is specifically applied to vegetables cut into thin, short stripes like matchsticks.

Junker [Ger.] Member of land-owning Prussian aristocracy noted for arrogance, militarism, exclusivity. *(YOONG-ker)*

junta [Sp.] Administrative council or committee, often with military power, exercising government, usually undemocratically or after revolution. Any ruling clique. *(JUN-ta, YUN-tah)*

jusquauboutisme [Fr.] Preparedness to see something through to the end. *(zhoo-skoh-boot-eesm)* From the French phrase **jusqu'au bout**, to the end. Also **jusquauboutiste** *(-eest)*, one who is prepared to see a thing through to its finish.

juste milieu [Fr.] Golden mean. Happy medium. *(joost meel-yur)*

juvenilia [Lat.] Works produced by artist in his youth. *(joo-ven-IL-ee-a)*

j'y suis, j'y reste [Fr.] Here I am and here I stay. *(zhee swee zhee rest)* Attributed to General MacMahon at fall of Sebastopol in Crimean War.

K

K. Abbreviation of **köchel.**

kabab, kabob Same as **kebab.**

kabuki [Jap.] Traditional popular Japanese drama, with music, song and stylised dancing, performed by men. *(kab-OO-ki)*

kaffeeklatsch [Ger.] Meeting for coffee and conversation, especially by women. *(KAF-ayk-lach)* Mainly American usage.

Kaffir [Arab.] (In South Africa) member of Bantu tribe. *(KAF-eer)* Derogatory term.

kaftan Same as **caftan.**

Kaiser [Ger.] (In Germany or Austria) emperor. *(KEYE-zer)*

kakemono [Jap.] Japanese picture on scroll so that it can be rolled up for storage when not unrolled for display or hanging. *(ka-ki-MOH-noh)*

Kamerad [Ger.] Comrade. Cry for mercy when surrendering. *(KAHM-er-ahdt)*

kamikaze [Jap.] Aircraft, sometimes loaded with explosives, deliberately crashed on to enemy target, with suicide of pilot. Pilot who does this. *(ka-mi-KAH-zi)*

kanaka [Hawaiian] Hawaiian or South Sea Islander, especially one employed by Australian or European. *(kan-AH-ka)*

kapellmeister [Ger.] Conductor of orchestra or choir. *(kap-EL-meye-ster)*

kaput [Ger.] Done for. Out of order. Useless. Smashed. Dead. Finished. *(kap-UT)* Slang. Correct German spelling is **kaputt.**

karate [Jap.] System of unarmed combat using bare hands and feet. *(kar-AH-teh)*

karma [Sanskrit] (In Buddhism and Hinduism) total of person's actions, which decides his destiny for his next incarnation. *(KAH-ma)*

kasbah See **casbah.**

kayak [Eskimo] Canoe consisting of light frame with covering which also laces round user's waist. *(KEYE-ak)*

kebab [Urdu] Small pieces of seasoned meat (sometimes with vegetables) cooked and/or served on skewer. *(ki-BAB)*

kendo [Jap.] Japanese type of fencing, with two-handed bamboo swords. *(KEN-doh)*

képi [Fr.] (In France) round military cap with straight sides, flat top and horizontal peak. *(kay-pee)*

kermesse [Fr.] (In Flanders and other low countries) village fair; annual carnival. *(kehr-mes)*

kermis [Dut.] Same as **kermesse.** *(KER-mis)* Also, in America, a charity bazaar.

K.G.B. [Russ.] (In Russia) state secret police. Abbreviation of Komitet Gosudarstvennoi Bezopasnosti.

khamsin [Arab.] Oppressive hot wind blowing from south in Egypt in spring. *(KAM-sin)*

khan [Turk.] Title of ruler or official in some Central Asian countries. *(kahn)*

khedive [Fr.] Title of Turkish viceroy in Egypt, 1867–1914. *(keh-DEEV)*

kibbutz [Heb.] (In Israel) collective farm or communal settlement. *(kib-UTS)* Plural **kibbutzim** *(kib-uts-EEM)*

kibbutznik [Heb.] Member of **kibbutz.** *(kib-UTS-nik)*

kibitzer [Yiddish] Meddlesome person who gives unwanted advice (especially such spectator of card-game). *(KIB-it-ser)*

kimono [Jap.] Long loose Japanese robe with wide (usually shortened) sleeves, and waist-sash. *(kim-OH-noh)*

kindergarden [Ger.] School for very young children below normal school age (i.e. less than five years old). *KIN-der-gah-ten)*

kirsch(wasser) [Ger.] Spirit distilled from cherries. Cherry brandy. *(KEERSH(vah-ser))*

kismet [Turk.] Fate. Destiny. *(KIZ-met)*

kitsch [Ger.] Cheap, tasteless, gaudy rubbish. Works of art which are pretentious and vulgar. *(kitch)*

Kiwi [Maori] New Zealander. *(KEE-wi)* Colloquial.

knesset [Heb.] Israeli parliament. *(kuh-NES-et)*

Köchel [Ger. name] Authoritative identification of composition by Mozart in Köchel's catalogue, by which Mozart's works are always numbered. *(KUR-khuhl)* Usually found in the expression **Köchel number**, normally abbreviated to **K.** in writing.

koh-i-noor [Pers.] Large diamond. Anything in a class of its own. *(KOH-i-noor)* Name of famous Indian diamond of 106 carats in British Crown Jewels.

Kohl [Arab.] Powder used as eye-shadow in Eastern countries. *(kohl)*

koine [Gk.] Language common to large area and several peoples. *(KOY-neh)* Also **Koine**, common language of ancient Greeks.

kolkhoz [Russ.] (In Russia) collective farm. *(KOL-koz)*

Kommandatura [Ger.] Headquarters of occupying military forces. *(kom-ahn-dat-OO-ra)*

Komsomol [Russ.] (In Russia) Communist league of youth. Member of this. *(KOM-som-ol)*

kope(c)k Same as **copeck.**

Koran [Arab.] Sacred book of the Muslims. *(kor-AHN)*

kosher [Heb.] (Of food) prepared in accordance with Jewish dietary laws. *(KOH-sher)* Colloquially, the word is applied to something that is legitimate, genuine, etc.

kowtow [Chin.] Show obsequiousness or subservience. *(kow-TOW)* Literally (in China), touch ground with forehead as sign of submission.

kraal [Afrikaans] (In S. Africa) native village of huts surrounded by fence, with central enclosure for animals. *(krahl)*

Kraft durch Freude [Ger.] Strength through joy. *(KRAHFT doorkh FROY-duh)* Name of Nazi organisation to provide mass recreation.

kraken [Norw.] Very large mythical sea-monster supposed to appear off Norwegian coast. *(KRAH-ken)*

krans, krantz, kranz [Afrikaans] (In geology) wall of rock. *(krahns, krahnts)*

Kraut [Ger.] German. *(krowt)* Derogatory word, originating in Second World War, from German fondness for **sauerkraut**.

krees Same as **kris.**

kremlin [Russ.] (In Russian town) citadel. *(KREM-lin)* Hence **Kremlin**, citadel of Moscow, seat of Russian government; the government itself.

kriegspiel [Ger.] Type of war-game, with pieces representing military forces moved about on map. Version of chess in which player is told, but does not see, opponent's move. *(KREEG-shpeel)*

kris [Malay] Malayan dagger. *(krees)*

kukri [Hind.] Curved knife with blade broadening towards point, used by Gurkhas. *(KOO-kri)*

kulak [Russ.] (In Russia) well-to-do peasant. *(KOO-lak)*

Kultur [Ger.] System of intellectual, moral, political and economic progress, involving subordination of the individual to the State, as a tenet of German imperialism. *(kool-TOOR)* The word, which does not mean culture, has overtones of militarism and racial arrogance.

Kulturkampf [Ger.] Struggle between civil authorities and Roman Catholic church (especially that in Prussia in nineteenth century), especially over control of education. *(kool-TOOR-kahmpf)*

kümmel, Kummel [Ger.] Sweet liqueur flavoured with caraway seeds. *(KOO-muhl)*

kung fu [Chin.] Chinese form of **karate.** *(kung-FOO)*

Kuomintang [Chin.] (In China) People's National Party, major political party between fall of Emperor and communist victory of 1948. *(KWO-min-tang)*

kursaal [Ger.] Public room(s) at health resort. *(KOOR-zahl)*

kwas(s) [Russ.] (In Russia) rye-beer. *(kvahs)*

kyrie Abbreviation of **kyrie eleison.**

kyrie eleison [Gk.] Lord have mercy. *(KEE-ree-eh el-AY-i-son)* Opening words of petition in Roman Catholic and Orthodox Mass, and in Communion Service of Anglican Church. Also applied to musical setting of this petition.

L

la [Fr.] the. *(lah)* Followed by surname of woman to signify disapproval of her over-bearing manner.

laager [Afrikaans] Camp, especially military or defensive encampment, within circle of wagons. *(LAH-ger)*

labarum [Lat.] Symbolic banner. *(LAB-ar-um)* Specifically applied to Constantine the Great's standard, showing both Roman and Christian symbols.

la belle France [Fr.] Beautiful France. *(la bel Frahns)* Common phrase applied to France without any strongly descriptive intention—rather like 'Merrie England'.

Lachryma Christi Same as **Lacrima Christi.**

Lacrima Christi [Lat.] Name of Italian red and white wines from area of Mount Vesuvius. *(LAK-ri-ma KRIS-ti)*

lacrymae rerum See **sunt lacrymae rerum.**

lacuna [Lat.] Missing portion, blank, gap (especially in manuscript, book, etc.). *(lak-YOO-na)*

La Girconda See **Gioconda.**

laissez-aller; laisser-aller [Fr.] Lack of restraint in speech, manner, etc. *(les-ay al-ay)*

laissez-faire; laisser-faire [Fr.] Governmental policy of non-intervention, especially in economic matters. *(les-ay FAIR)*

laissez-passer; laisser-passer [Fr.] Permit; pass. *(les-ay pah-say)*

lakh [Hind.] One hundred thousand. *(lahk)*

lama [Tibetan] (In Tibet) Buddhist priest or monk. *(LAH-ma)* See **Dalai Lama.**

La Manche [Fr.] The English Channel. *(la MAHṄSH)*

lamé [Fr.] (Fabric) with interwoven threads of silver or gold. *(LAH-may)*

Ländler, ländler [Ger.] Popular German dance in slowish waltz time. Music for this. *(LEND-ler)*

Langlauf [Ger.] Cross-country skiing. *(LANG-lowf)*

langouste [Fr.] Lobster. *(lahṅ-goost)*

langoustine [Fr.] Large prawn. Baby crawfish. *(lahṅ-goost-een)*

langue de chat [Fr.] Thin finger-shaped biscuit (or piece of chocolate). *(lahṅg-duh-shah)*

langue d'oc [Fr.] Medieval French as spoken south of Loire. Provençal. *(lahṅguh dok)*

langue d'oïl [Fr.] Medieval French as spoken north of Loire, the basis of modern French. *(lahṅguh duh-eel)*

la nostalgie de la boue See **nostalgie de la boue.**

lapis lazuli [Lat.] Bright blue mineral used as gem (or made into pigment). *(lap-is LAZ-yoo-lee)*

lapsus calami [Lat.] Slip of the pen. *(LAP-sus KAL-am-i)*

lapsus linguae [Lat.] Slip of the tongue. *(LAP-sus LING-weye* or *-wee* or *-wi)*

lares et penates [Lat.] Home. *(LAH-rays et pen-AH-tays)* Literally, household gods.

La Reyne le veult [Obsolete Fr.] The Queen wishes it. *(la ren luh vurlt)* Formula used in signifying Royal Assent to Act of Parliament during reign of a queen.

larghetto [It.] (Of music) slow and dignified, but less so than **largo.** *(lah-GET-oh)*

largo [It.] (Of music) slow, dignified in style. Piece of music in this manner. *(LAH-goh)*

l'art pour l'art [Fr.] Art for art's sake. *(lah poor lah)*

lasagna, lasagne [It.] Dish of pasta (in broad, flat pieces) with minced meat and sauce of cheese, tomato, etc. *(las-AN-ya, -yeh)*

Lascar [Urdu] East Indian sailor. *(LAS-kah)*

latifundia [Lat.] Large estates (especially in Spanish-speaking countries). *(lati-FUND-ee-a)*

la trahison des clercs. See **trahison des clercs.**

laudator temporis acti [Lat.] One who praises times past (and thus criticises times present). *(low-DAH-tor TEM-por-is AK-tee)* From Horace's *Ars Poetica.*

lavabo [Lat.] Ritual washing of priests' hands after offertory at Mass. Vessel used for this. Washing-place in monastery. *(lav-AH-boh)*

layette [Fr.] Set of clothes and other requisites for newly-born baby. *(lay-ET)*

lb. [Lat.] Pound(s) (weight). Abbreviation of **libra.**

lebensraum [Ger.] Territory which Nazi government claimed was necessary for Germany's development and enlarging population. Living space. *(LAY-benz-rowm)*

Leberwurst [Ger.] Liver-sausage. *(LAY-ber-voorst)*

lederhosen [Ger.] Leather shorts, usually with leather braces, as worn by men and boys in Bavaria, etc. *(LAY-der-hohz-en)*

legato [It.] (Of music) smoothly, with no break between notes. *(leg-AH-toh)*

Légion d'Honneur [Fr.] (In France) Legion of Honour. *(lay-zhoñ don-UR)* Honour awarded for civil or military distinction. Founded by Napoleon, 1802.

légionnaire, legionnaire [Fr.] Member of a legion, especially Foreign Legion. Legion of ex-servicemen. *(lay-zhon-air, lee-j'n-AIR)*

lei [Hawaiian] Wreath of flowers, worn round neck and presented as greeting. *(lay)*

leitmotiv or **-tif** [Ger.] Musical theme associated with particular person, place or sentiment and recurring throughout opera in that connexion. Any recurrent theme or central idea in any work of art. *(LEYE-t-moh-teef)* Term introduced by Wagner, whose operas illustrate it.

le mot juste See **mot juste.**

lento [It.] (Of music) played slowly. *(LEN-toh)*

leprechaun [Ir.] Tiny sprite supposed to do good to people who show good will to him. *(LEP-rek-orn)*

le roi est mort; vive le roi [Fr.] The king is dead; long live the king. *(luh rwah eh mor; veev luh rwah)*

le Roi Soleil [Fr.] The Sun King—Louis XIV of France. *(luh rwah sol-ay)*

le Roy le veult [Obsolete Fr.] The King wishes it. *(luh roy luh vurlt)* Formula used in signifying Royal Assent to Act of Parliament during reign of a king.

les [Fr.] The (applied to plural noun). *(lay)* Often used in title of group of performers (e.g. in circus or music hall) to suggest French **chic** or **panache.**

lèse-majesté [Fr.] Treason; offence against majesty of ruler or people. Any (supposed) impertinent or presumptuous conduct against person in authority. *(layz-MAZH-est-ay)* Term often used to imply criticism of pomposity of person in authority. Also anglicised to **lese-majesty** *(leez-MAJ-esti)*

les jeux sont faits [Fr.] (In roulette) no more stakes may be laid. *(lay zhur soṅ fay)*

le style est l'homme même [Fr.] Style in the man himself: a man's (especially a writer's) style reveals his personality. *(luh steel ay lom mehm)* Quotation from Buffon, *Discours sur le Style*, usually expressed as **le style, c'est l'homme.**

l'état, c'est moi [Fr.] I am the State. *(lay-tah, say mwah)* Attributed to Louis XIV.

lettre de cachet [Fr.] Document authorising summary imprisonment, arrest or exile. *(letr duh kash-ay)* Originally, written order from King of France for imprisonment without trial.

levée, levee [Fr.] Ceremonial reception of visitors by sovereign. *(luh-vay, LEV-i)* Originally, reception of visitors by sovereign on getting out of bed.

le vice anglais [Fr.] The English vice—homosexuality. *(luh vees ahṅ-glay)* Now often applied, humorously, to strike action.

lex talionis [Lat.] Law of retaliation, i.e. where punishment resembles crime. *(lex tali-OH-nis)*

liana, liane [Fr.] Climbing and twining plants found in tropical jungles. *(li-AH-na, li-AHN)*

libero [It.] (In football) designer of pattern of attack from mid-field position. *(LEE-ber-oh)*

liberté, égalité, fraternité [Fr.] Liberty, equality, fraternity. *(lee-ber-tay, ay-gal-ee-tay, frah-ter-nee-tay)* Motto of France; slogan of French Revolution.

libido [Lat.] (In psychology) the instinctual or psychic drive of human beings, especially the sexual urge. *(lib-EE-doh)*

libra [Lat.] Pound(s) weight or sterling. *(LIB-ra)* Normally abbreviated to **lb.** for weight and **£** (or **L.**) for sterling.

libretto [It.] Text to which a musical composition, especially opera or operetta, is set. *(lib-RET-oh)*

Liebfraumilch [Ger.] Mild, semi-sweet German white wine of modest quality. *(LEEP-frow-milkh)*

lied [Ger.] Song, especially German and Austrian song by classical composer in nineteenth century. *(leet)* Plural **lieder** *(LEED-er)*

lieder See above.

lignum vitae [Lat.] Wood of tropical American tree. Medicine from this. *(LIG-num VEE-tye* or *-ti* or *-tay)*

Limburger [Dut.] Soft cheese with strong flavour and smell. *(LIM-bur-ger)* Originally Made in Limburg, Belgium.

lingerie [Fr.] Women's underwear. *(LAṄ-zhuh-ree)*

lingua franca [It.] Mixture of Italian and some other Mediterranean languages, used in Eastern Mediterranean, especially for trading purposes, usually in ports. Any language used for communication among peoples of different nations. *(LIN-gwa FRAN-ka)*

l'istesso tempo [It.] (In printed music) maintain the same speed as before. *(lee-stes-oh TEM-poh)*

literati [It.] Literary people. The cultured or learned class. *(lit-er-AH-tee)*

literatim [Lat.] Literally. Letter by letter. *(lit-er-AH-tim)*

litotes [Gk.] Literary device of understatement, expressing something by the negative of its opposite (e.g. expressing *like* by the term *not unlike*). *(leye-TOH-tees)*

litterae humaniores [Lat.] Classics, especially as subject of study at Oxford. *(LIT-er-eye hyoo-mani-OAR-ays)*

littérateur [Fr.] Literary man. *(lit-ay-rat-UR)* Feminine **littératrice** *(-REES)*.

locale [Fr.] Locallity, place where something happens. *(loh-KAHL)*

loc. cit. Abbreviation of **loco citato.**

loco citato [Lat.] In the place or passage already quoted. *(LOK-oh sit-AH-toh)* Found especially in footnotes of scholarly books to avoid repetition of full title or other full details to which reader is being referred. Normally abbreviated to **loc. cit.** See also **opere citato.**

loco parentis See **in loco parentis.**

locum Abbreviation of **locum tenens.**

locum tenens [Lat.] Person performing professional duties of someone in his absence, especially absence of doctor or clergyman. *(LOH-k'm TEN-ens)* Usually shortened to **locum.**

locus classicus [Lat.] Most authoritative place, usually book, where a particular subject is expounded, exemplified, stated, etc. *(LOK-us KLAS-ik-us)*

locus in quo [Lat.] Scene of event. *(LOK-us in KWOH)*

locus standi [Lat.] Recognised position. (In law) right to appear in court. *(LOK-us STAND-ee* or *-eye)*

loden [Ger.] Thick woollen cloth. *(LOH-den)*

loge [Fr.] Box in theatre. *(lohzh)*

loggia [It.] Gallery or arcade with both sides (or one side) open. Covered, paved, open-sided area adjoining house as terrace, sun-porch, etc. *(LOH-* or *LO-ja* or *-jya)*

Logos [Gk.] The Word of God. *(LOG-os)* See below.

logos [Gk.] (In Greek philosophy) the divine mind or rational principle. *(LOG-os)* See above.

longueur [Fr.] Tediously lengthy passage (in play, book, speech, etc.). *(loṅ-GUR)*

loquitur [Lat.] (In stage direction of printed play) speaks. *(LOK-wit-ur)* Always followed by speaker's name.

lorgnette [Fr.] Pair of spectacles held to eyes by long handle. *(lorn-YET)*

louche [Fr.] Shifty, disreputable (especially in devious way). *(loosh)*

L.s.d. [Lat.] Pounds, shillings, pence. Abbreviation of **librae, solidi, denarii.**

luau [Hawaiian] Hawaiian or Hawaiian-style party or banquet. *(loo-OW)* Mainly American usage.

lucus a non lucendo [Lat.] Paradoxical explanation. Explanation of something (especially word) by the opposite of what it suggests. *(LOO-kus ah nohn look-END-oh)*

Luftwaffe [Ger.] German Air Force in Nazi times. *(LOOFT-vah-fuh)*

luge [Fr.] One-man toboggan, especially as used in competitive winter sport. *(loozh)*

lumpen [Ger.] Incapable of coherent action as a result of mental (or physical) poverty. *(LUMP-en)*

lumpenproletariat [Ger.] The common people, poor, uneducated but contented, not interested in or capable of bettering themselves (especially by revolution). *(LUMP-en-proh-let-AIR-ee-at)* Derogatory term.

lunette [Fr.] Arched aperture, or painting of semi-circular or crescent shape, in dome or vaulted ceiling. *(loo-NET)*

lustrum [Lat.] Period of five years. *(LUST-rum)* Plural **lustra.**

lusus (naturae) [Lat.] Freak of nature. *(LOO-sus nat-OOR* or *-YOOR-ee* or *-i* or *-eye)*

luxe [Fr.] Luxury. *(looks)*

lycée [Fr.] (In France) state secondary (usually grammar) school. *(LEE-say)*

M

M. Abbreviation of **Monsieur.**

macabre [Fr.] Gruesome. *(mak-AH-br)*

macaroni [It.] Type of **pasta** in tube form. *(mak-a-ROH-ni)* Also (now obsolete) the name given to a vicious fop in the late eighteenth century and subsequently.

macédoine [Fr.] Dish of mixed vegetables or fruit, cut into small pieces, especially cubes. *(ma-say* or *-si-DWAHN)*

Mach [Ger.] Speed of sound used as unit of measurement, especially in aircraft. *(mahk)* From Ernst Mach, Austrian physicist.

ma chère [Fr.] My dear. *(mah shair)* Applied only to women.

machete [Sp.] Heavy wide-bladed knife, wielded like axe or cutlass, used to cut stout plants (e.g. jungle undergrowth, sugar-cane) in America and W. Indies; also used as weapon. *(ma-CHEH-* or *-CHAY-teh)*

machismo [Sp.] Virility, masculinity. Display of this. Need to prove this by action. *(ma-CHIZ-* or *CHEEZ-moh)*

macho [Sp.] Aggressively or ostentatiously virile or masculine. *(MACH-oh, MAHCH-oh)* Also abbreviation of **machismo.**

machree Same as **mochree.**

machtpolitik [Ger.] Power politics. *(MAHKHT-pol-it-eek)*

Mâcon [Fr.] French wine, especially white, from region of Mâcon, Burgundy. *(MAH-kom̀)*

macramé [Turk.] Fringe or trimming of knotted thread. Technique of making this. *(mak-RAH-may)*

macushla Same as **acushla.**

Madame [Fr.] Proprietress of brothel. *(ma-DAM* or *-DAHM)* Also, in France, title given to married woman and, in many countries, title of respect given to women. In England, normally anglicised to **madam.** Plural **mesdames** *(may-dam).*

madeira [Port.] Blended dessert wine, fortified with brandy, from island of Madeira to west of N. African coast. *(mad-EER-a)*

madeleine [Fr.] Small rich cake. *(MAD-uh-len)*

Mademoiselle [Fr.] (In France) Miss. *(madm-wah-ZEL, mam-wah-ZEL)* Also, French governess in English family. Plural **mesdemoiselles** *(may-dem-wah-ZEL)*

madonna [It.] Virgin Mary. Picture or statue of Virgin Mary. *(ma-DON-a)*

maduro [Sp.] (Of cigar) full-flavoured. *(mad-OOR-oh)*

maestoso [It.] (Of music) played majestically. *(meye-STOH-zoh)*

maestro [It.] Masterly performer in any sphere. *(MEYE-*

stroh) Usually applied to performer, teacher or composer of serious music, and especially to conductor.

mafia, Mafia [It.] Secret organisation (especially in U.S.A.) originating among Italians and alleged to be involved in organised international crime. *(MAF-ee-a)*

mafioso [It.] Member of **mafia.** *(maf-ee-OH-so)* Plural **mafiosi.** *(-see)*

Magi See **magus.**

Magna Carta or **Charta** [Lat.] Great Charter of personal and political liberties granted by King John in 1215. *(mag-na KAH-ta)*

magna cum laude [Lat.] With great distinction. *(mag-na cum LOW-deh)* Usually applied to award of university degree or prize.

magna est veritas et praevalebit [Lat.] Truth is great and will prevail. *(mag-na est VER-it-ahs et preye-val-AY-bit)* A version of the same saying, with the verb **praevalet** (present tense) is found in the Vulgate Apocrypha.

Magnificat [Lat.] Prayer-book canticle beginning 'My soul doth magnify the Lord'. Musical setting of this. Any song of praise. *(mag-NIF-ik-at)* From Latin version of St Luke, Chapter 1, verse 46.

magnifico [It.] (Venetian) nobleman or magnate. *(mag-NIF-* or *man-YIF-ik-oh)*

magnifique [Fr.] Magnificent. Wonderful. *(man-yee-FEEK)* See **c'est magnifique mais ce n'est pas la guerre.**

magnum [Lat.] Bottle containing two quarts of wine or spirits, usually champagne. *(MAG-num)*

magnum opus [Fr.] Great work. Masterpiece. *(mag-num OP-us)* Usually applied to an artist's greatest work.

Magus, magus [Lat.] Member of priesthood of ancient Persia. *(MAY-jus)* Plural **magi.** *(MAY-jeye)*. Normally used in reference to the three wise men from the East who brought gifts for the new-born Christ.

Magyar [Hung.] Hungarian. *(MAG-yar* or *MUH-dyur)*

maharaja(h) [Hindi] Indian prince. *(ma-ha-RAH-ja)*

maharani, maharanee [Hindi] Wife or widow of **maharaja(h).** *(ma-ha-RAH-ni)*

maharishi [Hindi] Hindu sage. *(ma-ha-REE-shi)*

mahatma [Sanskrit] Buddhist sage. *(ma-HAT-ma)*

Mahdi [Arab.] Leader or messiah, both temporal and spiritual, expected by Muslims. Person who claims this title. *(MAH-* or *MAHKH-di)* Specially applied to main leader of revolution in Sudan 1883–5.

mah-jong(g) [Chin.] Board-game for four players. *(mah-JONG* or *-YONG)*

mahout [Hindi] Elephant-driver. *(ma-HOWT)*

maidan [Urdu] Open space in or near town used for sport or as parade-ground, etc. *(mi-DAHN)*

maillot [Fr.] Tights worn by dancer, gymnast, etc. One-piece bathing-costume for women. *(ma-YOH)*

maillot jaune [Fr.] Yellow jersey worn each day by current race-leader in **Tour de France** *(ma-yoh zhohn)*

maire [Fr.] (In France) Mayor. *(mair)*

mairie [Fr.] (In France) Town-hall. *(mair-ee)*

maison [Fr.] (As found on restaurant menu) of the house; as specially prepared by the restaurant's chef. *(mez-oṅ)* Always placed after the name of a dish.

maison de luxe [Fr.] High-class brothel. *(mez-oṅ duh looks)*

maître [Fr.] Master. Title of respect given to person eminent in scholarship, art, etc. *(met-ruh)*

maître-chef [Fr.] Head chef. Master cook. *(met-ruh SHEF)*

maître d'hôtel [Fr.] Head-waiter in hotel. *(meh-truh doh-TEL)* Sometimes applied to hotel-manager.

Majlis [Pers.] (In various N. African and Middle East countries, e.g. Iran) Parliament. *(MAHJ-lis)*

makimono [Jap.] Painted scroll, to be unrolled horizontally to show series of pictures. *(mak-i-MOH-noh)*

maladresse [Fr.] Clumsiness, tactlessness, awkwardness. *(mal-ad-RES)*

mala fide [Lat.] In bad faith. Intending to deceive or defraud. *(mah-la FEE-* or *FEYE-deh)*

Málaga [Sp.] Dark sweet wine from region of Málaga on southern coast of Spain. *(MAL-ag-a)*

malagueña [Sp.] Dance with improvised words, originating from Málaga, in southern Spain. *(mal-a-GEH-nyah)*

malaise [Fr.] Discomfort, uneasiness, sickness, without specifically identifiable cause. *(mah-lez* or *-LAYZ)*

mal à propos, malapropos [Fr.] Inopportune(ly). Inappropriate(ly). *(ma-la prop-OH)*

mal de mer [Fr.] Sea-sickness. *(mal duh MAIR)*

mal du siècle [Fr.] Weariness of life. Disillusionment at state of the world. *(mal doo see-EK-luh)*

mal-entendu, malentendu [Fr.] Misunderstanding. *(mal-ahṅ-tahṅ-doo)*

malgré lui [Fr.] In spite of himself. *(mal-gray LWEE)*

malgré tout [Fr.] In spite of everything. *(mal-gray TOO)*

mana [Maori] Power of personality. Supernatural or magical power. *(MAH-na)*

mañana [Sp.] Tomorrow. Some time in the future. *(man-YAH—*

na) Applied particularly to habit of dilatoriness supposed to be typical of Spanish, Spanish-speaking or Mediterranean people.

Manche See **La Manche.**

mandamus [Lat.] Command, issued as judicial writ (especially by superior court to inferior court, local government authority or individual person, ordering that something should be done). *(man-DAH-mus)*

manège, manege [Fr.] Riding-school. Movements of trained horse. Training in such movements. *(man-EHZH)*

manes [Lat.] Deified souls of departed ancestors. Shade, ghost, spirit of dead person deserving veneration. *(MAH-nayz)*

mannequin [Fr.] Fashion model. *(man-uh-KAṄ, MAN-i-kin, MAN-i-kwin)*

manqué [Fr.] Who might have been successful in that profession, trade, etc. *(mahṅ-kay)* Placed after the named profession.

mantilla [Sp.] Lace scarf worn over head and shoulders by Spanish women. *(man-TEE-lya, man-TIL-a)*

mantra [Sanskrit] Portion of ancient Hindu scripture used as incantation, prayer, etc. *(MAN-tra)*

manzanilla [Sp.] Pale, light, very dry Spanish sherry. *(man-sa-NEE-lya, man-za-NIL-a)*

maquette [Fr.] Small preliminary model (for piece of sculpture). Preliminary sketch (for painting, etc.). *(mak-ET)*

maquillage [Fr.] Make-up. Application of cosmetics. *(mahk-i-YAHZH)*

Maquis [Fr.] Member of secret army of French resistance in German-occupied France during Second World War. *(MAH-kee)* Also **maquisard, maquisarde**, man, woman belonging to this organisation.

marabou [Fr.] West African stork, with wing and tail having tufts of down used in trimming for women's hats, clothing, etc. *(MAR-ab-oo)*

marc [Fr.] Refuse (skins, pips, stalks) of pressed grapes after wine-making, used to make cheap brandy. *(mah, mahk)*

marcato [It.] (In music) marked; with each note emphasised. *(mah-KAH-toh)*

marchese, marchesa [It.] Marquis; marchioness. *(mah-KEH-seh, -sah)*

Mardi Gras [Fr.] Shrove Tuesday; last day of carnival (before Lent). Any festivity involving street carnival. *(mah-di GRAH)*

mare clausum [Lat.] Sea claimed as territorial water by country, and thus not open to general navigation. *(mah-ray KLOW-zum)*

mare liberum [Lat.] Sea open to all nations. *(mah-ray LEE-ber-um)*

mare nostrum [Lat.] The Mediterranean Sea. *(mah-ray NOS-trum)*

marginalia [Lat.] Notes in the margin. Matters of marginal importance. *(mah-jin-AH-lee-a)*

mariage de convenance [Fr.] Marriage of convenience; arranged marriage, usually for financial reasons. *(mar-i-ahzh duh koṅ-ven-ahṅs)*

marmite [Fr.] Earthenware cooking-pot. *(mah-MEET)*

marocain [Fr.] Fabric with crinkly texture, made of silk, cotton or wool. *(MA-rok-aṅ* or *-ayn)*

marque [Fr.] Make, brand (especially of high-class car). *(mahk)*

marquise [Fr.] Marchioness. (In jewellery) ring with gems in leaf-shape. *(mah-KEEZ)*

marquisette [Fr.] Light diaphanous fabric in cotton, rayon, silk, etc. used for curtains, etc. *(mah-kiz-ET)*

marron glacé [Fr.] Sweetmeat of chestnut preserved by sugar. Glazed or crystallised chestnut. *(mar-oṅ* or *-on GLAS-ay)*

Marsala [It.] Dark sweet fortified wine from Sicily. *(mah-SAH-la)*

Marseillaise [Fr.] French national anthem. *(mah-say-EZ* or *mah-sel-AYZ)* Originally a song of the French Revolution.

masseur [Fr.] Man who practises massage. *(mas-UR)* Feminine **masseuse.** *(mas-URZ)*

mastaba [Arab.] Ancient Egyptian tomb with flat roof and sloping sides. *(MAS-ta-ba)*

matador [Sp.] Bull-fighter who kills bull. *(MAT-a-dor)*

maté [Sp.] South American shrub, or its leaves; an infusion of tea made from them; the vessel in which this is made. *(MAH-teh)* The word is normally used to define a type of Paraguayan tea.

matelot [Fr.] Sailor. *(MAT-loh)*

matelote [Fr.] Fish stew with wine, onions, etc. *(mat-loht)*

Mater Dolorosa [Lat.] The Sorrowing Mother. *(MAH-ter dol-or-OH-sa)* Name given to Virgin Mary, in paintings, etc., in mourning, sorrow, etc.

materfamilias [Lat.] Woman head of family or household. *(MAH-ter fam-IL-i-ahs)*

materia medica [Lat.] Substances used in practice of medicine. Study of these. *(mat-EE-ri-a MED-ik-a)*

matérial [Fr.] Supplies, equipment, materials. *(mat-ay-ree-EL)* Specially applied to military supplies.

matinée, matinee [Fr.] Performance in theatre or cinema held in afternoon or at an unusual time. *(MAT-in-ay* or *-ee)*

matzo [Yiddish] Unleavened bread eaten at Jewish Passover. *(MAH-tso)*

mauvais goût [Fr.] Bad taste. *(moh-vay goo)*

mauvais sujet [Fr.] Rogue. Black sheep. *(moh-vay soo-zhay)*

mauvaise honte [Fr.] False shame. Painful shyness. *(moh-vayz orñt)*

mavourneen [Ir.] My darling. *(mav-OOR-neen)*

maxima cum laude [Lat.] With distinction. *(MAX-im-a kum LOW-deh)* Applied usually to university degrees.

maya, Maya [Sanskrit] (In Hinduism) illusion; confusion of reality and unreality. *(MAH-ya)*

mayonnaise [Fr.] Sauce of egg-yolk, oil, vinegar, salt, etc. used as dressing for cold vegetables, fish, etc. *(may-on-AYZ)*

mazel(-)tov [Yiddish] Congratulations. Cheers! Good luck. *(MAHZL-tohv* or *-tof)* Used as toast, etc.

mazurka [Pol.] Traditional Polish dance in lively waltz-time, with accent often on second beat. Music for this. *(maz-UR-kah)*

mea culpa [Lat.] The fault is mine. *(MAY-a KOOL-pa)* Also **mea maxima culpa**, I am grievously at fault.

Médoc [Fr.] Red wine of quality from the Bordeaux region of France. *(MAY-dok)* This wine is grown on the south side of the estuary of the Gironde.

meerschaum, Meerschaum [Ger.] Tobacco pipe with distinctive white bowl made from hydrated magnesium silicate. *(MEER-showm)* Also applied to the silicate itself.

Mein Kampf [Ger.] My Struggle. *(meye-n KAMPF)* Title of Hitler's autobiography.

Meistersinger [Ger.] Member of guild of lyric poets and musicians in Germany during late Middle Ages. *(MEYE-ster-sing-er)*

mélange [Fr.] Mixture. Medley. Miscellany. *(may-lahñzh)*

mêlée, melee [Fr.] Confused scuffle, fight, skirmish; disorderly scramble. *(MEL-ay)*

membrum virile [Lat.] Penis. *(MEM-brum vir-EE-leh)*

memento mori [Lat.] Reminder of death (e.g. skull). Emblem of mortality. *(mem-EN-toh MOH-ree)*

memoria technica [Lat.] System or device to assist memory. *(mem-OR-ee-a TEK-nik-a)*

memsahib [Anglo-Indian] (In India) European married woman. *(MEM-sah-eeb)* Normally found as form of address by Indian servant to European mistress. Also used as jocular or slang reference to one's wife.

ménage [Fr.] Household. *(may-nahzh)*

ménage à trois [Fr.] Household consisting of husband, wife, and lover of one of these, living together. *(may-nahzh a trwah)*

meno [It.] (In music) less. *(MAY-noh)*

Menshevik [Russ.] Member of the more moderate wing of Russian communist party, especially during early history of Russian communism. *(MEN-shuh-vik)*

mens rea [Lat.] Criminal intention. *(mens RAY-a)*

mens sana in corpore sano [Lat.] A healthy mind in a healthy body. *(mens SAH-na in KOR-por-eh SAH-noh)*

merci [Fr.] Thank you. *(mair-see)*

meringue [Fr.] Light confection of sugar and egg-white baked crisp. Small cake of this, often filled or served with cream. *(mer-ANG)*

mésalliance [Fr.] Marriage with person of inferior social standing. Unsuitable marriage. *(may-ZAL-i-ahn̈s)*

Mesdames See **Madame.**

Mesdemoiselles See **Mademoiselle.**

Messieurs See **Monsieur.**

mestizo [Sp.] Person of mixed Spanish and American-Indian blood. *(mes-TEE-soh)*

métayage [Fr.] System of land tenure by which farmer pays to owner part of produce in return for stock, seed, etc. *(mayt-ay-ahzh)*

métayer [Fr.] Tenant of land under system of **métayage.** *(mayt-ay-yay)*

métier [Fr.] Speciality; activity in which one is skilled. Trade, profession. *(may-tyay)*

métis, metis [Fr.] Person, especially child, of white (especially French) and American-Indian blood, especially in Canada. *(MAY-tee* or *-tis)*

Métro, Metro [Fr.] Underground railway in Paris. *(MAY-troh, MET-roh)*

metteur en scène [Fr.] Designer, producer or stage-manager of dramatic production. *(met-ur ahn̈ sehn)*

meum et tuum [Lat.] Mine and yours. *(MAY-um et TOO-um)* Used to express principle of rights of property. Sometimes **meum and tuum.**

mezuzah [Heb.] Scroll, inscribed with religious texts, enclosed in small metal tube, and attached to door-posts in Jewish homes. *(meh-ZOO-za)*

mezza voce [It.] (In music) medium (literally, half) volume of voice or sound. *(MET-sa* or *MED-za VOH-cheh)*

mezzo [It.] Medium. Moderately. Half. *(MET-soh* or *MED-zoh)*

mezzo forte [It.] Neither loud nor soft. *(MET-soh FOR-teh)* Usually abbreviated to **mf.**

mezzo piano [It.] Fairly soft. *(MET-soh pee-AH-noh)* Usually abbreviated to **mp.**

mezzo-rilievo [It.] (In sculpture) half-relief—the carving of figures, etc. on background, the figures projecting from the surface by half their true proportions. *(MET-soh ril-YAY-voh)* Compare **alto-rilievo, bas-relief, basso-relievo.**

mezzo-soprano [It.] (Woman with) voice between that of **soprano** and **contralto.** *(MET-soh sop-RAH-noh)*

mf. Abbreviation of **mezzo forte.**

mi-carême [Fr.] Mid-Lent. *(mee-kah-REHM)*

Midi [Fr.] Area of southern France consisting of coastal plain between Alps, Massif Central and Pyrenees. *(mee-dee)*

midinette [Fr.] Shop-girl, especially in Paris. *(mee-dee-NET)* Specially applied to dressmaker or to milliner's assistant.

mignon [Fr.] Small, delicate, dainty. Person with these characteristics. *(meen-yoṁ)* Feminine **mignonne** *(meen-yon).*

mikado [Jap.] Emperor of Japan. *(mik-AH-doh)*

miles gloriosus [Lat.] Boastful soldier. *(MEE-lays glori-OH-sus)*

milieu [Fr.] Environment. Surroundings. *(MEE-lyur)* Usually applied to social or intellectual surroundings, atmosphere, etc.

mille(-)feuille(s) [Fr.] Confectionery consisting of slices of puff pastry with cream and jam between them. *(meel-FUR-yuh)*

millefiori [It.] Type of mosaic glass. *(mee-leh-FYOR-i)*

minestrone [It.] Thick soup of vegetables with **pasta** and, usually, rice. *(min-est-ROH-neh)*

mir [Russ.] Village in pre-revolutionary Russia. *(meer)*

mirabile dictu [Lat.] Wonderful to tell, relate, say. *(mir-AH-bi-leh DIK-too)*

mirepoix [Fr.] Vegetables chopped and fried for use in sauce. *(meer-pwah)*

mis(e) en bouteille(s) au château or **dans nos caves** [Fr.] (On the labels or corks of French bottles of wine) bottled at the place where it is made *or* bottled in our cellars (not necessarily those of the grower). *(meez ahṅ boo-tay yoh shah-toh* or *dahṅ noh kahv)*

mis(e) en bouteille(s) au Domaine or **à la propriété** or **par le propriétaire** [Fr.] (Of wine) bottled at the place where it is made *or* by the grower. *(meez ahṅ boo-tay yoh doh-mehn* or *a la proh-pree-ay-tay* or *par la proh-pree-ay-tair)*

mise en scène [Fr.] Staging and production of a play. Setting, surroundings, background, of an event, story, happening, etc. *(meez ahṅ sen)*

misère [Fr.] (In card-playing) declaration that one will win no tricks. *(miz-AIR)*

miserere [Lat.] Have mercy. *(miz-er-AIR-i)* First word of Latin version of Psalm 51. Also applied to musical setting of this. Also used of projecting shelf on underside of hinged seat in choir-stall; when the seat was raised, the shelf gave some support to person standing in front of it.

miserere mei [Lat.] Have mercy on me, (Lord). *(miz-er-AIR-i MAY-ee)* First two words of Latin version of Psalm 51.

miserere nobis [Lat.] Have mercy on us, (Lord). *(miz-er-AIR-i NOH-bees)*

missa solemnis [Lat.] High Mass. *(MIS-a sol-EM-nis)*

mistral [Fr.] Strong, cold, dry north or north-west wind of Southern France, blowing from Massif Central towards Mediterranean. *(mee-strahl)*

mitrailleur [Fr.] Machine-gunner. *(mit-reye-UR)*

mitrailleuse [Fr.] Machine-gun with several barrels. *(mit-reye-URZ)*

Mitteleuropa [Ger.] Central Europe, especially the Balkans. *(mit-el-yoo-ROH-pa)*

Mlle Abbreviation of **Mademoiselle.**

Mlles Abbreviation of **mesdemoisells.**

MM Abbreviation of **Messieurs.**

Mme Abbreviation of **Madame.**

Mmes Abbreviation of **Mesdames.**

mochree [Ir.] My darling. *(muh-KREE)*

moderato [It.] (Of music) at a moderate speed. *(mod-er-AH-toh)*

modiste [Fr.] Dressmaker; milliner. Dress-designer, usually in high fashion. *(moh-DEEST)* Applied only to women.

modus operandi [Lat.] Method of working. Way in which a person or thing works. *(MOH-dus oper-AND-i* or *-ee* or *-eye)*

modus vivendi [Lat.] Arrangement by which people who have differences of opinion, etc. succeed in tolerating these differences while still living or working together. *(MOH-dus viv-END-i* or *-ee* or *-eye)* Literally, method of living.

moiré [Fr.] (Of silk) watered. Watered silk. (Fabric) with wavy markings or clouded appearance like watered silk. *(mwah-ray)*

moire antique [Fr.] Fabric, usually silk, which has been watered (i.e. moistened and pressed during manufacture to produce irregular wavy patterning). *(mwahr ahṅ-TEEK)*

molto [It.] (In directions for playing music) very. *(MOL-toh)* Followed (or preceded) by other words such as **allegro, vivace,** etc.

mon cher [Fr.] My dear. *(moṅ shair)* Applied only to men.

mondain [Fr.] Wordly. Belonging to fashionable society. *(moṅ-daṅ)*

mondaine [Fr.] Worldly woman. Woman of high society. *(moṅ-den)*

mon Dieu [Fr.] My God! Good heavens! *(moṅ dyur)*

monocoque [Fr.] Fuselage, hull or car-body manufactured as single entity, i.e. not built on separate chassis. *(MON-oh-kok)*

Monseigneur [Fr.] (In France) title given to important person such as cardinal, bishop, etc. *(moṅ-sen-yur)*

Monsieur [Fr.] (In France) Mr. *(muh-SYUR)* Also common mode of address to Frenchman, corresponding roughly to English Sir. Plural **messieurs.** *(mes-yur)*

Monsignor [It.] (In Roman Catholic Church) title given to some senior prelates. *(mon-SEEN-yor)*

monstre sacré [Fr.] Celebrated person, usually from world of public entertainment, with unorthodox elements in private or public life which nevertheless enhance his appeal. *(moństr sak-ray)*

mons Veneris [Lat.] Rounded fatty protruberance above pubic region of woman. *(monz VEN-er-is)*

montage [Fr.] Sequence of film created by editing. (Creation of) composite whole from various elements, especially piece of art made of fragments of painting, photography, three-dimensional articles, etc. *(mon-* or *moń-TAHZH)*

moonshee Same as **munshi.**

morbidezza [It.] (In art of painting) lifelike delicacy, especially in flesh-tints. *(mor-bid-ET-sa)*

morceau [Fr.] Short musical (or literary) composition. *(mor-soh)*

morendo [It.] (Of music) dying away. *(moh-REN-doh)*

mores [Lat.] Customs, habits, traditions, manners, conventions characteristic of a group, community, etc. *(MOH-rayz)*

morgue [Fr.] Haughtiness, superciliousness, arrogance. *(morg)* See below.

morgue anglaise [Fr.] Haughty demeanour as an English characteristic. *(morg ahń-glayz)*

morituri te salutant or **salutamus** [Lat.] Those (we) who are about to die salute you. *(mor-it-OO-ree tay sal-oo-TANT* or *-TAH-mus)* Salutation to Emperor by Roman gladiators on entering arena.

mosso [It.] (Of music) with speed. *(MOS-oh)*

mot Same as **bon mot.**

mot juste [Fr.] Word or expression that conveys the exact shade of meaning required. *(moh zhoost)*

moto [It.] (In music) motion, movement. *(MOH-toh)*

moto perpetuo [It.] Perpetual motion. *(MOH-toh per-PET-oo-oh)* Sometimes used as title of, or to describe, piece of music with rapid sequence of notes continuously repeated.

motu proprio [Lat.] Of one's own accord. *(moh-too PROP-ree-oh)*

mouchoir [Fr.] Handkerchief. *(moo-shwahr)*

moue [Fr.] Pout. *(moo)*

moujik [Russ.] Russian peasant. *(MOO-zhik)*

moule [Fr.] Mussel. *(mool)* Also **moules marinière**, mussels served with a sauce of seasoned vegetables. *(mool mar-in-YAIR)*

moulin [Fr.] Vertical or near-vertical shaft in glacier, formed by action of water in ice. *(moo-laṅ)* Not to be confused with **moulin (à vent)**, windmill.

moulinette [Fr.] Piece of kitchen equipment for pulping soft substances, such as cooked vegetables. *(moo-lin-ET)*

mous(s)aka [Gk.] Greek dish of minced meat with vegetables, especially aubergines, etc. *(moo-SAH-ka)*

mousse [Fr.] (In cookery) light dessert of whipped cream or eggs or similar substance, flavoured with chocolate, fruit, etc. Paste of fish (or meat) whipped with cream. *(moos)*

mousseux [Fr.] (Of wine) sparkling, frothy. *(moos-ur)*

moutarde [Fr.] Mustard. *(moo-tard)*

mouton [Fr.] Sheep. Mutton. *(moo-toṁ)*

mouvementé [Fr.] Animated. *(moov-mahṅ-tay)*

mouzhik Same as **moujik.**

mozzarella [It.] Mild white soft Italian cheese. *(mos-ar-EL-a)*

mp. Abbreviation of **mezzo piano.**

mudéjar [Sp.] Spanish architectural style with strong Moorish influence. Christianised Moor in Spain. *(mood-AY-hahr)*

muezzin [Arab.] Muslim crier who calls people to prayer at prescribed hours, usually from minaret. *(MUZ-in* or *moo-EZ-in)*

mufti [Arab.] Plain clothes, as distinct from uniform or other official dress. *(MUF-ti)*

mullah [Arab.] Muslim religious teacher. *(MUL-a)*

multum in parvo [Lat.] Much in little; a great deal in a small space. *(MUL-tum in PAH-voh)*

munshi [Urdu] (In India) secretary. Teacher of language. *(MOON-shee)*

Muscadet [Fr.] Dry white wine grown near mouth of the River Loire on western coast of France. *(moos-ka-day)*

musique concrète [Fr.] Concrete music: music created by arrangement, editing, etc. of recorded sounds, real or artificial. *(moo-zeek koṁ-kreht)*

mutatis mutandis [Lat.] With appropriate changes. *(moo-TAH-tees moo-TAN-dees)* Used when applying an existing rule, etc. to fit a different set of circumstances.

muu-muu [Hawaiian] Loose, brightly coloured, straight dress worn by Hawaiian woman. *(moo-moo)*

muzhik Same as **moujik.**

myrtille [Fr.] Bilberry. *(meer-TEEL)*

mystique [Fr.] Air of mystery or reverence surrounding some activities, pursuits, professions, skills, doctrines or people, usually created and cultivated by persons associated with them to impress the layman. *(mis-TEEK)*

N

naïf [Fr.] Simple, ingenuous man or boy. *(nah-EEF)* Also used as male equivalent of **naïve.**

naïve [Fr.] Simple, ingenuous, artless, innocent, natural, unaffected. *(nah-EEV)* This is technically the feminine form of **naïf**. In practice, it is generally used as an adjective, irrespective of gender, and **naïf** is used, much more rarely, of men only.

naïveté [Fr.] State of being **naïve** (or **naïf**). *(nah-EEV-uh-tay)*

narghile [Pers.] Same as **hookah.** *(NAH-gil-eh)*

nature [Fr.] Plain. *(nat-oor)* Always placed after noun: thus an **omelette nature** is one without any filling.

Nazi [Ger.] (Member) of the German National Socialist Party, 1920-1945. *(NAH-tsi)* First two syllables of German word meaning National Socialist.

nawab [Urdu] (In India) title of governor or noble. (In Pakistan) title of distinguished Muslim. *(nwahb* or *nworb)*

N.B. Abbreviation of **nota bene.**

née [Fr.] Born. *(nay)* Always followed by a surname, which indicates the maiden name of a married woman.

négligé(e) [Fr.] Loose, informal garment, especially light, diaphanous dressing-gown, worn by women. *(NAY-glee-zhay)*

négociant [Fr.] (On French wine bottles) name of a shipping house which buys wine until it is ready to bottle or ship. *(nay-goh-see-ahṅ)*

négociant-éleveur [Fr.] Merchant who buys wine for re-sale after caring for it in his own cellars. *(nay-goh-see-ahṅ ay-luh-vur)*

nem.con. Abbreviation of **nemine contradicente.**

nemine contradicente [Lat.] Unanimously. *(NEM-ini KON-tra-dik* or *-dis* or *-dich-EN-ti)*

nemo me impune lacessit [Lat.] No-one injures me with impunity. *(NAY-moh may im-POO* or *-PYOO-neh lak-ES-it)* Motto of Scotland.

ne plus ultra [Lat.] Furthest or highest point attainable. Perfection. *(nay ploos UL-trah)*

nero antico [It.] Kind of black marble found in Roman ruins. *(NAIR-oh ahn-TEE-koh)*

netsuké, netsuke [Jap.] Small carved ornament worn by Japanese at waist. *(net-SOO-kay)*

névé [Fr.] Snow at head of glacier, not yet compressed into ice. *(nay-vay)*

nihil ad rem [Lat.] Irrelevant. *(NI-hil ad rem)*

nihil obstat [Lat.] Official approval. *(NI-hil OB-stat)* Formula used by Roman Catholic church authorities to certify that a book has been approved for publication.

nil desperandum [Lat.] Never despair. *(nil des-per-AND-um)*

Nippon [Jap.] Japan. *(NIP-on)* Also **Nipponese**, Japanese.

nirvana [Sanskrit] (In Buddhism and Hinduism) state of beatitude achieved by sublimation or extinction of one's individual existence, desires, etc. *(nur-VAH-na)*

nisi [Lat.] Coming into effect after a stated time provided certain conditions are met. *(NEYE-seye)* Usually found in grant of decree nisi in legal action for divorce.

nisi prius [Lat.] Trial of civil cases by judges in Crown Court. *(NEYE-seye PREYE-us)*

Nō See **Noh.**

noblesse [Fr.] People of aristocratic rank. *(noh-BLES)*

noblesse oblige [Fr.] The aristocracy must behave according to their obligations. Rank entails responsibility. *(noh-BLES ob-LEEZH)*

nocturne [Fr.] Musical composition, especially for piano, suggesting romantic beauty of night; slow, graceful, sleepy music. *(NOK-turn* or *-toorn)*

noël [Fr.] Christmas. *(noh-EL)*

Noh [Jap.] (In Japan) traditional, classical, highly stylised drama, with dance, song and lavish costume. *(noh)*

noisette [Fr.] Small piece of meat. *(nwah-ZET)*

nolens volens [Lat.] Whether willing or not. Willy-nilly. *(NOH-lenz VOH-lenz)*

noli me tangere [Lat.] Warning or prohibition against meddling, interference, approach, etc. *(NOH-li may TANG-* or *TANJ-eri)* Also used as title of paintings showing Christ appearing to Mary Magdalene at sepulchre and forbidding her to touch him (St John, Chapter 20, verse 17).

nolle(-pros) American abbreviation of **nolle prosequi.**

nolle prosequi [Lat.] Abandonment of suit, or part of it, by plaintiff or prosecutor in court. *(noli PROS-ik-wi)*

nolo episcopari [Lat.] Refusal of high office. *(NOH-loh ep-isk-op-AH-ri)*

nom de guerre [Fr.] Pseudonym adopted by person in some enterprise or action (e.g. sport, literature). *(nom duh GAIR)*

nom de plume [Fr.] Pseudonym of writer. *(nom duh PLOOM)*

non compos (mentis) [Lat.] Of unsound mind. *(non* or *nohn KOM-pos MEN-tis)*

non est (inventus) [Lat.] (In law) statement that defendant cannot be found. *(non* or *nohn est in-VEN-tus)*

non grata [Lat.] Unacceptable. *(non* or *nohn GRAH-ta)* Applied only to people. Abbreviation of **persona non grata.**

non nobis (Domine) [Lat.] Not unto us (O Lord). *(non* or *nohn NOH-bis DOM-in-eh)* Opening words of Latin version of Psalm 115.

non placet [Lat.] Expression used to signify negative vote in learned assemblies (e.g. university, church). *(non* or *nohn PLAK* or *PLAS-et)*

non possumus [Lat.] (In law) plea of inability to act in a matter. *(non* or *nohn pos-OO-mus)*

non sequitur [Lat.] Illogical statement or conclusion. Conclusion that does not follow from premisses. *(non* or *nohn SEK-wit-er)*

nostalgie de la boue [Fr.] Yearning of civilised man for (especially sexual) degradation. *(nos-tal-zhee duh lah boo)* Literally, home-sickness for the gutter.

nostrum [Lat.] Quack medicine prepared by person selling it. Any pet scheme or panacea, especially one savouring of charlatanism. *(NOS-trum)*

nota bene [Lat.] Note well. Please take careful note. *(NOH-ta BEN-eh)* Normally found as abbreviation **n.b.**

Notre Dame [Fr.] Our Lady. *(notr DAM)*

noumenon [Gk.] Object of purely intellectual intuition. *(NOO-men-on)*

nous [Gk.] Common sense. *(nows)*

nouveau [Fr.] New. *(noo-voh)*

nouveau riche [Fr.] Person who has recently become rich. *(noo-voh reesh)* The phrase implies that the person's humble origins are still evident, or that the wealth is vulgarly advertised. Plural **nouveaux riches** (same pronunciation).

nouvelle [Fr.] Short novel. *(noo-VEL)*

nouvelle vague [Fr.] New trend. *(noo-vel vahg)* Specially applied to style of film-making in France in 1960s, with hand-held camera, amateur actors, low budgets, etc.

nova [Lat.] New star, especially one that exhibits sudden and temporary increase in brightness. *(NOH-va)*

novella [It.] Short novel or narrative tale. *(nov-EL-a)*

novena [Lat.] (In Roman Catholic Church) devotion consisting of prayers or services on nine successive days. *(nov-EE-na)*

noyade [Fr.] Execution by drowning. *(nwah-YAHD)* Especially in France during Reign of Terror, 1794.

noyau [Fr.] Liqueur of brandy flavoured with kernels of certain fruits. *(NWAH-yoh)*

nuance [Fr.] Slight variation or difference in or shade of meaning, opinion, feeling, expression, colour, shade, tone, etc. *(NOO-ahṅs)*

nulla bona [Lat.] Legal statement that debtor has no goods for seizure. *(NUL-a BOH-na)*

nullah [Hindi] Ravine, stream, gully, watercourse (especially dry one). *(NUL-a)*

nulli secundus [Lat.] Second to none. *(NUL-ee sek-UN-dus)*

numerus clausus [Lat.] Fixed number, especially of vacancies at learned institution, etc. *[NOO-mer-us KLOW-sus)*

Nunc Dimittis [Lat.] Prayer-book canticle (best known in service of Evening Prayer in Church of England) beginning 'Lord, now lettest thou thy servant depart in peace'. *(nunk DIM-it-is)* Opening words of Latin version of St Luke, Chapter 2, verse 29.

nuncio [It.] Pope's permanent diplomatic representative in a country. *(NUN-see-oh* or *-shoh)*

nux vomica [Lat.] Seed of tree in East India from which strychnine is obtained. *(nuks VOM-ik-a)*

O

ob. Abbreviation of **obiit.**

obiit [Lat.] (He, she) died. *(OB-i-it)* Always followed by date of death.

obbligato [It.] (In directions for playing of music) not to be omitted. *(ob-lig-AH-toh)* Normally applied to decorative part by solo instrument in an accompaniment or orchestral piece.

obiter dictum [Lat.] Incidental remark. *(OB-it-er DIK-tum)* Also applied, in law, to judge's remarks which are not part of his judgement and therefore not legally binding. Plural **obiter dicta.** *(DIK-ta)*

objet Abbreviation of **objet d'art.**

objet d'art [Fr.] Work of art, usually small (e.g. pottery, jewellery, etc.). *(OB-zhay DAH)* Plural **objets d'art** (same pronunciation).

objet trouvé [Fr.] Object (usually natural, e.g. piece of wood or stone) found at random and presented as attractive, rare or artistic. *(OB-zhay TROO-vay)* Plural **objets trouvés** (same pronunciation).

obligato Same as **obbligato.**

obscurum per obscuris [Lat.] Same as **ignotum per ignotus.**

octroi [Fr.] Duty levied on goods entering towns in certain countries. Local tax-office where, or officials to whom, such duty is payable. *(ok-TRWAH)*

odalisque [Fr.] Female slave or concubine in the East, especially in harem of Turkish Sultan. *(OD-al-isk)*

oderint dum metuant [Lat.] Let them hate, as long as they fear. *(OH-der-int dum MET-oo-ant)* Quotation from Cicero *(Philippic I, 14)* and others.

odi et amo [Lat.] I hate and I love. *(OH-dee et AM-oh)* Quotation from Catullus *(Carmina LXXXV)*.

odium aestheticum, scholasticum See **odium theologicum.**

odium theologicum [Lat.] Acrimony supposed to be characteristic of theologians when in disagreement with one another. *(OH-di-um thee-ol-OJ-ik-um)* The phrases **odium aestheticum** *(eye-STET-ik-um)* and **odium scholasticum** *(skol-AST-ik-um)* are applied to similar acrimony supposed to be characteristic of artists and scholars respectively, when is dispute among themselves.

œil-de-bœuf [Fr.] Small round window. *(ur-y-duh-burf)*

œillade [Fr.] Meaning look, especially amorous glance. *(ur-yahd)*

œuvre [Fr.] Total output of writer, artist, composer, etc. *(urv-ruh)*

olio [Sp.] Stew of various meats and vegetables. Medly, hotchpotch. *(OH-li-oh)*

olla podrida [Sp.] Same as **olio.** *(OL-ya pod-REE-da)*

oloroso [Sp.] Full-bodied medium-sweet sherry. *(ol-oh-ROH-soh)*

omadhaun [Ir.] Fool. *(OM-ad-orn)* Term of abuse in Ireland.

ombré [Fr.] (Fabric) woven with gradual shading of colour. *(ORṀ-bray)*

ombudsman [Swedish] Official appointed to investigate citizens' complaints against public authorities. *(OM-buds-man)*

omega [Gk.] Last letter of Greek alphabet. *(OH-meg-a)* Also applied to anything that is last in series.

omnia vincit amor [Lat.] Love conquers everything. *(OM-nee-a VIN-* or *WIN-kit AM-or)* From Virgil's, *Aeneid.*

on dit [Fr.] Item of gossip. *(orṁ dee)*

onus probandi [Lat.] Burden of proof. *(OH-nus proh-BAN-di* or *-dee)*

oomiak Same as **umiak.**

op. Abbreviation of **opus.**

op.cit. Abbreviation of **opere citato.**

opéra bouffe [Fr.] Comic opera. *(op-ay-ra boof)*

opera buffa [It.] Same as **opéra bouffe.** *(OP-er-a BOO-fa)*

opéra comique [Fr.] Opera which includes spoken dialogue. *(op-ay-ra kom-eek)* Not to be confused with comic opera, but to be distinguished from grand opera, which is entirely set to music.

opera seria [It.] Serious opera. *(OP-er-a SAY-ree-a)* As opposed to **opera buffa.**

opere citato [Lat.] In the work already quoted. *(OP-ay-ray sit-* or *kit-AH-toh)* Almost always abbreviated to **op.cit.** and found in footnotes of learned books to avoid full repetition of title of a book previously referred to or quoted.

opus [Lat.] Composition. Work. *(OP-* or *OHP-us)* Often used, with abbreviation **op.**, followed by a number, to indicate musical composition, the number referring to order of publication or composition.

opus Dei [Lat.] The work of God. *(OP-us DAY-ee)* Also used as title of powerful, traditionally-minded society within Roman Catholic church.

ora pro nobis [Lat.] Pray for us. *(OH-ra proh NOH-bees)*

orare est laborare, laborare est orare [Lat.] To pray is to work, to work is to pray. *(oh-RAH-re est lab-or-AH-re)*

oratorio [Lat.] Extended musical composition for orchestra, soloists and chorus, usually based on scriptural theme. *(or-at-OH-ree-oh)* Normally semi-dramatic in character, but without scenery, costume, movement, etc.

orbis terrarum [Lat.] The earth. *(OR-bis ter-AH-rum)*

oriflamme [Fr.] Flag, standard, etc. serving as rallying-point in struggle. Ideal, cause, inspiration, etc. having similar function. *(o-ri-flam)*

origami [Jap.] Art of folding or cutting paper into decorative patterns. *(o-rig-AH-mi)*

O sancta simplicitas [Lat.] O holy simplicity. *(oh SANK-ta sim-PLIS-it-ahs)*

ostinato [It.] (In music) short figure, melody or theme running through whole or part of a musical composition, normally in the bass. *(os-tin-AH-toh)*

O tempora, O mores! [Lat.] What times, what (moral) standards! *(oh TEM-por-a oh MOH-rays)* Complaint about contemporary behaviour, events, etc. in society.

Ostpolitik [Ger.] Western European country's foreign policy as regards a communist Eastern European country. *(ost-pol-it-EEK)*

ottava rima [It.] (In poetry) stanza of eight lines, each of ten syllables, the first six lines rhyming alternately, the last two with each other. *(ot-AH-va REE-ma)*

oubliette [Fr.] Secret dungeon with entrance only by trapdoor in ceiling. *(oo-blee-ET)*

ou sont les neiges d'antan? [Fr.] Where are the snows of yesteryear?

(oo soñ lay neh-zh dahñ-tahñ) Quotation from Villon's *Ballade des Dames du Temps Jadis.*

outré [Fr.] Eccentric, extravagant, bizarre, exaggerated, outrageous; outside normal convention. *(oo-tray)*

outre(-)mer [Fr.] Overseas. *(oo-truh-mair)*

ouvreuse [Fr.] (In France) woman who unlocks boxes in theatre, or who shows members of audience to their seats. *(oo-vrurz)*

ouzo [Gk.] Aniseed-flavoured spirit made in Greece. *(OO-zoo)*

oyer and terminer [Fr.] Commission granted to judges on circuit, directing them to hold courts. *(OH-yay and TER-mee-nay)* The shorter form **oyer** is applied to a criminal trial taking place by virtue of this commission.

P

p. Abbreviation of **piano.**

pace [Lat.] At the risk of offending. With apology to. *(PAH-chay)* Always followed by person's name. Used to introduce contradiction of him, or difference of opinion.

padre [It.] Chaplain in armed services. Any Anglican clergyman. *(PAH-dray* or *-ri)*

paella [Sp.] (In cookery) dish of rice with chicken, shellfish and other meats. *(peye-EL-ya)*

pair [Fr.] (In roulette) even number. *(pair)* See **impair.**

palaestra [Lat.] Athletic training-quarters, especially wrestling-school. *(pal-EYE-stra)*

palais (de dance) [Fr.] Dance-hall. *(PAL-eh duh DAHṄ-s)* Also applied to public ice-skating rinks.

palazzo [It.] (In Italy) palace. Mansion. *(pal-AHT-soh)*

paletot [Fr.] Cloak, often with sleeves. *(PAL-uh-toh)*

pallium [Lat.] Large rectangular cloak as worn by ancient Greeks and others. Ecclesiastical vestment worn by archbishops, etc. consisting of woollen shoulder-band with front and rear pendants. *(PAL-i-um)*

palmette [Fr.] (In art, architectural decoration, archeology, etc.) ornament of radiating petals rather like palm-leaf. *(pal-MET)*

palomino [Sp.] Horse of golden or cream colour with light-coloured tail and mane. *(pal-oh-MEE-noh)*

pampas [Sp.] (In South America, especially Argentina) extensive treeless plains south of Amazon. *(PAM-pas)* Also, with same meaning, in singular **pampa**. Also **pampas-grass**, gigantic ornamental grass from same area.

panache [Fr.] Swagger, verve. *(pan-ASH)*

panada [Sp.] Thick sauce forming base of most fish, meat or vegetable creams. *(pan-AH-da)* May be made with a **roux.**

panatella [Sp.] Long thin cigar. *(pan-at-EL-a)*

panem et circenses [Lat.] Bread and circuses (i.e. games or sport in the circus or hippodrome). *(PAH-nem et keer-KEN-ses)* Quotation from Juvenal's *Satires* referring to what the common people need to be given by politicians in order to satisfy their needs.

panzer, Panzer [Ger.] (In German army of Second World War) tanks. *(PAN-tser)* Normally found in plural to signify armoured troops.

papabile [It.] Suitable for election as Pope. *(pap-AH-bil-eh)* Also applied, colloquially, to person thought (or thinking himself) to be suitable for any high office.

paparazzo [It.] Free-lance news photographer of type notorious for invasion of privacy. *(pa-pa-RAH-tsoh)* Plural **paparezzi** *(pa-pa-RET-see).*

papier-mâché [Fr.] Paper pulp, used for moulding into shapes (e.g. for theatrical properties). *(pap-yay- MASH-ay)*

paprika [Hung.] Red pepper. *(PAP-rik-a* or *pap-REE-ka)*

paramo [Sp.] High treeless plateau in tropical South America. *(PAR-a-moh)*

par excellence [Fr.] Pre-eminently. *(pah EK-sel-ahṅs)*

par exemple [Fr.] For example *(pah eks-AHṄ-pluh)*

parfait [Fr.] (In cookery) iced dessert of whipped cream, eggs, fruit, etc. *(PAH-fay)*

parfum [Fr.] Perfume. *(pah-furṅ)*

pariah [Tamil] (In India) member of lowest caste. *(par-EYE-a)* Hence any social outcast, human or animal.

pari mutuel [Fr.] Type of betting in which winners share all money staked by losers. *(pah-ree moo-too-el)*

pari passu [Lat.] In step. Simultaneously. At an equal rate. Without preference to one side or another. *(pa-ri PAS-oo)*

Paris vaut bien une messe [Fr.] Paris is well worth a mass. *(PAH-ree voh byaṅ oon MES)* Attributed to the protestant Henry of Navarre who became the Roman Catholic Henry IV of France. Used to signify cynically that material gain is worth a dereliction of (religious) principles.

parka [Russ.] Waterproof hooded jacket, with fur lining or trim. *(PAH-ka)*

parlando [It.] (In music) speaking, rather than singing, the words of a song. *(pah-LAN-doh)*

parterre [Fr.] Garden with formal, symmetrical arrangement of flower-beds. *(pah-TAIR)* Plural **parterres** (same pronunciation).

parti [Fr.] Marriageable person. *(pah-TEE)*

partie carré [Fr.] Party of four people, usually two men and two women. *(pah-tee kar-ay)*

parti pris [Fr.] Preconceived opinion. *(pah-tee PREE)*

partita [It.] Suite of music. Air with variation. *(pah-TEE-ta)*

parturient montes, nascetur ridiculus mus [Lat.] The mountains will be in labour, and an absurd mouse will be born. *(pah-TOO-ri-ent MON-tays nas-KAY-toor rid-IK-oo-lus mus)* Quotation from Horace's *Ars Poetica*, referring to trivial results of much fuss and bother. Also **parturiunt**, are in labour.

parvenu, parvenue [Fr.] Man, woman of humble origin who has gained wealth or position. Upstart. *(PAH-ven-oo)* The word carries overtones of vulgarity.

pas de chat [Fr.] (In ballet) jump in which each foot in turn is lifted to opposite knee. *(pah duh shah)*

pas de deux [Fr.] (In ballet) dance for two persons. *(pah duh dur)* Also **pas de quatre, pas de trois**, dance for four, three persons. *(katr, trwah)*

pas devant les enfants [Fr.] Not in front of the children. *(pah duh-vahṅ layz ahṅ-fahṅ)* Warning to others not to continue an indiscreet or unsuitable conversation in the presence of children; it is assumed that the latter will not understand the warning.

pas glissé [Fr.] (In dance) sliding step, usually using flat of foot. *(pah glee-say)*

pasha [Turk.] Turkish title of officer or official of high rank. *(PAH-sha)* Placed after his name.

paso doble [Sp.] Ballroom dance in march-time, in Latin-American style. Music for this. *(PAH-soh DOH-blay)*

passacaglia [It.] Same as **chaconne.** *(pas-a-KAH-lya)*

passé [Fr.] Out of fashion. Behind the times. Past one's prime. *(PAH-say)*

passementerie [Fr.] Trimming of gold or silver lace, braid, beads, etc. *(PAS-ment-ri)*

passe-partout [Fr.] Master-key. Picture-frame (usually for photograph) consisting of glass and backing held together by adhesive tape around edges. Adhesive tape or strip of paper suitable for this. *(pas-par-TOO)*

pas seul [Fr.] (In ballet) solo dance. *(pah surl)*

passim [Lat.] In many places. *(PAS-im)* Often found in footnote of scholarly work, placed after title of a book, to indicate that an idea, allusion, phrase, etc., may be found throughout that book.

passionné [Fr.] Devotee. *(pas-yon-ay)*

pasta [It.] (In cookery) mixture of flour and water in various shapes (e.g. macaroni, spaghetti). *(PAS-ta)*

pasticcio [It.] Same as **pastiche.** *(pahs-TEE-chee-oh)*

pastiche [Fr.] Musical, literary or other composition in imitation of the style of some well-known practitioner, sometimes for humorous effect. *(pas-TEESH)* Also used to mean a medley drawn from the work of various composers, writers, artists, etc.

pastrami [Yiddish] Meat, usually beef, smoked and seasoned. *(pas-TRAH-mi)*

patchouli [Tamil] Strong perfume from Eastern India. *(pa-CHOO-li)*

pâté [Fr.] Paste (of meat or fish). *(PAH-tay* or *PAT-ay)*

pâté de foie gras. [Fr.] **Pâté** of fatted goose liver. *(PAH-tay duh fwah grah)*

paterfamilias [Lat.] Father of a family; head of household. *(PA-* or *PAH-ter fam-IL-i-as)* Normally used jocularly.

paternoster [Lat.] The Lord's Prayer. *(pat-er NOS-ter)* Literally, 'Our Father'.

patio [Sp.] Paved area immediately adjoining house and used for open-air dining, etc. *(PAT-ee-oh)*

pâtisserie [Fr.] Pastry shop. Cake, usually rich or elaborate. *(paht-EE-ser-ee)*

patois [Fr.] Local dialect. *(PAT-wah)*

patron [Fr.] Proprietor, usually of café or hotel. *(PAT-roṁ)* Feminine **patronne** *(pat-RON).* Not to be confused with the English word, and normally printed in italics to distinguish it.

pavane [Fr.] Majestic slow dance. Music for this. *(pav-AHN)* Sometimes spelt **pavan.**

pavé [Fr.] (In France) cobbled street. Cobble-stone. Method of setting jewels close together. *(pah-vay)*

pax Britannica [Lat.] Peace imposed by British rule. *(paks brit-AN-ik-a)*

pax Romana [Lat.] Peace imposed by Roman rule. *(paks roh-MAH-na)*

pax vobiscum [Lat.] Peace be with you. *(paks voh-BIS-kum)*

paysage [Fr.] Landscape painting. Landscape; countryside. *(pay-ee-zahzh)*

Pays-Bas [Fr.] Belgium and Holland. *(pay-ee bah)*

peau-de-soie [Fr.] Smooth silk or rayon fabric with satin appearance. *(poh-duh-SWAH)*

peccavi [Lat.] I have sinned. *(pek-AH-vi)* Jocular apology.

pêche Melba [Fr.] Confection of ice-cream and peaches, perhaps with a liqueur. *(pesh MEL-ba)*

peignoir [Fr.] Woman's loose dressing-gown. *(pen-wahr)*

peine forte et dure [Fr.] Death by being pressed under heavy weights. *(pen fort ay doo-r)* Former punishment for persons refusing to plead to charge of felony.

pelota [Sp.] Basque game played in walled court using ball and wicker racket fastened to hand. *(pel-OH-ta)*

penchant [Fr.] Inclination, liking. *(PAHṄ-shahṅ)*

pendente lite [Lat.] (In law) while a suit is pending. During litigation. *(pen-DEN-ti LEE-ti)*

penetralia [Lat.] Innermost parts. *(pen-et-RAY-lee-a)* Usually applied to building, especially to innermost shrine of temple.

pensée [Fr.] Thought or reflection expressed in literary form. *(pahṅ-say)*

pension [Fr.] (In France and some other European countries) boarding-house, providing all or some meals, at fixed price. *(pahṅ-syorṅ)*

pentimento [It.] (In art) alteration (made by a painter while executing work) which later becomes apparent when overlying paint becomes transparent with age. *(pen-ti-MEN-toh)*

peon, peón [Sp.] (In Spanish America, especially Mexico) day-labourer, peasant, serf. Debtor held in servitude by creditor until debt is paid or worked off. (In India) messenger, attendant. *(PEE-on, pay-ON)*

peplum [Lat.] Short flounce at hem of woman's blouse, bodice or jacket, worn outside skirt. *(PEP-lum)*

per [Lat.] For each. *(pur)*

per annum [Lat.] For each year. *(pur AN-um)*

per capita [Lat.] For each person. *(pur KAP-it-a)*

per cent., percent Abbreviation of **per centum.** *(pur SENT)*

per centum [Lat.] In every hundred. *(pur SENT-um)*

percheron [Fr.] Strong, swift breed of horse, originally bred in Normandy. *(PAIR-sher-orṅ)*

per contra [Lat.] On the opposite side (of argument, financial accounts, etc.). *(pur KON-trah)*

per diem [Lat.] For each day. *(pur DEE-em)*

père [Fr.] The father. Senior. *(pair)* Placed after a name to distinguish between father and son of same name. See **fils.**

perfecto [Sp.] Large thick cigar with both ends tapered. *(per-FEK-toh)*

perfide Albion [Fr.] Perfidious England *(pair-feed al-byorṅ)* Traditional French view of England.

pergola [It.] Covered walk or arbour formed by trailing plants over trellis-work. *(PUR-gol-a)*

per impossibile [Lat.] By means of something that is not in fact possible. *(pur im-pos-EE-bil-ay)*

per incuriam [Lat.] (In law) by oversight, carelessness, negligence. *(pur in-KYOH-ree-am)*

peripeteia [Gk.] Sudden change of fortune, especially as an element in drama. *(peh-ri-pet-EE-* or *-EYE-a)*

per mensem [Lat.] For each month. *(pur MEN-sem)*

permis de sejour [Fr.] Written permission to stay in a place, granted by police or other authority in certain countries. *(pair-mee duh say-zhoor)*

perpetuum mobile [Lat.] Same as **moto perpetuo.** *(pur-PET-oo-um MOH-bil-eh)*

per pro. Abbreviation of **per procurationem.**

per procurationem [Lat.] By proxy. By an agent. *(pur prok-yoo-rah-ti-OH-nem)* Used at end of letter (usually in abbreviation **per pro.** or **p.p.**) signed by a subordinate on behalf of a superior. The expression, followed by the name of the superior, is typed, etc. after the signature of the subordinate or agent.

Perrier [Fr.] Bottled water from natural spring near Nîmes in southern France. *(peri-yay)*

perruque [Fr.] Periwig. *(per-OOK)*

perruquier [Fr.] Wig-maker. *(per-OOK-ee-ay)*

per se [Lat.] By or in itself. Essentially, intrinsically. *(pur say)*

persiennes [Fr.] Outside window-shutters or blinds with horizontal light laths resembling those of Venetian blinds. *(pers-YEN)*

persiflage [Fr.] Banter. Light raillery. Frivolity of manner in treating subject. *(PER-see-flahzh)*

persona [Lat.] Aspect of personality, character, etc. as presented by a person to other people. *(pur-SOH-na)*

persona grata [Lat.] Person who is acceptable to others. *(pur-SOH-na GRAH-ta)* Applied particularly to a person's diplomatic or legal status in a foreign country.

persona non grata [Lat.] Person who is not acceptable to others. *(pur-SOH-na nohn GRAH-ta)* See **persona grata.**

pesante [It.] (Of music) heavily. *(pes-ANT-eh)*

pétard [Fr.] (Of art) designed to shock. *(pay-tar)*

pétillant [Fr.] (Of wine) semi-sparkling. *(pay-tee-yahṅ)*

petit beurre [Fr.] Plain sweet biscuit. *(puh-tee bur)*

petit bourgeois [Fr.] Member of lower middle class. *(puh-tee boor-zhwah)* Often used derogatorily to indicate limited cultural or intellectual horizons.

petite [Fr.] Small and dainty. *(puh-TEET)* Applied only to women's figure.

petite bourgeoisie [Fr.] Lower middle classes. *(puh-teet boor-zhwah-zee)* See **petit bourgeois.**

petit four [Fr.] Very small fancy cake or biscuit, eaten after meal with coffee or liqueur. *(puh-tee foor)* Normally found in plural **petits fours** (same pronunciation).

petitio principii [Lat.] Begging the question. *(pet-ISH-i-oh prin-SIP* or *-KIP-i-ee)*

petit maître [Fr.] Dandy. *(puh-tee MEH-truh)*

petit mal [Fr.] Mild form of epilepsy, with no loss of consciousness. *(puh-tee mal)*

petit point [Fr.] Embroidery consisting of small stitches on canvas. *(puh-tee pwañ)*

petits fours See **petit four.**

petits pois [Fr.] Small green peas. *(puh-tee pwah)*

petits soins [Fr.] Small attentions. *(puh-tee swañ)*

petit verre [Fr.] Glass of liqueur. *(puh-tee vair)*

pharos [Gk.] Lighthouse. *(FAIR-os)*

pianissimo [It.] (In music) very softly. *(pee-ahn-IS-im-oh)* Normally abbreviated to **pp.** See **piano.**

piano [It.] (In music) softly. *(pee-AH-noh)* Normally abbreviated to **p.** See **pianissimo.**

piastre, piaster [Fr.] (In Middle East, especially Turkey) small coin. *(pi-AS-ter)*

piazza [It.] Public square or market place. *(pi-ATS-a)* Especially in Italy, but also found elsewhere.

pibroch [Gael.] Set of variations, especially martial or funeral, on bagpipe. *(PEE-brok* or *-brokh)*

picador [Sp.] (In bull-fighting) horseman with lance. *(PIK-ad-or)*

picaresque [Fr.] Dealing with the adventures of rogues. *(pik-ar-ESK)* Applied specially to type of literature.

pickelhaube, Pickelhaube [Ger.] Spiked helmet worn by German soldiers in First World War. *(PIK-el-how-buh)*

picot [Fr.] Small loop of twisted thread in lace-edging. *(PEE-koh)*

pièce de résistance [Fr.] Most important, remarkable, praiseworthy achievement in a series. *(pyes duh ray-zees-tahñs)*

pied-à-terre [Fr.] House, flat or other accommodation, usually small and near place of work, convenient for temporary occupation when needed, but not one's principal residence. *(pyay-da-tair)*

pied noir [Fr.] European settler in Algeria. (In France) former settler in Algeria, now back in France. *(pyay nwahr)* Plural **pieds noirs** (same pronunciation).

pietà [It.] (In art) representation of Virgin Mary holding dead body of Christ, usually in her lap. *(pyeh-TAH)*

pietas [Lat.] Respect for ancestor, forerunner, dead friend, etc. *(PEYE-et-ahs)*

pilaf(f), pilau, pilav, pilaw [Turk.] (In cookery) oriental dish of rice with meat, fish or poultry, with spices. *(pil-AF)*

pimento, pimiento [Sp.] Sweet pepper. *(pim-EN-toh, pimi-EN-toh)*

pince-nez [Fr.] Pair of spectacles held in place by clip for nose. *(pańs-nay)*

pinto [Sp.] (Of horse) piebald. *(PIN-toh* or *PEEN-toh)*

pinx(it) [Lat.] Painted (this). *(PINKS-it)* Used with name and inscribed on painting to identify painter.

piolet [Fr.] Ice-axe with two blades, used in mountaineering. *(PEE-oh-lay)*

piquant [Fr.] Sharp (to the taste). Stimulating (to the mind). *(PEE-kahń, PEE-kahnt)* Always indicates pleasure.

pique [Fr.] Irritation, resentment, ill-feeling. *(peek)* See also **piquet.**

piqué [Fr.] Fabric, usually cotton, with raised pattern. *(PEE-kay)*

piquet [Fr.] Game for two players, with 32 cards. *(PEE-kay)* Also **pique** *(peek)*, the scoring of 30 points at this game before one's opponent scores.

pirouette [Fr.] Rapid turn of whole body, usually more than once. *(pi-roo-ET)* Also used as verb.

pis aller [Fr.] Last resort. *(pee-zal-ay)*

piscina [Lat.] Stone basin with drain, normally found in wall near altar in church, for ritual ablution. *(pis-EE-na)* Occasionally, a fish-pond or an ancient Roman bathing-pool.

piscine [Fr.] Swimming-pool. *(pis-EEN)*

pisé [Fr.] Gravel with clay or earth, and rammed as building-material. *(pee-zay)*

pissaladière [Fr.] (In cookery) dish of bread dough spread with onions, anchovies, black olives and, sometimes, tomatoes. *(pee-sal-ad-yair)*

pissoir [Fr.] Public urinal. *(PEE-swahr)*

pistachio [Sp. and It.] Nut with green edible kernel. Flavouring made from this. *(pist-ASH-* or *ACH-ee-oh)*

piste [Fr.] Ski-run. Race-track. *(peest)*

piton [Fr.] (In mountaineering) short peg to be driven in rock-face, etc. to support climber or rope. *(PEE-tom̀, PEE-ton)*

più [It.] (In music) more. *(pyoo)*

pizza [It.] (In cookery) flat piece of dough covered with various ingredients such as cheese, tomato, anchovy, herbs, etc., then baked. *(PEET-sa)*

pizzeria [It.] Place where **pizza** is made or sold. *(peets-er-EE-a)*

pizzicato [It.] (Of music) played by plucking string of instrument instead of using bow. *(pits-ik-AH-toh)*

placebo [Lat.] Medicine given to please rather than to cure patient. *(plas-EE-boh)*

placet [Lat.] Affirmative vote in church or university assembly. *(PLA-set)*

plafond [Fr.] Ceiling, especially ornamental or decorated with paintings. *(pla-foṅ)*

plage [Fr.] Beach, especially at continental resort. *(plahzh)*

planchette [Fr.] Small board on castors, with pencil attached to it, so that letters may be traced out when people place their fingers on the board, the resultant letters or words being supposed demonstrations of psychic phenomena. *(plahṅ-SHET)*

plaque [Fr.] Tablet of metal, wood, stone, etc., used as ornamentation, or with inscription to commemorate event, etc. Gambling counter. Bacterial film on teeth. *(plahk)*

plat [Fr.] Dish of food. *(plah)*

plat du jour [Fr.] (On certain restaurant menus) dish that happens to be available on that particular day. Dish given special prominence, or specially recommended, on a particular day. *(plah doo joor)*

plaza [Sp.] Market-place. Square. *(PLAH-za)*

plebs [Lat.] Common people. *(plebs)*

plein air [Fr.] (In art) attempting to represent, in painting, the light, atmosphere, etc. of the outdoors. *(plen air)*

plié [Fr.] (In ballet) bending of knees with toes turned outwards. *(plee-ay)*

plus ça change Abbreviated form of the following.

plus ça change, plus c'est la même chose [Fr.] The more things change (apparently), the more they remain the same (in fact). *(ploo sa shahṅzh, ploo say lah mehm shohz)*

p.m. Abbreviation of **post meridiem.**

poco [It.] (In music) little; a little. *(POH-koh)*

poco a poco [It.] (In music) little by little. *(POH-koh a POH-koh)*

podestà [It.] Judge or magistrate in Italian town. *(pod-est-AH)* In former times, chief magistrate, elected annually.

pogrom [Russ.] Organised massacre. *(POG-rom)* Applied especially to massacre of Jews.

poilu [Fr.] French private soldier. *(pwah-loo)* Colloquial usage.

point d'appui [Fr.] Point of support. Standpoint. Basis of argument. *(pwaṅ dap-wee)*

pointillé [Fr.] (Of painting) made up of innumerable small dots of paint. *(pwaṅ-tee -yay)* Also used of gilt dots decorating book.

pointillisme, pointillism [Fr.] Impressionist style of painting using dots of various colours which are blended by the eye. *(pwaṅ-tee-yeez-muh, PWAN-til-ism)*

pointilliste [Fr.] Painter of **pointillism.** *(pwañ-tee-yeest, PWAN-til-ist)*

poisson [Fr.] Fish. *(pwah-somñ)*

polder [Dut.] Piece of land reclaimed from sea or river, especially in Netherlands. *(POL-der)*

polenta [It.] Thick porridge made of maize. *(pol-EN-ta)*

politburo [Russ.] Main committee of a communist party. *(POL-it-byoo-roh)*

politesse [Fr.] Formal politeness; good manners. *(pol-ee-TES)*

politico [Sp.] Politician. *(pol-IT-ik-oh)*

polonaise [Fr.] Slow, stately Polish dance. Music for this. *(pol-on-EZ)*

pommes frites [Fr.] Chipped potatoes. *(pom freet)*

poncho [Sp.] Cloak consisting of square or rectangular piece of cloth with centre slit or hole for head. *(PON-choh)*

pons asinorum [Lat.] Anything that is difficult for beginners or for the slow-witted. *(pons as-in-OH-rum)* Originally applied to Euclid's proposition that angles at base of isosceles triangle are equal.

pontifex maximus [Lat.] Pope. *(PON-ti-feks MAK-sim-us)*

portamento [It.] (In music) gliding from one note to another without gaps (i.e. in **legato** style) when singing, or playing a bowed instrument or other instrument (e.g. trombone) capable of this effect. *(port-am-EN-toh)*

porte-cochère [Fr.] Gateway and passage for vehicles through house, usually to internal courtyard. *(port kosh-air)*

portière [Fr.] Curtain over door or doorway. *(por-tyair)*

portmanteau [Fr.] Large suitcase; small trunk. *(port-MAN-toh)* Also used to describe a word made up of parts of two other words and drawing its meaning from both, e.g. **franglais.**

Port Salut [Fr.] Type of mild French cheese. *(por sal-oo)*

posada [Sp.] (In Spain or Spanish-speaking countries) inn, tavern. *(poh-SAH-da)*

poseur [Fr.] Person who behaves affectedly, artificially. *(poh-ZUR)* Feminine **poseuse** *(poh-ZURZ)*

poste restante [Fr.] Post-office department where letters are kept until called for. *(post REST-ahñt)*

post hoc, ergo propter hoc [Lat.] After that (thing), and so because of it. *(pohst hohk, UR-goh PROP-ter hohk)* Statement of fallacy that, because something precedes something else, it causes it.

postiche [Fr.] Counterfeit. Something inappropriately added to a finished work. *(post-eesh)* Especially applied to coil of false hair worn as adornment or to cover thinness of hair.

post meridiem [Lat.] After noon. *(pohst mer-ID-i-em)*

post(-)mortem [Lat.] After death. Medical examination of corpse to determine cause of death. *(pohst MOR-tem)* Also, colloquically, the discussion of an event after its conclusion, especially if event has been unsuccessful.

post obit(um) [Lat.] Taking effect after death. *(pohst OB-it(-um))*

post scriptum [Lat.] Postscript. *(pohst SKRIP-tum)* Normally abbreviated to **P.S.**

pot au feu [Fr.] Boiled beef cooked in vegetable broth. *(poht oh fur)*

poteen, potheen [Ir.] (In Ireland) whisky illicitly brewed. *(pot-EEN)*

pot(-)pourri [Fr.] Musical (or literary) medley. Mixture of spices and dried flowers kept in jar to spread perfume. *(poh-poo-ree)*

pouf, pouffe [Fr.] Low seat consisting of box-shaped or flat, round case of cloth or other material stuffed with kapok, foam, etc. *(poof)* Sometimes mispronounced *poo-fay*.

poujadiste [Fr.] (Person) reflecting the political opinions and attitudes supposed to be typical of small shopkeepers. *(poo-zhad-EEST)* After Pierre Poujade, a French political leader of the 1950s, whose views were thought to be petty, reactionary, demagogic; he was opposed to the growth of big industry and of workers' salaries.

poulet [Fr.] (In cookery) chicken. *(poo-lay)*

poult-de-soie [Fr.] Fine corded silk. *(poo-duh-swah)*

pourboire [Fr.] Gratuity. Tip. *(poor-bwahr)*

pour encourager les autres [Fr.] To encourage other people (by frightening them). *(poor ahň-koo-rah-zhay layz oh-tr)*

pour épater les bourgeois [Fr.] To startle the (conventional, Philistine) middle classes. *(poor ay-pah-tay lay boor-zhwah)* See **bourgeois.**

pourparler [Fr.] Informal discussion before formal conference, negotiation, etc. *(poor-pah-lay)*

pour prendre congé [Fr.] To say farewell. *(poor prahň-druh korň-zhay)* Normally abbreviated to **p.p.c.** and written on visiting card left at farewell visit.

pourriture noble [Fr.] Natural moulding and withering of certain grapes on the vine, allowing the juice to evaporate, concentrating the sugar content of the grape, and enabling the production of specially good wine. *(poo-rit-oor NOB-luh)* The phrase implies that the process is not one of rottenness but of nobility.

pousse-café [Fr.] Liqueur taken with or after coffee after a meal. *(poos-kaf-ay)*

pou sto [Gk.] Place to stand; base of operation. *(poo STOH)*

pp. Abbreviation of **pianissimo.**

p.p. Abbreviation of **per pro.**

p.p.c. Abbreviation of **pour prendre congé.**

praesidium [Lat.] Chief executive committee of government of U.S.S.R. *(pr-eye-ZID-i-um)*

prahu [Malay] (In Malaya) boat with triangular sail and outrigger, resembling canoe's, at one side. *(PRAH-oo)* Also spelt **proa.**

praline [Fr.] Sweetmeat or flavouring made by browning nuts in boiling sugar. *(PRAH-leen)*

praliné [Fr.] Browned in boiling sugar. With burnt almonds. *(prah-lee-nay)*

précieuse [Fr.] Woman affecting refinement of speech or manner. *(pray-syurz)* Masculine **précieux** *(pray-syur)*

préciosité [Fr.] Behaviour which is affected to an absurd extent. *(pray-syos-ee-tay)*

predikant [Dut.] Minister of Dutch Protestant Church, especially in South Africa. *(pray-dik-AHNT)*

premier cru [Fr.] (In Burgundy) wine of good quality, but second to **grand cru**. (In Bordeaux) wine of first growth. *(prum-yay kroo)*

premier danseur, première danseuse [Fr.] Male, female leading dancer in ballet company. *(prum-yeh dahn̓-sur, prum-yair dahn̓-surz)*

première [Fr.] First performance (of film, play, etc.). *(PREM-yair)*

prestissimo [It.] (Of music) very quickly. *(pres-TIS-im-oh)*

presto [It.] (Of music) quickly. *(PRES-toh)*

prêt-à-porter [Fr.] Ready to wear. *(pret-a-por-tay)*

pretzel [Ger.] Crisp salty biscuit, in shape of knot, eaten with beer. *(PRET-zel)*

preux chevalier [Fr.] Gallant knight. *(prur shev-al-yay)*

prie-dieu [Fr.] Prayer-desk, with low shelf to kneel on, and higher shelf for book or to rest arms on. *(pree-dyur)*

prima ballerina [It.] Chief female dancer in ballet. *(pree-ma bal-er-EE-na)* The additional title **assoluta** *(as-ol-OO-ta)* is occasionally added as signal honour.

prima donna [It.] Principal female singer in opera (company). *(pree-ma DON-a)* Also applied to temperamental person.

prima facie [Lat.] At first sight. Strong enough to justify judicial proceedings, further investigation, etc. *(pree-ma FAY-si* or *-shi)*

primo [It.] First. Upper part in duet. *(PREE-moh)* See below. See also **secondo, tempo primo.**

primo [Lat.] Firstly. *(PREE-moh)* See above. See also **secundo.**

primum mobile [Lat.] Prime source of motion or action. *(pree-mum MOH-bil-eh)*

primus inter pares [Lat.] First among equals: chairman, spokesman, etc., of a group of people with same status. *(pree-mus in-ter PAH-rayz)*

Privatdozent, Privat-docent, privat-dozent [Ger.] (In German university) lecturer recognised but not on salaried staff. *(pree-vaht-doh-TSENT)*

prix fixe [Fr.] (Of meal) at fixed price. *(pree feeks)* As opposed to **à la carte.**

P.R.N. Abbreviation of **pro re nata.**

pro [Lat.] In favour of. *(proh)* Usually found in phrase **the pros and cons** (see **con**), the arguments for and against.

proa [Malay] Same as **prahu.** *(PROH-a)*

pro bono publico [Lat.] For the public good. *(proh BON- or BOH-noh PUB-lik-oh)*

procès [Fr.] Lawsuit. *(proh-say)*

procès-verbal [Fr.] Written report of proceedings. (In French court) written evidence supporting criminal charge. *(proh-say ver-BAHL)*

procul este, profani [Lat.] Keep your distance, you who are uninitiated. *(proh-kul es-teh proh-FAH-ni)*

profiteroles [Fr.] Dessert of balls of **choux** pastry filled with cream and served with hot chocolate sauce. *(prof-EE-ter-ol)*

pro forma [Lat.] As a matter of form. As a legal or business requirement. *(proh FOR-ma)* Now usually found, often as a single word, as an elaborate synonym for 'form (to be filled in)'.

prognosis [Gk.] Forecast. *(prog-NOH-sis)*

pro hac vice [Lat.] For this occasion only. *(proh hahk VEYE-si or VEE-si or VEE-chi)*

prolegomenon [Gk.] Preliminary discourse prefixed to book. *(pro-leg-OM-en-on)* Plural **prolegomena**, introductory comments.

proneur [Fr.] Flatterer. *(pron-UR)*

pronto [Sp.] Quickly. *(PRON-toh)* Slang.

pronunciamento [Sp.] Proclamation. *(pron-un-sya-MEN-toh)*

pro patria [Lat.] For one's country. *(proh PAT-ree-a)*

propriétaire-récoltant [Fr.] (On wine labels) owner-manager. *(proh-pree-ay-tair ray-kol-tahn̉)*

pro rata [Lat.] Proportional. Proportionally. *(proh RAH-ta)*

pro re nata [Lat.] For an unexpected occasion that has arisen. *(proh ray NAH- or NAY-ta)* Usually abbreviated to **P.R.N.** and applied to medicine given by nursing staff in hospital, as distinct from prescribed medicine.

prosciutto [It.] Raw Parma ham. *(pro-SHOO-toh)*

prosit [Lat.] Good health! *(PROH-sit)* Usually found as **prost.**

prost [Ger.] Abbreviation of **prosit.** *(prohst)* Used as toast.

pro tanto [Lat.] To that or such an extent. So far; so much. *(proh TAN-toh)*

protégé [Fr.] Person who is under the protection, patronage or tutelage of another (usually older, or of greater experience, superior position, etc.). *(PROT-ay-zhay)* Feminine **protégée** (same pronunciation)

pro tem. Colloquial abbreviation of **pro tempore.**

pro tempore [Lat.] For the time being. *(proh TEM-poh-reh)*

prox. Abbreviation of **proximo.**

prox. acc. Abbreviation of **proxime accessit.**

proxime accessit [Lat.] Runner-up to prize-winner. *(prox-im-eh ak-SES-it)*

proximo [Lat.] Of next month. *(PROK-sim-oh)* Found only in old-fashioned commercial correspondence.

P.S. Abbreviation of **post scriptum.**

psyche [Lat.] Soul, spirit. Mind. *(SEYE-ki)*

psychosis [Lat.] Severe mental derangement. *(seye-KOH-sis)* Plural **psychoses** *(-seez)*.

pucka Same as **pukka(h).**

pudenda [Lat.] Genitals, especially female. *(pyoo-DEN-da)* Also found in singular **pudendum.**

pueblo [Sp.] (In Latin America or Spain) village, settlement. *(PWEH-bloh)*

puissance [Fr.] (In show-jumping) test of horse's strength and skill in jumping high obstacles. *(pwee-sahṅs* or *-sns)*

pukka(h) [Hindi] Genuine. Permanent. Reliable. *(PUK-a)*

pundit [Hindi] Expert. (In India) Hindu learned in Sanskrit, religion and law. *(PUN-dit)*

punica fide [Lat.] Treacherously. *(POO-ni-ka FEE-deh)* Also **punica fides**, treachery *(-dayz)*.

punkah [Hindi] Large swinging blind, moved up and down by rope, usually by servant, to create draught. *(PUN-ka)*

purdah [Hindi] Indian system of secluding women of rank from public view. *(PUR-da)* Colloquially, any imposed seclusion.

purée [Fr.] Pulp of fruit, vegetables, etc., obtained by passing them through sieve or food-mixer to reduce them to creamy, uniform consistency. *(PYOO-ray)*

pur sang [Fr.] Pure-blooded. Through and through. *(poor sahṅ)* Placed after noun or adjective, usually one indicating nationality, outlook, etc.

putsch, Putsch [Swiss Ger.] Revolutionary attempt or attack against political authority or opponents. *(putsch, pootch)*

puttee [Hindi] Long strip of cloth wound round leg from ankle to knee as protection and support. *(PUT-i)* Worn by British soldiers in First World War.

putto [It.] Figure of child, usually cherub, often naked, found in painting or sculpture of **renaissance.** *(PUT-oh)* Plural **putti** *(PUT-ee)*

Q

Q.E.D. Abbreviation of **quod erat demonstrandum.**

Q.E.F. Abbreviation of **quod erat faciendum.**

qua [Lat.] In the capacity of. As. Considered as. *(kwah, kway)*

quadriga [Lat.] Chariot drawn by four horses abreast. *(kwod-REE-ga)*

quadrille [Fr.] Square dance for four couples, with five movements. Music for this. *(kwod-RIL)* Now obsolete. The word is also the name of an eighteenth-century card-game, also obsolete, for four persons.

quadrivium [Lat.] (In medieval universities) course of arithmetic, geometry, astronomy and music. *(kwod-RIV-i-um)*

Quai d'Orsay [Fr.] French Foreign Ministry. *(kay dor-SAY)* Name of street in Paris where Ministry is located.

quand même [Fr.] All the same. Even so. Despite any consequences. *(kahṅ mehm)*

quantum [Lat.] Unit of energy proportional to frequency of radiation. *(KWON-tum)*

quantum sufficit [Lat.] As much as is sufficient. *(KWON-tum suf-EE-kit)*

quartette [Fr.] Musical composition for four instruments or voices. Performers of this. Quartet. *(kwor-TET)*

quartetto [It.] Same as **quartette.**

quartier [Fr.] (In France) particular district in town or city. *(kar-tyay)*

Quartier latin [Fr.] Latin quarter: area on south bank of Seine in Paris where students, also writers and artists, live. *(kar-tyay lat-aṅ)*

quasi [Lat.] Virtually. Almost. Apparent(ly) but not real(ly). *KWAY-zeye, KWAH-zi)* Normally followed by adjective or noun, and linked to it with hyphen.

quattrocento [It.] The fifteenth century. Art, especially Italian, of that period. *(kwah-troh-CHEN-toh)*

quenelle [Fr.] (In cookery) fried ball of shredded meat or fish with seasoning. *(kwen-EL)*

que sera sera (or **será**) [Sp.] What will be will be. *(kay ser-AH ser-AH)*

quiche [Fr.] (In cookery) open tart with savoury (or sweet) filling. *(keesh)*

quiche Lorraine [Fr.] (In cookery) open tart with filling of smoked bacon, cream and eggs. *(keesh lor-AYN)*

quidnunc [Lat.] Busybody, gossip. *(KWID-nunk)*

quid pro quo [Lat.] One thing in exchange for another. *(kwid proh KWOH)*

quietus [Lat.] Discharge from debt. Death. *(kwee-AY-tus, kweye-EE-tus)*

quinquennium [Lat.] Period of five years. *(kwin-KWEN-i-um)*

quis custodiet (ipsos custodes) [Lat.] Who is going to control (people in control, people in authority themselves). *(kwis kus-TOH-dee-et IP-sohs kus-TOH-days)*

qui s'excuse s'accuse [Fr.] He who makes excuses for himself accuses himself (i.e. admits responsibility). *(kee seks-kooz sak-ooz)*

qui vive [Fr.] Alert. *(kee veev)* Only in the expression 'on the *qui vive*', on the alert.

quod erat demonstrandum [Lat.] Which was what had to be proved. *(kwod er-AT dem-on-STRAN-dum)* Normally abbreviated to **Q.E.D.** and used to clinch an argument, or a mathematical proof.

quod erat faciendum [Lat.] Which was what had to be done or made. *(kwod er-AT faki-END-um* or *fashi-END-um)* Sometimes abbreviated to **Q.E.F.** and appended to demonstration of geometrical proof.

quod erat inveniendum [Lat.] Which was what had to be found. *(kwod er-AT in-ven-i-END-um)*

quodlibet [Lat.] Subtle point or argument. Quibble. *(KWOD-lib-et)* Originally, an exercise in philosophical or theological disputation.

quod vide [Lat.] Which see. Refer to this. *(kwod VEE-di* or *-day)* Used in footnotes of scholarly books, usually in abbreviation **q.v.**, to advise reader that he should consult the work thus indicated.

quondam [Lat.] Former. *(KWON-dam)*

quot homines, tot sententiae [Lat.] There are as many opinions as there are people. *(kwot HOM-in-ayz tot sen-TENT-ee-eye)*

quo vadis? [Lat.] Where are you going? *(kwoh VAH-dis)* Latin version of St Peter's words to Christ (St John Chapter 13, verse 36).

q.v. Abbreviation of **quod vide.**

R

R. Abbreviation of **regina** and **rex**, used as part of sovereign's signature.

raconteur [Fr.] Person good at telling anecdotes. *(rak-oñ* or *-on-TUR)* Feminine **raconteuse** *(-TURZ)*

ragoût, ragout [Fr.] Thick stew of meat and vegetables with lots of seasoning. *(rag-oo)*

raison d'état [Fr.] Reason having to do with state security. *(ray-zoñ day-tah)*

raison d'être [Fr.] Reason for existing. Justification for being. *(ray-zoñ dehtr)*

raj [Hind.] Sovereign rule. *(rahj)* Especially applied to British rule of India.

raja(h) [Hind.] Indian king, prince or nobleman. *(RAH-ja)*

rallentando [It.] (Of music) becoming slower. *(ral-ent-AND-oh)*

Ramadan [Arab.] Ninth month of Muslim year, when daily fast is observed between sunrise and sunset. *(ram-ad-AHN)*

ranee [Hindi] Hindu queen. Wife or widow of **raja(h).** *(RAH-nee)*

rani [Hindi] Same as **ranee.**

ranz-des-vaches [Swiss Fr.] Swiss herdsman's song, or melody played on **alpenhorn.** *(rahñs-day-vahsh)*

rappel [Fr.] (In mountaineering, rock-climbing) descent of sheer rock-face by using double rope secured to it. Descend by this means. *(rap-EL)* The word is also found on French road-signs to mean 'reminder'.

rapport [Fr.] Affinity. Harmonious relationship, communication, connexion, understanding. *(rap-OR)*

rapporteur [Fr.] Person who prepares account of discussion for reporting to some other body. *(rap-or-TUR)*

rapprochement [Fr.] Coming together. Establishment or re-establishment of harmonious relations, especially between countries. *(rap-ROSH-mahñ)*

rara avis [Lat.] Rare bird. Person or thing seldom encountered. *(rah-ra AY-* or *AH-vis)*

ratatouille [Fr.] Vegetable stew with aubergines, sweet peppers, onions, tomatoes and (sometimes) courgettes and potatoes. *(rat-at-wee)*

Rathaus [Ger.] (In Germany) town hall. *(RAHT-hows)*

ravioli [It.] (In cookery) small cases of **pasta** containing meat (or savoury substance). *(rav-i-OH-li)*

re [Lat.] Concerning. *(ree)*

realpolitik, Realpolitik [Ger.] Politics based on realities, practicalities, material factors, rather than on ideals. *(ray-al-pol-it-EEK)*

réchauffé [Fr.] (In cookery) warmed-up, re-heated, re-hashed. *(ray-shoh-fay)* Also applied to concoction of stale literary material.

recherché [Fr.] Recondite. Far-fetched. Obscure. Rare. Unusual. *(ruh-SHAIR-shay)*

recitativo [It.] Recitative: form of vocal composition imitating speech inflexions, with little attention to melody or fixed rhythm, frequently used for narrative or dialogue parts of opera, oratorio, etc. *(res-it-at-EE-voh)*

réclame [Fr.] Notoriety. Deliberate achievement of this. *(ray-klahm)*

récolte [Fr.] Vintage. *(ray-kolt)*

recto [Lat.] Right-hand page of open book. Front of leaf of book. *(REK-toh)* See **verso.**

reculer pour mieux sauter [Fr.] Retreat in order to make more effective advance. *(ruh-koo-lay poor myur soh-tay)*

redingote [Fr.] Woman's long coat. *(RED-in-goht)*

reductio ad absurdum [Lat.] Disproof of proposition by proving that its logical conclusion is absurd. Carrying of anything to absurd lengths. *(red-UK-ti-oh ad ab-SUR-dum)*

reflet [Fr.] Lustre, especially on pottery. *(ruh-flay)*

reggae [W. Indian] West Indian style of music with heavy accent on subsidiary beats. *(REG-ay)*

régie [Fr.] (In France) state monopoly, especially in control of tobacco. *(ray-zhee)*

régime [Fr.] System of government. System of control for purposes of diet, punishment, etc. *(ray-ZHEEM)*

Regina [Lat.] The reigning Queen. (In lawsuits) the Crown, the State. *(rej-EYE-na)*

régisseur [Fr.] Stage-manager who rehearses items in repertory of ballet-company. *(ray-zhees-UR)*

Regius [Lat.] Appointed by the Crown to professorship founded by sovereign (principally by Henry VIII at Oxford and Cambridge). *(REE-jus)*

Reich [Ger.] (In Germany) state, empire, commonwealth. *(reye-kh* or *-k)* Normally applied to Third Reich, the Nazi régime of 1933–45.

relai (routier) [Fr.] (In France and, to a much smaller extent, in a few other European countries) one of chain of restaurants and hotel-restaurants offering simple but substantial fare at reasonable prices. *(ruh-lay roo-tyay)* Originally intended for and still much favoured by lorry drivers. Plural **relais routiers** (same pronunciation).

religieuse [Fr.] Nun. *(ruh-lee-zhurz)*

religioso [It.] (Of music) played in a devotional manner. *(rel-iji-YOH-soh)*

reliquiae [Lat.] Remains, especially fossil remains of animals or plants. *(rel-IK-wi-ee)*

remoulade [Fr.] (In cookery) sauce made of eggs, vinegar, mustard, salt, pepper, olive oil and herbs. *(ruh-moo-lad)*

renaissance [Fr.] Rebirth, regeneration, revival, especially in the arts, after period of stagnation or decay. *(ruh-nes-ahṅs, ren-ES-ns)* The **Renaissance** is the period of revival in the fourteenth to fifteenth centuries under the influence of classical models in art and literature.

rendez-vous [Fr.] Agreed meeting-place and -time. Meet by agreement. *(rahṅ-* or *ron-day-voo)*

rentier [Fr.] Person who lives on income from property or investments. *(rahṅ-tyay)* Used contemptuously, with implication that person is parasite who does no work.

repêchage [Fr.] (In rowing, etc.) contest, heat, race in which runners-up in eliminating heats compete for place in final. *(rep-uh-sharzh)*

repertoire [Fr.] Stock of pieces which a performer or company of performers is able or willing to perform. *(REP-er-twahr)* Also used, more generally, to indicate the extent of a person's skill in other respects.

répétiteur [Fr.] Tutor of musicians, especially opera-singers, in rehearsal. *(rep-et-it-UR)*

repiano Mis-spelling of **ripieno.**

répondez, s'il vous plaît [Fr.] Please reply. *(ray-poṁ-day seel voo play)* Abbreviated to **R.S.V.P.** and used on invitation cards.

reportage [Fr.] Documentary reporting for press, book, television, etc. *(rep-or-tahzh)*

repoussé [Fr.] (Metal) hammered into relief from reverse side, for artistic, decorative purposes. *(ruhp-oo-say)*

reprise [Fr.] (In music) recapitulation section. Repeated song or piece in musical programme, especially operetta or musical comedy. *(ruhp-REEZ)*

requiem [Lat.] Mass for the dead. Musical setting for this. *(REK-wi-em)* Opening word of Latin version of Mass.

requiescat in pace [Lat.] May he (she) rest in peace. *(rek-wi-ES-kat* or *-chat in PAH-keh* or *-cheh)* Plural **requiescant.** Abbreviated to **R.I.P.** and found on grave-stones, etc.

restaurateur [Fr.] Owner or manager of restaurant. *(rest-tuh-rat-UR)*

résumé [Fr.] Summary. *(RAY-zoo-may)*

retournons à nos moutons Version of **revenons à nos moutons.**

retroussé [Fr.] (Of nose) turned up. *(ruh-TROO-say)*

retsina [Gk.] Resin-flavoured wine of Greece. *(ret-SEE-na)*

revanchisme [Fr.] Policy of seeking to recover lost territory. *(ruh-VAHṄ-sheez-muh)* Increasingly anglicised to **revanchism** *(rev-AHN-shism)*, and derived from **revanche** *(ruh-VAHṄ-sh)*, revenge, especially the French desire to regain Alsace-Lorraine after its loss to Germany in 1870.

revenant [Fr.] One who returns from the dead. *(ruhv-en-ahṅ)*

revenons à nos moutons [Fr.] Let us return to the subject. *(ruhv-en-oṅ a noh moo-toṅ)* Based on catch-phrase in early French comedy in which judge has to prevent witness from digressing from subject, which is ill-treatment of sheep.

rex [Lat.] The reigning King. *(reks)* See **regina.**

ría [Sp.] Long narrow inlet formed by submergence of valley. *(REE-a)*

ricochet [Fr.] Bouncing of projectile (e.g. bullet) off obstacle, causing it to change direction. Bounce thus. *(RIK-oh-shay)*

rien ne va plus [Fr.] (In roulette) no more bets accepted. *(ree-yaṅ nuh vah ploo)*

Riesling [Ger.] Type of grape. White wine made from this, especially in Alsace, Germany, Italy and Yugoslavia. *(REE-sling)*

rifacimento [It.] Remodelled form of literary (or musical) work. *(rif-ahch-im-EN-toh)*

rigor mortis [Lat.] Stiffening of body after death. *(ri-ger MOR-tis)*

rilievo [It.] (In sculpture) relief. *(ril-YAY-voh)*

rinderpest, Rinderpest [Ger.] Cattle-plague. *(RIN-der-pest)*

Rioja [Sp.] Wine, mainly red, from area on banks of River Ebro in north west Spain. *(ree-OKH-a)*

R.I.P. Abbreviation of **requiscat in pace.**

ripiano Mis-spelling of **ripieno.**

ripieno [It.] (In music) instruments which do not play solo parts, and which perform only in full passages. *(rip-YAY-noh)* Now found only in brass and military band music, usually in clarinet and trumpet sections, for parts which are supplementary to the leading ones.

riposte [Fr.] (Make) quick counterstroke. Prompt retort. *(rip-OST)*

Risorgimento [It.] Movement to unite Italy, and gain its independence, in nineteenth century. *(ris-orj-im-ENT-oh)*

risotto [It.] (In cookery) Italian dish of rice with vegetables and meat broth. *(riz-OT-oh)*

risqué [Fr.] Slightly indecent, obscene, suggestive. *(rees-kay)* Usually applied to anecdote, etc.

rit. See **ritardando.**

ritardando [It.] Same as **rallentando.** *(rit-ahd-AND-oh)* Usually abbreviated to **rit.**

ritenuto [It.] (Of music) played more slowly. *(rit-en-OO-toh)* Indicates immediate change to slower speed, not gradual change indicated by **rallentando** and **ritardando.**

rive gauche [Fr.] District on left (i.e. south) bank of River Seine in Paris, also known as **Quartier latin.** *(reev gohsh)*

riviera [It.] Coastal district, especially one with agreeable climate and scenery. *(ri-vi-AIR-a)* Specially applied to Mediterranean coast in south east France and north west Italy, and to Cornish coast.

rivière [Fr.] Necklace, especially one with more than one string, of precious stones. *(riv-YAIR)*

robe de chambre [Fr.] Dressing-gown. *(rob duh shahṅ-bruh)* Especially applied to woman's gown suitable for wearing about the house.

rocaille [Fr.] Style of decoration, popular in eighteenth century, using shapes of shells and rocks. *(rok-EYE)*

rococo [Fr.] (Of architecture, furniture, etc.) florid, highly ornamented in style. *(rok-OH-koh)*

rodeo [Sp.] (Open-air) exhibition of cowboys' skills. *(ROH-day-oh* or *roh-DAY-oh)* Also applied to rounding-up of cattle on ranch for inspection, branding, etc.

roi fainéant [Fr.] Nominal king; king who does nothing. *(rwah fay-nay-ahṅ)* Applied especially to nineteenth-century French kings whose powers had been usurped. Plural **rois fainéants** (same pronunciation).

Roi Soleil See **le Roi Soleil.**

rôle [Fr.] Role. Actor's part. Person's function. *(rohl)*

roman(-)à(-)clef [Fr.] Novel describing real people or actual events in fictitious terms. *(rom-ahṅ a klay)*

roman(-)à(-)thèse [Fr.] Novel seeking to express a particular philosophy or point of view. *(rom-ahṅ a tehz)*

roman-fleuve [Fr.] Novel, or series of novels, about life of one person, family or group of characters. *(rom-ahṅ flurv)*

rondeau [Fr.] Verse-form of ten or thirteen lines with only two rhymes. *(RON-doh)*

rondo [It.] (In music) piece with returning theme. *(RON-doh)*

rond-point [Fr.] Circus where a number of streets meet. *(roṁ-pwaṅ)*

Roquefort [Fr.] Soft sharp cheese made from sheep's milk in French town near Nîmes. *(rok-for)*

rosé [Fr.] (Of wine) pink. *(roh-zay)*

Rosh Hashanah [Heb.] Jewish New Year. *(rohsh ha-SHAH-na)*

rosso [It.] Red *(ROS-oh)* Normally applied to wine.

rôti [Fr.] (In cookery) roast, roasted. *(roh-tee)*

rôtisserie [Fr.] Place where roast meat and other cooked foods are sold. Oven, or part of oven, where meat may be cooked on rotating spit. Barbecue attachment for cooking meat on rotating spit. *(roh-tee-ser-ee)*

rotunda [Lat.] Circular building or hall, usually domed. *(roh-TUN-da)*

roturier [Fr.] Person of low social rank. *(roh-too-ree-ay)*

Rotwein [Ger.] Red wine. *(ROHT-veye-n)*

roué [Fr.] Debauched person. *(roo-ay)*

rouge [Fr.] Red make-up for cheeks and lips. Apply this. Red powder used for polishing metal. Red wine. *(roozh)*

rouge-et-noir [Fr.] Card-game in which players gamble by placing stakes on red and black marks on table. *(roozh-ay-nwahr)*

roulade [Fr.] (In music) long elaborate running passage in singing, usually of one syllable (e.g. in music of Handel, Bach and other composers of seventeenth and eighteenth century). *(roo-lad)*

route nationale [Fr.] (In France) major road. *(root nas-yon-ahl)* Usually abbreviated to **R.N.** or **N.**

routier [Fr.] Restaurant (sometimes hotel) in France, serving simple, wholesome meals at reasonable price. *(root-yay)* See **relais.**

roux [Fr.] (In cookery) mixture of butter (or other fat) and flour as basis for sauce, etc. *(roo)*

R.S.V.P. See **répondez s'il vous plaît.**

rubato [It.] (In music) with variation of speed to suit expression. *(roo-BAH-toh)*

ruche [Fr.] Frilling of material, especially lace, to decorate woman's dress, blouse, etc. *(roosh)*

Rudesheimer [Ger.] White Rhine wine. *(ROO-des-heye-mer)* Named after the town of Rudesheim, Germany.

rumba [Sp.] Lively dance of Cuban negro origin. Music for this. *(RUM-ba)*

Rum baba See **baba.**

rupee [Hind.] Monetary unit of India, Pakistan and some other countries. *(roo-PEE)*

rusé [Fr.] Sly. Cunning. *(roo-zay)* Feminine **rusée** (same pronunciation).

rus in urbe [Lat.] The country in the town. *(roos in OOR-beh)* Reference to attempt to create rural atmosphere (e.g. park, garden) in urban setting.

S

s. Abbreviation of **solidus** or its plural **solidi**, in £. s. d., etc.

S.A. Abbreviation of **Société Anonyme.**

sabot [Fr.] Shoe made from single piece of wood, hollowed out. Shoe with wooden sole. Clog. *(sab-oh)*

sabotage [Fr.] Deliberate destruction. Render useless. *(SAB-oh-tahzh)*

saboteur [Fr.] Person who commits **sabotage.** *(sab-oh-TUR)*

sachet [Fr.] Small packet (e.g. of shampoo). Small perfumed bag. *(sash-ay).*

saeter [Norw.] (In Scandinavia) high summer pasture. *(SAY-ter)*

safari [Swahili] Journey, especially for hunting or exploring, in wild territory, particularly Africa. *(saf-AH-ri)*

Sahib [Hind.] Title of respect to superior (usually European) by Indians; also added after superior's name as title of respect. *(SAH-ib)*

sake [Jap.] Japanese alcoholic beverage made from fermented rice. *(SAH-keh)*

salaam [Arab.] Peace. *(sal-AHM)* The word also describes an Indian salutation, in which the word is spoken with a low bow, with the palm of the right hand placed on the forehead.

salade niçoise [Fr.] Salad of cooked vegetables, uncooked cucumber and tomato, olives, anchovy, and small pieces of cooked tuna, ham, chicken or prawns, with French salad dressing. *(sal-ad nee-SWAHZ)* There are numerous variations of the recipe.

salami [It.] Very thick spicy Italian sausage, usually garlic-flavoured. *(sal-AH-mi)*

salina [Sp.] Salt-lake. *(sal-EE-na)*

salé [Fr.] Salted. *(sal-ay)*

salle-à-manger [Fr.] Dining-room. *(sal a mahn̊-zhay)*

salle d'attente [Fr.] Waiting room. *(sal dat-ahn̊t)*

salmi, salmis [Fr.] A **ragoût** of game. *(sal-mee)*

salon [Fr.] Reception room in large house. Gathering of intellectuals there and elsewhere. Room or establishment where clients are received by **couturier**, hairdresser, etc. *(SAL-on̊)* Also **Salon**, annual exhibition of paintings by living artists.

saltarello [It.] Italian and Spanish dance with lively movement, including skips. Music for this. *(sal-ta-REL-oh)*

saltimbanque [Fr.] Mountebank. Quack. *(sal-tam-bahn̊k)*

salve [Lat.] Welcome. *(SAL-vay or -way)* Addressed to one person.

salvete [Lat.] Welcome. *(sal-VAY* or *-WAY-teh)* Addressed to several people.

sal volatile [Lat.] Solution of ammonium carbonate used as restorative when person faints. *(sal vol-AT-il-eh)*

samba [Port.] Lively Brazilian Negro dance. Music for this. *(SAM-ba)*

samovar [Russ.] Russian pot, with interior heating arrangement, for making tea. *(SAM-oh-vah)*

sampan [Chin.] Small boat, usually with oar(s) at stern, or with sail, used in Far East. *(SAM-pan)*

samurai [Jap.] (In Japan) army officer; member of military caste. *(SAM-oo-reye)*

sanbenito [Sp.] (During the Spanish Inquisition) long yellow garment with diagonal red cross on front and back, worn by penitent heretic. Similar black garment, decorated with flames and devils, worn by unrepentant heretic at **auto-da-fé.** *(san ben-EE-toh)*

sancta simplicitas [Lat.] Holy simplicity. Well-meant naivety. *(sank-ta sim-PLIS-it-ahs)*

sanctum [Lat.] Holy place. *(SANK-tum)* Hence, any private inner retreat. See below.

sanctum sanctorum [Lat.] Holy of Holies in Jewish temple. *(sank-tum sank-TOH-rum)* Hence, any specially important or private inner retreat, into which no-one enters uninvited. See above.

Sanctus [Lat.] Hymn which closes preface to Eucharist or Mass. *(SANK-toos)* From the first word of the Latin version of 'Holy, holy, holy'.

sang-de-bœuf [Fr.] Deep red colour found in porcelain, especially Chinese. *(sahṅ-duh-burf)*

sang froid [Fr.] Composure, self-possession, in circumstances of tension, pressure, danger, etc. *(sahṅ frwah)*

sangría [Sp.] Cold drink of red wine and fizzy lemonade, etc. with sliced fruit. *(san-GREE-a)*

sans blague [Fr.] Seriously; without joking. *(sahṅ blahg)*

sans cérémonie [Fr.] With neglect of formalities. *(sahṅ say-ray-mon-ee)*

sansculotte [Fr.] Republican, revolutionary. *(sahṅ-koo-lot)* Originally applied to lower-class revolutionaries in French Revolution who did not wear knee-breeches *(culotte)*

sans façon [Fr.] Outspokenly. Unceremoniously. *(sahṅ fas-oṅ)*

sans(-)gêne [Fr.] Familiarity; absence of constraint. *(sahṅ-zhehn)*

sans peur et sans reproche [Fr.] Without fear and above reproach. Chivalrous. *(sahṅ pur ay sahṅ ruh-prosh)*

sans phrase [Fr.] In a word. Without qualification. *(sahṅ frahz)*

sans-souci [Fr.] Light-hearted unconcern. *(sahṅ soo-see)*
santé [Fr.] Good health. *(sahṅ-tay)* Used as toast.
sari [Hindi] Common female dress of Hindu women, comprising long length of material, usually cotton or silk, wound round body. *(SAH-ri)*
sarong [Malay] (In Malaysia) man's or woman's garment, consisting of strip of cloth, usually brightly patterned, wound round body. *(sar-ONG)*
satori [Jap.] (In Buddhism) sudden enlightenment. *(sat-OH-ri)*
satsuma [Jap.] Kind of mandarin orange originally grown in Japan. *(sat-SOO-ma)* From the name of a Japanese province. Also applied, with capital letter, to type of Japanese pottery from same region.
Saturnalia [Lat.] Ancient Roman festival of Saturn in December, marked by feasting and revelry, and supposed to be the predecessor of Christmas. *(sat-ur-NAY-li-a)* Hence **saturnalia**, any period or scene of wild revelry or licence.
satyagraha [Sanskrit] Passive resistance. *(saht-YAH-gra-hah)* Especially applied to political philosophy of Gandhi.
sauerkraut [Ger.] German dish of chopped pickled cabbage. *(SOW-er-krowt)*
Saumur [Fr.] French white wine. *(soh-moor)* From name of town in Loire region.
sauna [Finn.] Steam-bath based on Finnish model. *(SOR-na)* After the body is cleansed by the action of steam, it is toned up by exposure to cold water.
sauté [Fr.] (In cookery) quickly fried in a little hot fat. *(soh-tay)*
Sauternes [Fr.] Sweet white wine from Bordeaux region of France. *(soh-tairn)*
sauve qui peut [Fr.] Hasty flight to escape trouble. *(sohv kee pur)*
savant [Fr.] Learned man. *(sav-ahṅ)* Feminine **savante** *(sav-ahṅt)*
savoir(-)faire [Fr.] Ready ability to know and do what is appropriate in the circumstances, especially socially. *(sav-wahr FAIR)*
savoir(-)vivre [Fr.] Good breeding; behaving with instinctive correctness in society. *(sav-wahr VEE-vruh)*
scagliola [It.] Plaster painted to resemble stone, marble, etc. *(skag-LYOH-la)*
scampi [It.] (In cookery) large prawns. *(SKAM-pi)* Also known as Dublin Bay prawns, though found in the Mediterranean and elsewhere.
scena [It.] (In opera) long vocal solo, usually dramatic. *(SHAY-na)*
scenario [It.] Outline of plot of play or film, scene by scene. *(sen-AH-ri-oh)* Also used as a synonym for 'expected happenings' in the sense of an imagined sequence of future events.

schadenfreude [Ger.] Malicious enjoyment of another's misfortune. *(SHAH-den-froy-duh)*

scherzando [It.] (Of music) played jokingly, playfully. *(sker-TSAND-oh)*

scherzo [It.] Instrumental piece, especially movement of symphony, sonata, string quartet, etc., in lively, quick triple-time. *(SKERT-so)*

schlemiel [Yiddish] Unlucky, uncomplaining man. *(shluh-MEEL)*

schlock [Yiddish] Of poor quality; cheap and inferior. *(shlok)* Slang.

Schloss [Ger.] (In Germany) castle. *(shlohs)*

schmaltz [Yiddish] Exaggerated, sugary or off-putting sentimentality. *(shmalts)*

schnapps [Ger.] Strong Dutch gin. *(shnaps)*

Schnauzer [Ger.] German breed of dog with wiry coat. *(SHNOWT-ser)*

schnitzel [Ger.] Veal cutlet. *(SHNIT-sl)* *See* **wiener schnitzel.**

schnorrer [Yiddish] Beggar. *(SHNOR-uh)* Slang.

schottische [Ger.] Slow polka. Music for this. *(shot-EESH)*

Schuhplattler [Ger.] Bavarian folk-dance in which male dancers slap their feet and thighs. *(SHOO-plaht-luh)*

schuss [Ger.] (In ski-ing) straight downhill run. Make this. *(shoos)*

scire facias [Lat.] Writ to warn of pending enforcement or annulment of judgement, patent, etc. *(seye-ri FASH-i-as)*

scirocco Same as **sirocco.**

scriptorium [Lat.] Room set aside for writing, especially in monastery. *(skrip-TOAR-i-um)*

sculps(it) [Lat.] Carved (this). *(SKULP-sit)* Always accompanied by name, and engraved on sculpture to identify sculptor.

séance [Fr.] Meeting for exhibition, observation or investigation of spiritualistic phenomena. *(SAY-ahńs)*

sec [Fr.] (Of wine) dry. *(sek)*

sécateur, secateurs [Fr.] Pair of pruning scissors or clippers. *(say-kat-ur, sek-at-URZ)* The second, anglicised form is now normal.

secco [It.] (Of Italian wine) dry. (In art) painting on dry plaster. *(SEK-oh)*

secondo [It.] Second. Lower part in duet. *(sek-ON-doh)* See **primo** [It.].

secrétaire, secretaire [Fr.] Writing-desk, bureau, **escritoire.** *(sek-ret-AIR)*

secundo [Lat.] Secondly. *(sek-UN-doh)* See **primo** [Lat.].

securus iudicat (or **judicat) orbis terrarum** [Lat.] The verdict of the world is conclusive. The whole world cannot be wrong.

(sek-OO-rus YOO- or *JOO-dik-at OR-bis ter-AH-rum)* Quotation from St Augustine, *Contra Epistolam Parmenides*, iii, 24.

sederunt [Lat.] Sitting of ecclesiastical or other body, or of company of people for conversation, etc. *(SED-er-unt)*

sedia gestatoria [It.] Ceremonial papal chair, carried on shoulders of bearers. *(SAY-dya jest-at-or-EE-a)* Abandoned by recent popes.

sedilia [Lat.] Seats, usually three, in south wall of chancel of church, often decorated, for use of clergy. *(sed-IL-i-a)* Singular **sedile** *(sed-EE-li)*

segno [It.] Sign (:S:) used in printed music. *(SAYN-yoh)* See **dal segno, al segno, da capo al segno.**

seguidilla [Sp.] Ancient Spanish dance in quick triple time, resembling bolero, with singing and castanets, still widely performed in Andalusia and throughout Spain. *(seg-ee-DEEL-ya)*

seicento [It.] Seventeenth century, especially the Italian art and architecture of that century. *(say-CHEN-toh)*

seiche [Swiss Fr.] Oscillation of lake water, rather like tidal wave, caused by change in barometric pressure. *(saysh)*

seigneur [Fr.] Feudal lord (especially in France). *(sehn-YUR)* See **grand seigneur.**

semper eadem [Lat.] Always the same. *(sem-per ay-AH-dem)* Motto of Queen Elizabeth I and others.

semper fidelis [Lat.] Always trustworthy. *(sem-per fid-AY-lis)*

semplice [It.] (In music) to be played simply. *(SEM-plee-cheh)*

sempre [It.] (In music) throughout. *(SEM-preh)*

senhor; senhora; senhorita [Port.] (In Portugal, Brazil, etc.) Mr, sir, man; Mrs, madam, lady; Miss, young unmarried lady. *(say-NYOR, say-NYOR-a, say-nyor-EE-ta)*

se non è vero, è molto ben trovato [It.] If it is not true, it is a happy invention. *(say nohn ay VEH-roh ay MOL-toh ben troh-VAH-toh)*

señor; señora; señorita [Sp.] (In Spain and Spanish speaking countries) same as **senhor** etc. *(sen-YOR, sen-YOR-a, sen-yor-EE-ta)*

sensorium [Lat.] Seat of sensation in the brain. *(sen-SOR-i-um)*

senza [It.] Without *(SENT-sa)*

sepoy [Hind.] Native Indian soldier under European, especially British, command. *(SEE-poy)*

seq. [Lat.] Abbreviation of **sequens**, the following.

sérac, serac [Fr.] Pinnacle of ice on glacier caused by intersection of crevasses. *(say-RAK)*

seraglio [It.] Same as **harem**. Turkish palace, especially that of Sultan in Constantinople. *(ser-AHL-yoh)*

serein [Fr.] Fine evening rain falling from cloudless sky in tropical areas. *(ser-AṄ)*

serenata [It.] Dramatic **cantata**. Suite of music, light in character, for orchestra or wind-band. *(ser-en-AH-ta)*

seriatim [Lat.] One by one, in order. *(ser-i-AY* or *-AH-tim)*

Sèvres [Fr.] Fine porcelain made at Sèvres, France. *(SEHV-ruh)*

Sf. Abbreviation of **sforzando.**

sforzando [It.] (Of note or chord in music) to be played suddenly loud. *(sforts-AND-oh)*

sfumato [It.] (Of painting) with indistinct outlines, the colours merging gently into one another. *(sfoo-MAH-toh)*

sgraffito [It.] (In architecture and pottery) method of decorating by scratching a surface to reveal a different colour beneath. *(sgrahf-EE-toh)*

shah [Pers.] King of Iran. *(shah)*

shaik(h) See **sheikh.**

shalom [Heb.] Peace. *(shah-LOHM)* Used as salutation among Jews.

shaman [Russ.] Priest or witch-doctor among primitive tribes. *(SHA-man)*

shantung [Chin.] Heavy silk fabric originating from Shantung province, China. *(shan-TUNG)*

shebeen [Ir.] Unlicensed house selling alcoholic drink. Hence, any low public house. *(shi-BEEN)* In Ireland only.

sheikh [Arab.] (In Arab countries) chief; leader; head of tribe or village. *(shayk, sheek)*

shemozzle [Yiddish] Brawl. Uproar. Quarrel. Muddle. *(she-MOZL)*

shiksa [Yiddish] Non-Jewish girl or woman. Non-practising Jewish girl or woman. *(SHIK-sa)*

Shinto [Jap.] Japanese religion based on worship of ancestors. *(SHIN-toh)*

shish kebab [Turk.] Small pieces of meat and vegetable cooked on skewer. *(SHISH kuh-bab)*

Shiva [Sanskrit] Hindu god, associated by some with destruction. *(SHEE-va)*

shnorrer Same as **schnorrer.**

shogun [Jap.] (In Japan) hereditary commander-in-chief and, until mid-nineteenth century, virtual ruler. *(SHOH-gun)*

sic [Lat.] Thus spelt; thus written; thus said. *(sik)* Used, in brackets, after a quotation to indicate that it is accurately reproduced, i.e. to make it clear that any error (e.g. of grammar), nonsense, etc. in the quotation is in the original, and is not caused by inaccurate copying. A method of drawing attention to error, nonsense, etc. in the original.

sic semper tyrannis [Lat.] Thus be it (i.e. the fate) of tyrants ever.

(sik SEM-per tir-AN-is) Motto of Virginia, U.S.A. Used by assassin as he shot Abraham Lincoln.

sic transit gloria mundi [Lat.] Thus passes away the glory of the (i.e. this) world. *(sik TRAN-sit GLOAR-i-a MUN-dee)* Based on words of Thomas à Kempis, *Imitation of Christ.*

Sieg heil! [Ger.] Victory, hail! *(zeek HEYE-l)* Nazi chant.

sierra [Sp.] Long range of mountains with serrated peaks in Spain, South America, etc. *(see-ER-a)*

siesta [Sp.] Afternoon nap or rest, especially in hot countries. *(see-ES-ta)*

siffleur [Fr.] Performer skilled in whistling. Person hired to barrack performance, speech, etc. *(see-FLUR)* Feminine **siffleuse** (-FLURZ)

signore; signora; signorina [It.] (In Italy) same as **senhor**, etc. *(seen-YOR-eh; seen-YOR-a; seen-yor-EE-na)*

si jeunesse savait, si vieillesse pouvait [Fr.] If (only) youth knew, if (only) old age could. *(see zhur-nes sav-ay, see vyay-yes poo-vay)*

s'il vous plaît [Fr.] Please. *(seel voo play)*

si monumentum requiris, circumspice [Lat.] If you seek (need) a monument, look around you. *(see mon-oo-MENT-um rek-WEE-ris sur-kum SPIK-eh)* Epitaph of Sir Christopher Wren in St Paul's Cathedral, which he designed.

simoom, simoon [Arab.] Hod dry sand-laden wind blowing at intervals in deserts, especially Arabian. *(sim-OOM or -OON)*

simpatico [It.] Congenial. Likeable. Helpful. *(sim-PAH-tee-koh)* Feminine **simpatica.**

simpliciter [Lat.] Absolutely; without limitation. *(sim-PLIS-it-er)*

simulacrum [Lat.] Image, representation, imitation, not the real thing; deceptive likeness or substitute. *(sim-ul-AHK-rum)*

sine die [Lat.] Indefinitely; without any date being fixed. *(see-nay DEE-ay)*

sine qua non [Lat.] Indispensable thing (or person) necessary for achievement of some purpose, condition, etc. *(see-nay kwah nohn)*

sinfonia [It.] Symphony. Symphony orchestra. *(sin-FOH-ni-a)*

sinfonietta [It.] Small-scale symphony. Small symphony orchestra. *(sin-fohn-i-ET-a)*

Singspiel [Ger.] Light opera, with spoken dialogue and interpolated songs. *(ZING-shpeel)*

Sinn Fein [Ir.] Irish patriotic movement and party, founded 1905, to bring about cultural development and political independence. *(shin FAYN)*

sirdar [Hind.] Commander; leader. *(SUR-dah)*

sirocco [It.] Hot south wind blowing from Africa to Italy. *(sir-OK-oh)*

sitar [Hind.] Long-necked musical instrument of India, resembling guitar. *(SIT-ah* or *sit-AH)*

Siva Same as **Shiva.** *(SEE-va)*

sjambok [Afrikaans] Heavy whip of rhinoceros hide. Flog with this. *(SHAM-bok)*

skål [Norw.] See **skoal.**

skean dhu [Gael.] Dagger kept in stocking as part of Highland costume. *(skeen DOO)*

skijöring, ski-joring [Norw.] Sport in which skier is towed by animal or vehicle. *(SKEE-jor-ing, shee-UR-ing)*

skoal [Scandinavian] Good health! *(skohl)* Used as a toast. Properly spelt **skål.**

slalom [Norw.] Downhill ski-race over zigzag course marked out by poles. *(SLAH-luhm)* Also applied to race over zigzag course in other sports, e.g. water-skiing, canoeing.

smörgåsbord, smorgasbord [Swedish] Meal with variety of (cold) savouries on open sandwiches. *(SMUR-gohs-boord, SMOR-guhs-bord)*

sobriquet [Fr.] Assumed name. Nick-name. *(soh-brik-ay)*

Société Anonyme [Fr.] Joint-stock company. *(sos-yay-tay an-on-eem)* Equivalent to the English *& Co.* and found, normally abbreviated to **S.A.**, as part of the name of French companies.

soi-disant [Fr.] Self-styled. *(swah-deez-ahṅ)* Implies deceit.

soigné, soignée [Fr.] (Of man, woman respectively) well-groomed. *(swahn-yay)*

soirée [Fr.] Evening party, especially for intellectual purpose, music or conversation. *(swah-ray)*

soirée musicale [Fr.] Evening gathering to play or listen to music. *(swah-ray moo-zeek-ahl)*

solarium [Lat.] Room, or open space protected from wind, for taking the sun. *(sol-AH-ri-um)*

sola topi [Hindi] Sun-helmet made from pith of E. Indian swamp plant. *(SOH-la TOH-pi)* The word *sola* has nothing to do with *solar* or the sun.

solidi Plural of **solidus.**

solidus [Lat.] Shilling. Roman gold coin. (In typography or writing) oblique stroke (/). *(SOL-i-dus)*

solitaire [Fr.] Single precious stone set in ring, etc. Card-game or board-game for one person. *(sol-it-AIR)*

solus [Lat.] Alone. *(SOH-lus)*

soma [Sanskrit] Intoxicating drink used in Vedic religious ritual. *(SOH-ma)*

sombrero [Sp.] Wide-brimmed felt or straw hat worn in Spain, South America, etc. *(som-BRAIR-oh)*

sommelier [Fr.] Wine-waiter. *(som-uh-lyay)*

sonata [It.] Musical composition, normally in four movements, for solo instrument (e.g. piano, organ, harpsichord) or for instrument (e.g. violin, flute) accompanied by piano, etc. *(son-AH-ta)*

sonatina [It.] Musical composition resembling **sonata** but shorter, easier or lighter. *(son-a-TEEN-a)*

son et lumière [Fr.] Entertainment at night, at historic building, etc., illustrating its history with lighting effects, recorded sound, music (and sometimes actors). *(son ay loom-yair)*

soprano [It.] Highest-pitched human singing voice. *(sop-RAH-noh)* Also applied to instrument of highest pitch in a family (e.g. soprano saxophone).

Sorbonne [Fr.] Ancient university in Paris. *(sor-BON)*

sordino [It.] Mute for musical instrument. *(sor-DEE-noh)*

sortes [Lat.] Divination by selection from book, which is opened at random, the first word or phrase on which the eye chances being taken as prophetic. *(SOR-tez)* Hence **sortes Biblicae** *(BIB-lik-eye* or *BIB-lis-ee),* **sortes Homericae** *(hoh-MER-ik-eye* or *hoh-MER-is-ee),* such divination using Bible, Homer's works, etc.

sortie [Fr.] Sudden attack, especially on beleaguered garrison. Operational flight by military aircraft. *(SOR-ti)*

sostenuto [It.] (In music) with notes played in a sustained manner, with lengthened value and smooth style. *(sos-ten-OO-toh)*

sotto voce [It.] In an undertone; in a low voice; aside. *(sot-oh VOH-cheh)*

sou [Fr.] Coin of little value. *(soo)*

soubrette [Fr.] Maidservant or similar character in play, especially comedy, with conventional pertness, flirtatiousness, proneness to intrigue, etc. Actress in this style, or accustomed to play such parts. *(soo-BRET)*

soubriquet [Fr.] Same as **sobriquet.** *(soo-brik-ay)*

soufflé [Fr.] (In cookery) dish made with whipped egg-whites and other ingredients, baked until light and frothy. *(soo-flay)*

soupçon [Fr.] Very small quantity. Slight trace. Dash. *(soop-soṅ)*

soupe [Fr.] Soup. *(soop)*

soutane [Fr.] Cassock of Roman Catholic priest. *(soo-TAHN)*

souteneur [Fr.] Man living on prostitute's earnings. *(soo-tuh-nur)*

souterrain [Fr.] Underground room. (In archaeology) underground chamber or passage. *(soo-ter-aṅ)*

soviet [Russ.] Elected council in Russia, either in particular district, or as governing body of the whole country (Supreme Soviet). *(SOHV-* or *SOV-i-et)*

spaghetti [It.] Form of **pasta** in long sticks which become soft when boiled. *(spag-ET-i)*

spaghetti bolognese [It.] Spaghetti served with sauce of liver or minced beef with vegetables, notably tomato. *(spag-ET-i bol-on-AYZ)*

spaghetti milanese [It.] Spaghetti served with sauce of mushroom, ham and tomato. *(spag-ET-i mil-an-AYZ)*

spalpeen [Ir.] Rascal. Youngster. *(spal-PEEN)*

spécialité de la maison [Fr.] Dish which is the speciality of the chef at a particular restaurant. *(spehs-yal-ee-tay duh la may-zoṁ)*

spiccato [It.] (Of music for string instruments) to be played **staccato**, with clear separation of notes by a bouncing movement of the bow. *(spik-AH-toh)*

spiel [Ger.] Long story, especially glib or persuasive one (e.g. patter of salesman). Reel off such a story. *(shpeel)*

Sprechgesang [Ger.] Speech-song: use of singing voice tinged with speech quality in some modern songs of experimental or **avant-garde** nature. *(SHPREKH-guh-sang)* See below.

Sprechstimme [Ger.] Use of speaking voice tinged with singing quality in some modern songs of experimental or **avant-garde** nature. *(SHPREKH-shtim-uh)* See above.

springbok [Afrikaans] Type of antelope, found in South Africa, with habit of springing upwards when excited or disturbed. *(SPRING-bok)*

spumante [It.] (Of wine) sparkling. *(spoo-MAN-teh)*

sputnik [Russ.] (Russian) space satellite. *(SPOOT-nik)*

S.S. Abbreviation of **Schutz-Staffel**, Nazi special police force.

Stabat Mater [Lat.] (In Roman Catholic liturgy) Latin hymn on the agony of the Virgin Mary at the Crucifixion. Musical setting of this. *(STAB-at MAH-ter)* Literally, 'The Mother stood', i.e. at the Cross.

staccato [It.] (Of music) to be played with the notes sharply separated from one another, the value of the notes being cut short. *(stak-AH-toh)*

stakhanovite [Russ.] Worker who increases production to gain extra pay and approbation. *(stak-AH-noh-veye-t)*

Stalag [Ger.] German prisoner-of-war camp in Second World War. *(STAL-ag)*

status quo [Lat.] Present state of affairs. Prevailing, existing conditions. *(stay-tus KWOH)* Always used in connexion with continuation of existing state of affairs.

status quo ante [Lat.] Previous state of affairs. *(stay-tus kwoh AN-*

teh) Always used in connexion with reversion to former position, state of affairs, condition, etc.

stein [Ger.] (In Germany, Austria, etc.) large earthenware drinking-mug, especially beer-mug, often richly decorated and with ornate lid. *(sht-eye-n)*

stela [Lat.] (In archaeology) upright slab or pillar, often decorated, with inscription (e.g. as gravestone, milestone). *(STEEL-a)* Plural **stele** *(STEEL-eh)*

steppe [Russ.] Flat, grassy, treeless plain, especially in south-east Europe and Siberia. *(step)*

stet [Lat.] Ignore the alteration: let the original stand. *(stet)* Used when proof-reading, or when annotating manuscript, draft typescript, etc., to indicate that a correction, deletion or alteration is to be ignored in favour of the original.

stigmata [Lat.] Marks, sometimes including bleeding, corresponding to wounds on body of Christ when crucified, which sometimes appear on bodies of devout people. *(STIG-ma-ta* or *stig-MAH-ta)*

stoa [Gk.] Roofed colonnade in ancient Greek buildings. *(STOH-a)*

stoep [Dut.] Verandah or terrace at front of house. *(stoop)*

strega [It.] Italian liqueur. *(STRAY-ga)*

stretto [It.] (In music) becoming faster. *(STRET-oh)*

stria [Lat.] (In architecture) narrow band between flutes of column. *(STREE-ah)*

strudel [Ger.] Baked flaky pastry with filling, usually sweet. *(stroodl)* See **apfelstrudel.**

stucco [It.] Plaster or smooth cement used for coating walls or architectural decoration (e.g. cornices, mouldings). *(STUK-oh)*

Sturm und Drang [Ger.] Storm and stress: period of tumult in person's development or in national life, especially ideological. *(shtoorm oont drahng)* Title of play by von Klinger (1775) applied to German literary movement in late eighteenth century, characterised by expression of violent passion.

sub judice [Lat.] Not yet decided. Still being considered. (In law) under consideration by a court of law; having been referred for legal judgement (so that all other public deliberation of or comment on a matter is prohibited, e.g. by newspapers). *(sub JOO-dis-i* or *YOO-dik-ay)*

subpoena [Lat.] Writ demanding person's attendance in court under pain of penalty. Issue or serve such writ. *(sub-PEE-na)*

sub rosa [Lat.] In confidence; secretly. *(sub ROH-za)* Applied to communications, consultations, etc.

sub specie aeternitatis [Lat.] In relation to God, eternity, the timelessness of things, without reference to the temporal, actual, changing conditions of everyday life. *(sub SPEK-i-eh* or *SPEE-sheh it-er-nit-Ah-tis)*

succedaneum [Lat.] Substitute (often drug), usually of inferior quality. *(suk-sed-AY-ni-um)*

succès de scandale [Fr.] Success (e.g. of book) achieved through notoriety or scandal. *(sook-say duh skahṅ -dahl)*

succès d'estime [Fr.] Success (of work of art) in the eyes of experts, critics or the discerning, but not in popular or financial terms. *(sook-say des-teem)*

succès fou [Fr.] Success marked by wild enthusiasm. *(sook-say foo)*

succubus [Lat.] Evil spirit, especially feminine one supposed to have sexual intercourse with men during their sleep. *(SUK-yoo-bus)*

suggestio falsi [Lat.] Deliberate misrepresentation not involving direct lie. *(suj-est-i-oh FAL-si)*

sui generis [Lat.] Of its own kind; in a class by itself; unique. *(soo-i JEN-* or *GEN-er-is)*

summa [Lat.] Summary of what is known about a subject. *(SUM-a)*

summa cum laude [Lat.] With the highest distinction. *(sum-a kum LOW-deh)* Applied to examination success.

summum bonum [Lat.] The supreme good. *(sum-um BON-* or *BOHN-um)*

sumo [Jap.] Type of Japanese wrestling. Practitioner of this. *(SOO-moh)*

sunt lacrymae rerum [Lat.] There is sadness in life. Life is tragic. *(sunt LAK-rim-eye REH-rum)* From Virgil, *Aeneid*, I, 462.

supressio veri [Lat.] Suppression of the truth; misrepresentation by concealment. *(sup-res-i-oh VEAR-i)*

supra [Lat.] Above. Previously mentioned. *(SOO-* or *SYOO-pra)* Found in footnotes of learned books to refer reader to earlier passage.

suprême [Fr.] (Of cookery) served in rich cream sauce. *(soo-prehm)*

supremo [Sp.] Supreme leader, ruler, authority, commander, supervisor, etc. especially one combining a number of responsibilities. *(soo* or *syoo-PREE-moh)*

Sûreté [Fr.] Criminal investigation department of French police, especially that of Paris. *(syoor-tay)*

sursum corda [Lat.] Lift up your hearts. *(soor-* or *sur-sum KOR-da)* From the Latin version of the Roman Catholic Mass.

Sutra [Sanskrit] Part of Hindu and Buddhist sacred literature. *(SOO-tra)*

svelte [Fr.] Elegant, graceful. Slim, lissom. *(svelt)*

swami [Hindi] Hindu religious teacher. *(SWAH-mi)*

swaraj [Sanskrit] Indian self-government. *(swar-AHJ)*

sympathique [Fr.] Same as **simpatico.** *(sahṅ-pat-eek)*

T

tableau vivant [Fr.] Group of people, silent and motionless, arranged to represent a scene, incident, painting, etc. *(tab-loh vee-vahn̍)* Plural **tableaux vivants** (same pronunciation).

table d'hôte [Fr.] Restaurant meal at fixed price with little or no choice of dishes. *(tah-bluh doht)*

tabouret [Fr.] Low seat or stool without back or arms. *(tab-oo-ray, TAB-er-et)*

tabula rasa [Lat.] Human mind with no innate ideas, preconceptions, etc. and therefore able to receive information about a subject. *(tab-yoo-la RAH-za* or *-sa)*

tacet [Lat.] (In music) remain silent. *(TAS-it)* Direction that voice or instrument is to remain silent during a particular portion of the music.

tachisme [Fr.] Style of painting originating after Second World War, using technique of pouring, smearing or throwing paint on canvas in random way. *(tash-eesm)* Sometimes known as 'action painting'.

taedium vitae [Lat.] Weariness of life. *(tee-di-um VEE-teye* or *VEYE-tee)*

Tafelwein [Ger.] Ordinary table wine. *(TAH-fl-veye-n)*

tagliatelle [It.] Ribbon-shaped form of **pasta**. *(tahl-yah-TEL-i)*

taiga [Russ.] Siberian coniferous forest. *(TEYE-gah)*

taipan [Chin.] (In China) head of a foreign business. *(TEYE-pan)* There is also an aboriginal word, identically spelt and pronounced, for a large, venomous Australian snake.

taj [Arab.] Tall conical hat worn by dervish. *(tahj)*

Talmud [Heb.] Body of Jewish laws and traditions. *(TAL-mood)*

tambour [Fr.] Pair of hoops for holding material stretched in place so that it can be embroidered. *(tahn̍-boor, TAM-boor)*

tandoori [Hind.] Food cooked over charcoal. *(TAND-oor-i)*

tant mieux [Fr.] So much the better. *(tahn̍ myur)*

tant pis [Fr.] So much the worse. *(tahn̍-pee)*

Tantum Ergo [Lat.] Opening words of hymn by St Thomas Aquinas, used in various services but especially Benediction. Musical setting of this hymn. *(tan-tum UR-goh)* The best known English version begins 'Therefore we, before Him bending'.

Taoiseach [Ir.] Prime Minister of Irish Republic. *(TEE-shakh)*

tapis [Fr.] Found only in the phrase **on the tapis**, under discussion. *(ta-pee)*

taramasalata [Gk.] Smoked cod's roe, usually served as first course of meal. *(tah-ra-mah-sal-AH-ta)*

tarantella [It.] Very rapid whirling dance, originating in southern Italy. Music for this. *(tar-an-TEL-a)* Once believed to be cure for malady caused by bite of **tarantula** spider, named after seaport Tarento in heel of Italy.

tarantula [Lat.] Large black spider found in southern Europe and having mildly poisonous bite. *(tar-ANT-tyoo-la)* See **tarantella.**

tarboosh [Arab.] Tasselled cap, usually red, resembling fez and worn by Moslem men. *(tah-BOOSH)*

tartare [Fr.] (In cookery) name of sauce of eggs, oil, vinegar, gherkin and spices, specially used with fish. *(tah-tah)* Often anglicised to **tartar** *(TAH-tah)*

tastevin [Fr.] Shallow silver dish, often worn on ribbon round neck, used by wine-taster. *(tast-vañ)*

Te Deum [Lat.] Thee, God. Opening words of Latin version of hymn of thanksgiving sung at morning service and on special occasions. Music for this hymn. *(tee DEE-um, tay DAY-um)* The fuller version is **'Te Deum, laudamus'**, We praise thee, O God.

teepee Same as **tepee.**

tempera [It.] (In art) method of painting in which pigments are bound together with egg-yolk. *(TEM-per-a)*

tempo [It.] Speed. *(TEM-poh)*

tempo primo [It.] (In music) at the original speed. *(TEM-poh PREE-moh)* Direction found at end of passage played more quickly or slowly than original speed.

tempora mutantur et nos mutamur in illis [Lat.] Times change, and we change with them. *(TEM-por-a moo-TAN-toor et nohs moo-TAH-moor in IL-ees)*

tempo rubato [It.] Same as **rubato.**

tempura [Jap.] Japanese dish of fried fish or shellfish with vegetables. *(TEM-poo-ra)*

tempus edax rerum [Lat.] Time, the devourer of all things. *(TEM-pus ED-aks RAY-rum)*

tempus fugit [Lat.] Time flies. *(TEM-pus FYOO-jit* or *FOO-git)*

ten. Abbreviation of **tenuto.**

tenuto [It.] (Of music) note(s) to be sustained to full value or even a little more. *(ten-OO-toh)*

tepee [American Indian] Conical tent, wigwam, made of skins, etc. on frame of poles. *(TEE-pee)*

tequila [Sp.] Strong Mexican drink distilled from fermented agave. *(tek-EE-la)*

terminus ad quem [Lat.] Finishing-point (of argument, etc.) *(TUR-min-us ad KWEM)*

terminus a quo [Lat.] Starting-point (of argument, policy, etc.) *(TUR-min-us ah KWOH)*

terra alba [Lat.] Pipeclay. *(ter-a AL-ba)*

terra cotta [It.] Hard, unglazed brownish-red pottery. *(ter-a KOT-a)*

terrae filius [Lat.] (At Oxford University) satirical orator who used to be allowed licence on certain occasions. *(ter-eye FIL-i-us)*

terra firma [Lat.] Firm ground; dry land (as distinct from sea). *(ter-a FUR-ma)*

terra incognita [Lat.] Unknown territory. *(ter-a in-KOG-ni-ta)*

terrazzo [It.] Flooring-material of chips of marble or stone set in cement and given smooth finish. *(ter-ATS-oh)*

terrine [Fr.] Earthenware cooking pot, usually rectangular with lid and without handle, used for cooking of **pâté.** *(ter-EEN)* Hence, in cookery, the name of the dish has become applied to the food cooked in it, and a terrine is also a pâté prepared in the dish (as distinct from being prepared in a crust, sausage, etc.).

tertium quid [Lat.] Something intermediate between two opposite or incompatible things. *(TER-ti-um* or *TUR-shum KWID)*

terza rima [It.] Verse-form consisting of three-line stanzas: the first and third lines rhyme with each other and with the second line of the previous stanza. *(TAIR-tsa REE-ma)*

tessitura [It.] Range (e.g. high, middle, low) within which lie most of the notes in the vocal part of a piece of music. *(tes-it-OOR-a)*

testudo [Lat.] Military formation of Roman soldiers in ancient times, consisting of number of soldiers in close array with shields held side by side, both above and around the array, for protection. Machine or siege-engine affording protection to attacking troops. *(tes-TOO* or *-TYOO-doh)*

tête-à-tête [Fr.] Private or intimate conversation between two people. Privately. *(tet-a-tet)*

tête-bêche [Fr.] (Postage stamp) printed upside down or sideways relative to others on same sheet. *(tet-besh)*

thé dansant [Fr.] Afternoon tea-party with dancing. *(tay dahṅ-sahṅ)*

tic douloureux [Fr.] Severe form of neuralgia with habitual spasmodic twitching of facial muscles. *(tik doo-luh-RUR)*

tiers état [Fr.] Third estate: the common people, including their parliamentary representatives, before the French Revolution. *(tyez ay-tah)* The first two 'estates' were the nobility and clergy.

tilde [Sp.] Mark (˜) placed over letters in some languages, especially Spanish (to indicate that *n* is pronounced *ny* when marked *ñ*) and

Portuguese (to indicate nasalisation of certain vowels). *(teel-deh)*

timbale [Fr.] Drum-shaped dish or mould, of copper, tin or china, for preparation of food. *(tañ-bahl)*

timbre [Fr.] Distinctive quality or character of sound produced by voice or musical instrument. *(tahñ-bruh)*

timeo Danaos et dona ferentes [Lat.] I fear the Greeks even when they are bringing gifts. *(tim-AY-oh dan-AH-ohs et DON-a* or *DOH-na fer-EN-tays)* Warning to mistrust apparent generosity of one's enemies. From Virgil's *Aeneid.*

timpani [It.] Kettle-drums. *(TIM-pan-i)*

tirailleur [Fr.] Sharp-shooter. Soldier trained as skirmisher. *(tee-reye-ur)*

toccata [It.] Composition for piano or organ, in rapid **tempo**, fantasia-like in style. *(tok-AH-ta)*

toga [Lat.] (In Ancient Rome) citizen's normal outer garment consisting of long loose robe. *(TOH-ga)*

toga praetexta [Lat.] **Toga** with wide purple border worn by magistrates, etc. *(TOH-ga pree-TEKS-ta)*

toga virilis [Lat.] Adult **toga** donned by Roman boys at age of fourteen as sign of manhood. *(TOH-ga vir-EE-lis)*

toilette [Fr.] Process of dressing, arranging hair, etc. *(twah-LET)*

Tokay [Hung.] Sweet Hungarian dessert wine. *(tok-AY)*

ton [Fr.] Fashionable style, society, mode. *(toñ)*

tondo [It.] Circular painting or relief. *(TON-doh)*

topee See **topi.**

topi [Hindi] Sun-helmet. *(TOH-pi)* Sometimes spelt **topee.**

toque [Fr.] Hat (normally worn by women) of pill-box shape. *(tok)*

Torah [Heb.] Mosaic law. Book containing Jewish law. *(TOR-a)*

torchère [Fr.] Tall stand for candle or lamp. *(tor-SHAIR)*

toreador [Sp.] Bull-fighter. *(TOH-ray-a-dor)* See below.

torero [Sp.] Bull-fighter. *(toh-REH-roh)* This is now the normal word used in Spain. See above.

torii [Jap.] Gateway to Shinto shrine in Japan, consisting of two uprights, each with two cross-pieces, the upper one curving upwards. *(TOR-i-i)*

toro [Sp.] Bull. *(TOH-roh)*

torque [Fr.] Necklace of twisted metal, especially as worn by ancient Celtic people. *(tork)* Also (from Lat.) quantity and system of forces tending to cause rotation (in engine, etc.).

tortilla [Sp.] (In Mexico) thin flat cake of maize. (In Spain) omelette. *(tor-TEEL-ya)*

tot homines quot sententiae Same as **quot homines tot sententiae.**

Totentanz [Ger.] Same as **danse macabre.** *(TOH-tuhn-tahnts)*

toties quoties [Lat.] On each occasion. *(tot-* or *toht-i-ez* or *tosh-i-eez kwot-* or *kwoht-i-ez* or *kwosh-i-eez)*

toto caelo [Lat.] By a very considerable amount. *(toh-toh KEYE-* or *SEE-loh)*

touché [Fr.] (In fencing) expression used to acknowledge a hit by an opponent. Hence used to acknowledge valid point or accusation against one made by another person in argument, discussion, etc. *(TOO-shay)*

toujours la politesse [Fr.] It is always best to be polite. *(too-zhoor la pol-eet-es)*

tour de force [Fr.] Outstanding achievement in skill, strength, etc. *(toor duh fors)*

Tour de France [Fr.] Annual cycle-race by road around large area of France. *(toor duh France)*

tour d'horizon [Fr.] General survey. *(toor dor-ee-zoṁ)*

tournedos [Fr.] Steak fillet. *(toor-nuh-doh)*

tout comprendre c'est tout pardonner [Fr.] To understand everything is to forgive everything. *(too coṁ-prahṅ-druh say too pah-don-ay)*

tout court [Fr.] Briefly. Peremptorily. Without explanation. *(too koor)* Implies discourtesy or unhelpfulness.

tout de suite [Fr.] Immediately. *(toot dsweet)*

tout ensemble [Fr.] Thing viewed as a whole. General effect. *(toot ahṅ-sahṅ-bl)*

tout le monde [Fr.] Everybody. *(too luh moṅd)* Especially, anybody who is anybody.

tovarish [Russ.] Comrade. *(tov-AH-rish)*

trahison des clercs [Fr.] Betrayal by the intellectuals (in compromising their own standards). *(trah-ee-zoṁ day klair)*

tramontana [It.] Cold north wind blowing from mountains. *(trah-mohn-TAH-na)*

tranche [Fr.] Slice. Portion (e.g. of income, payment, etc.). *(trahṅsh)*

trattoria [It.] Italian eating-house. *(trah-toh-REE-ah)*

trecento [It.] The fourteenth century, especially the Italian art and architecture of that period. *(treh-CHEN-toh)*

tremolo [It.] (In music) very rapid reiteration of one note by agitation of bow in playing stringed instrument. In singing, rapid continuous change of pitch of a single note, producing tremulous effect. *(TREM-ol-oh)*

trente-et-quarante [Fr.] Same as **rouge et noir**. *(trahṅt ay kah-rahṅt)*

triclinium [Lat.] (In ancient Rome) couch running round three sides of dining-table. Dining-table or room thus furnished. *(tri-KLIN-i-um)*

tricolor(e) [Fr.] French national flag having vertical stripes of red, white and blue. *(tree-kol-or)*

tricorn(e) [Fr.] (Cocked hat) with brim turned up on all three sides. *(tree-korn)*

tricot [Fr.] Knitted fabric. *(tree-koh)*

tricoteuse [Fr.] Frenchwoman who knitted while watching execution of aristocrats by guillotine during French Revolution, or while encouraging revolutionary excesses. *(tree-koht-urz)*

triennale [It.] (Festival, exhibition, etc.) held every three years. *(tree-en-AH-leh)*

triforium [Lat.] Gallery over arches of nave, choir, etc. in church. *(tr-eye-FOR-i-um)*

trio [It.] (In music) composition for three voices or instruments. Second section of minuet, march or scherzo (after which first section is repeated). Any set of three persons or things. *(TREE-oh)*

trivia [Lat.] Trivialities. *(TRIV-i-a)*

trivium [Lat.] University course of grammar, logic and rhetoric in medieval times. *(TRIV-i-um)*

troika [Russ.] Russian carriage or sled drawn by three horses. Any group of three persons, authorities, nations, etc. acting jointly or exercising joint control. *(TROY-ka)*

trompe-l'œil [Fr.] (Painting) in fine detail intended to deceive the spectator into thinking that what is depicted is real. *(trom̃p lur-y)* Especially applied to painting giving impression of three-dimensional effect.

troppo [It.] (In music) Too; too much. *(TROP-oh)* Usually found in negative; **non troppo**, not too much; **allegro (ma) non troppo**, quickly (but) not too much so.

trottoir [Fr.] Pavement at side of street. *(trot-wahr)*

troubadour [Fr.] (In middle ages) lyric poet of southern France and adjacent regions of Spain and Italy, who composed and sang poems of gallantry, chivalry and courtly love, sometimes as wandering minstrel. Hence, any writer or performer of ballads. *(TROO-bad-oor)*

trou normand [Fr.] Drink of **calvados** after meal. *(troo nor-mahñ)*

troupe [Fr.] Company of actors or other performers. *(troop)*

trousseau [Fr.] Clothes, household linen, etc. collected by bride to begin married life. *(TROO-soh)*

trouvaille [Fr.] Lucky find. Windfall. *(troo-veye)*

trouvère [Fr.] (In medieval times) epic poet of northern France. *(troo-vair)*

truite [Fr.] Trout. *(trweet)*

tsar, tsarevitch, tsarina [Russ.] Same as **czar, czarevitch, czarina**, and pronounced in same way.

tsetse [Bantu] African fly carrying disease, especially sleeping-sickness. *(TSET-si)*

tsunami [Jap.] Large wave or series of waves caused by disturbance (e.g. earth tremor, volcanic movement) of ocean flow. *(tsoon-AH-mi)*

tuan [Malay] Sir. Master. *(too-AHN)* Respectful form of address by Malay-speakers.

tulle [Fr.] Fine net fabric of silk, etc. used for dresses, veils, hats, etc. *(tyool)*

tundra [Lappish] Flat, treeless Arctic region in northern Russia, etc. *(TUN-dra)*

tu quoque [Lat.] You too. *(too KWOK-weh* or *KWOH-kwi)* Retort that the accusation(s) made by the accuser apply to him too.

tutti [It.] (In music) to be played or sung by all the performers together. *(TUT-i)*

tutti-frutti [It.] Confection, especially ice-cream, made or flavoured with a number of fruits. *(too-ti-FROO-ti)*

tutu [Fr.] Short, projecting, frilled skirt worn by ballet-dancer *(TOO-too)*

tympanum [Lat.] (In architecture) semi-circular space between lintel of doorway and surrounding arch. Similar triangular space forming centre of pediment. *(TIM-pan-um)*

tzar, tzarevitch, tzarina Same as **czar, czarevitch, czarina**, and pronounced in same way.

tzigane [Fr.] Hungarian gypsy. *(tsig-AHN)*

U

Übermensch [Ger.] Superman. *(OO-buh-mensh)*

uhlan [Ger.] Cavalryman armed with lance in some European armies, especially German. *(OO-lan)*

Uitlander [Afrikaans] (In South Africa) foreigner; alien settler. *(AYT-lon-der, OYT-lan-der)*

ukase [Russ.] (In Tsarist Russia) government edict. *(oo-KAYS, oo-KAHS)* Hence, any arbitrary order.

ukelele [Hawaiian] Small four-stringed guitar. *(yoo-kuh-LAY-li)*

ult. Abbreviation of **ultimo.**

ultima ratio [Lat.] The final argument. *(ULT-i-ma RAH-ti-oh)* Usually applied to the use of force to settle a difference.

ultima Thule [Lat.] Far-away unknown land, supposed by the ancients to be an island or point of land six days' sail north of Britain and to be the extreme northern limit of the world. The end of the world. *(ULT-im-a THYOO-lee* or *TOO-leh)*

ultimo [Lat.] Of last month. *(ULT-im-oh)* Used in commercial correspondence, normally abbreviated to **ult**. (e.g. *your letter of 15th ult.).* This usage is now seldom found.

ultra [Lat.] Extreme. Extremely. *(ULT-ra)* Often prefixed to adjective *(ultra-modern)*, adverb or noun in this sense.

ultra vires [Lat.] Beyond (legal) power or authority of person, council, etc. *(ult-ra VEYE-reez* or *-rayz* or *VEE-rayz)*

umbra [Lat.] Total shadow in an eclipse. Dark central part of sunspot. *(UMB-ra)*

umiak [Eskimo] Large open boat of skin stretched over wooden frame. *(OOM-yak)*

umlaut [Ger.] Mark (¨) used over certain vowels in German, indicating pronunciation. *(UM-laut)*

uomo universale [It.] Universal man: one who is comprehensively cultured, educated and gifted. *(WOR-moh oo-ni-ver-SAH-leh)*

Upanishad [Sanskrit] One of a series of philosophical treatises in Ancient Hindu scripture. *(oo-PAN-ish-ad)*

urbi et orbi [Lat.] To the city (Rome) and to the world. *(OOR-bi et OR-bi)* Blessing or proclamation by the Pope.

Ursa [Lat.] Bear. *(UR-sa)*

Urtext [Ger.] Original text (of piece of literature, etc.). *(OOR-text)*

usquebaugh [Ir. and Scottish Gael.] Whisky. *(US-kwi-bor)*

ut infra [Lat.] See further below. *(ut IN-fra)* Found in footnotes of learned books to refer reader to later portion.

uti possidetis [Lat.] Principle that leaves belligerents in possession of what they have acquired. *(oo-ti pos-id-EE-* or *AY-tis)*

ut supra [Lat.] See further above. *(ut SOO-pra)* Found in footnotes of learned books to refer reader to earlier portion.

V

v. Abbreviation of **versus** and **vide.**

vade mecum [Lat.] Handbook, suitable for carrying about with one for ready reference. *(vah-deh MAY-kum)*

va-et-vient [Fr.] To-ing and fro-ing. Commotion. *(va ay vyañ)*

vae victis [Lat.] Woe to the vanquished. *(veye VIK-tees)*

vale [Lat.] Farewell. *(VAH-leh)*

Valenciennes [Fr.] Rich kind of lace. *(val-uhn-syenz)*

valet [Fr.] Gentleman's personal servant. Hotel employee with similar duties. *(VAL-ay)*

valet de chambre [Fr.] Same as **valet.** *(VAL-ay duh CHAHM-bruh)*
valete [Lat.] Farewell. *(val-AY-teh)*
Valhalla [Lat.] (In Scandinavian mythology) hall in the celestial regions for those slain in battle, who spend eternity there in joy and feasting. *(val-HAL-a)*
valise [Fr.] Suitcase, usually small. *(val-EEZ)*
Valkyrie [Old Norse] (In Scandinavian mythology) one of the twelve nymphs who entered battlefields, selected those destined to die, and conducted them to **Valhalla.** *(VAL-ki-ri)*
vallum [Lat.] Defensive rampart as used by ancient Romans. *(VAL-um)*
vaporetto [It.] Small passenger-boat (especially in Venice). *(vap-or-ET-oh)*
vaquero [Sp.] (In Spanish America) herdsman, cowboy. *(vah-KEH-roh)*
variorum [Lat.] (Of book, especially literary text) with notes of various previous commentators, editors, etc. *(vair-i-OAR-um)*
vaudeville [Fr.] Variety entertainment with songs, sketches, dances, etc. *(voh- or vor-duh-vil)*
V.D.Q.S. See **vin délimité de qualité supérieure.**
veau [Fr.] Veal. *(voh)*
Veda [Sanskrit] Collection of ancient Hindu sacred writings. *(VEE- or VAY-da)*
vedette [Fr.] Small passenger-boat (especially for sight-seers on River Seine in Paris). *(vuh-det)*
veilleuse [Fr.] Night-light, especially low light in corridor of hotel. Sanctuary-lamp. *(vay-yurz)*
veldt, veld [Afrikaans] (In South Africa) open country or pasture-land. *(felt, velt)*
velours [Fr.] Plush-like fabric used for hats, furnishing, etc. *(vel-OOR)*
velouté [Fr.] (In cookery) white sauce made of white stock (e.g. chicken, veal) with **roux** of butter and flour. *(vel-oo-tay)*
vendetta [It.] (In Corsica, southern Italy, etc.) blood feud between families, usually involving revenge for injury. *(ven-DET-a)* Normally applied to any exhibition of malicious, prolonged hostility.
vendeuse [Fr.] Saleswoman, especially in dress-shop. *(vahn̄-durz)*
Veni, Creator Spiritus [Lat.] Come, Creator Spirit: eighth-century Whitsuntide hymn, found in the Book of Common Prayer in the service for the Ordering of Priests in a translation beginning 'Come, Holy Ghost, our souls inspire', and sung on other notable occasions. *(VAY-ni kray-AH-tor SPI-rit-us)*
Venite [Lat.] O come: first word of Latin version of Psalm 95, sung

at Morning Prayer in English version beginning 'O come, let us sing unto the Lord'. *(ven-EYE-ti, ven-EE-teh)*

veni, vidi, vici [Lat.] I came, I saw, I conquered. *(VAY* or *WAY-ni, VEE* or *WEE-di, VEE* or *WEE-ki)* Attributed to Julius Caesar after one of his victories.

ventre à terre [Fr.] At full speed. *(vahn̄tr-a-tair)*

venue [Fr.] Appointed place of meeting. *(VEN-yoo)*

verbatim [Lat.] Word for word. *(ver-BAY-tim)*

verboten [Ger.] Forbidden. *(fer-BOH-ten)*

verb. sap. Abbreviation of **verbum sapienti sat est.**

verbum sapienti sat est [Lat.] A word is enough for a wise person. *(VER-bum sap-i-ENT-tee sat est)* Used, normally in abbreviation **verb. sap.**, to indicate that the preceding words are to be taken as a warning or strong hint.

verb. sat. [Lat.] Abbreviation of **verbum satienti.**

verbum satienti [Lat.] A word is enough. *(VER-bum sati-EN-ti)* Usually abbreviated to **verb. sat.**, with meaning similar to **verb. sap.**

verglas [Fr.] Thin coating of ice. *(vair-glah)*

verismo [It.] Realism. *(veh-REEZ-moh)*

verité [Fr.] Truth. Realism (especially in cinema or television work). *(vay-ree-tay)*

Verkrampte [Afrikaans] (In South Africa) white man or woman of stern reactionary or right-wing views. *(fer-KRAMPT-uh)*

verligte [Afrikaans] Of progressive views, especially with regard to sympathetic attitude towards Negroes. *(fer-LIKH-tuh)*

vermicelli [It.] Variety of **pasta** in long, very thin threads. *(vehr-mi-CHEL-i)*

vers de société [Fr.] Light, witty, topical verse. *(vair duh sohs-yay-tay)*

vers libre [Fr.] Free verse, without rhyme or lines of regular length and pattern, with variable rhythm instead of metre. *(vair lee-bruh)*

verso [Lat.] Left-hand page of open book. *(VER-soh)* See **recto.**

versus [Lat.] Against. *(VER-sus)* Normally abbreviated to **v.** and used, for example, of two teams in opposition.

vertu Same as **virtu.**

via [Lat.] By way of. *(VEYE-a, VEE-a)*

Via Crucis [Lat.] The Way of the Cross. Stations of the Cross, a devotion performed in Church or in the open air before fourteen successive representations (paintings, statues, etc.) of incidents in Passion of Christ, especially at Easter. *(vee-a KROO-chis* or *-kis)*

via dolorosa [Lat.] Jesus' route to the Crucifixion. Hence, any succession of anguished experiences. *(vee-a dol-or-OH-sa)*

via media [Lat.] Middle way or course between extremes or conflicting opposites. *(vee-a MAY-di-a)*

viaticum [Lat.] Eucharist administered to person dying or in danger of dying. *(veye* or *vee-AT-ik-um)*

vibrato [It.] (In music) rapid slight fluctuation of pitch of a note, especially in the playing of stringed instruments (where it is caused by rapid movement of the left hand while holding down the string(s) with the finger(s), which remain in position), but also applied to a tremulous effect in the singing voice. *(vib-RAH-toh)*

vice [Lat.] In succession to; in place of. *(VEYE-si)*

vice anglais See **le vice anglais.**

vice versa [Lat.] The other way round. Conversely. *(veye-si VER-sa)*

Vichy [Fr.] Effervescent mineral water. *(vee-shi)* Named from the spa town in central France.

vichyssoise [Fr.] Cold soup of creamed potatoes and leeks. *(vee-shi-swahz)*

victor ludorum [Lat.] The winner of the games: the most successful competitor in an athletics contest. *(vik-tor loo-DOR-um)*

vicuña [Sp.] South American type of llama with fine silky wool. Fabrics made from this wool. *(vi-KOO-nya)* Increasingly spelt without the **tilde** and pronounced *vi-KOO-na* or *vi-KYOO-na)*.

vide [Lat.] See. Consult. *(VEE-deh, VID-ay)* Found in footnotes of learned book to direct reader's attention to passage, reference, etc. elsewhere in book or in another book.

videlicet [Lat.] In other words. That is to say. Namely. *(vid-AY-li-ket)* Used, in abbreviation **viz.**, to introduce specific explanation of something generally stated in preceding words.

vieux jeu [Fr.] Old-fashioned. *(vyur zhur)*

vigilante [Sp.] Member of self-appointed body for maintenance of law and order, safety, etc. *(vij-il-AN-ti)*

vigneron [Fr.] Vine-grower. *(vee-nyer-orn̊)*

villanelle [Fr.] Verse form with nineteen lines and only two rhymes. *(vil-an-EL)*

villeggiatura [It.] Holiday or retirement spent in the country. *(vil-ej-a-TOO-ra)*

ville lumière [Fr.] City of light—Paris. *(veel loom-yair)*

vinaigrette [Fr.] (In cookery) dressing of oil and wine vinegar. Dish made or served with this. Pair of small bottles, sometimes ornamental, sometimes on stand, for holding oil and vinegar. *(vin-ay-gret, vin-ig-RET)*

vin blanc [Fr.] White wine. *(van̊ blon̊)*

vin délimité de qualité supérieure [Fr.] (On labels of French wine-bottles as) guarantee that wine is authentic. *(vañ day-lee-mee-tay duh kal-ee-tay soo-pay-ree-ur)* Often abbreviated to **V.D.Q.S.** Designates, in general terms, wine of second quality. See **appellation contrôlée.**

vin de pays [Fr.] Wine classified by the French system as being of third quality. *(vañ duh pay-ee)* See **appellation contrôlée** and **vin délimité de qualité supérieure.**

vin de table [Fr.] Wine of inferior quality, classed as fourth-grade in the French system. *(vañ duh tah-bluh)* See **appellation contrôlée, vin délimité de qualité supérieure** and **vin de pays.**

vin d'honneur [Fr.] Reception in honour of distinguished guest(s), with consumption of and toasting in wine. *(vañ don-UR)*

vin du pays [Fr.] Wine from the local region. *(vañ doo pay-ee)* Compare **vin de pays.**

vingt-et-un [Fr.] Card-game now commonly known as pontoon. *(vañt-ay-erñ)*

vin mousseux [Fr.] Sparkling wine. *(vañ moos-ur)*

vino [It.] Wine. *(VEE-noh)*

vin ordinaire Same as **vin de table.** *(vañ or-dee-nair)*

vin rosé [Fr.] Pink wine. *(vañ roh-zay)*

vin rouge [Fr.] Red wine. *(vañ roozh)*

virement [Fr.] Power to transfer items from one financial account to another. *(VEER-mahñ)* Now rapidly becoming anglicised and pronounced as if it were an English word, the first syllable rhyming with *fire.*

virgo intacta [Lat.] Woman who is physically a virgin. *(VER-goh in-TAK-ta)*

virtù [It.] Artistic excellence. Importance in workmanship, antiquity, rarity, etc. *(ver-TOO)* Usually found in the expression **objects of virtu.**

virtuoso [It.] Person highly skilled in performance, especially of music. Showing a high degree of skill. *(ver-tyoo-OH-soh)*

vis-à-vis [Fr.] In relation to. Opposite to. *(veez-ah-vee)*

viticulteur [Fr.] (In France) vine-grower. *(vee-tee-kool-TUR)*

viva [It.] Long live . . .! *(VEE-va)* See also **viva voce.**

vivace [It.] (Of music) played vivaciously, in a brisk and lively way. *(viv-AH-cheh)*

vivandière [Fr.] Woman attached to regiment of continental (especially French) army, selling provisions. Female camp-follower. *(veev-ahñ-dyair)*

vivat [Lat.] Long live . . .! (VEYE- or *VEE-vat)* See below.

vivat regina or **rex** [Lat.] Long live the Queen or King. *(VEYE-vat rej-EYE-na* or *reks)*

viva voce [Lat.] Orally. Oral examination. *(veye-va VOH-cheh)* Sometimes colloquially abbreviated to **viva**, and used as verb.

vive la différence [Fr.] Long live the difference (between the sexes). *(veev la dee-fay-rahn̄s)*

vive le roi [Fr.] Long live the King. *(veev luh rwah)*

vivo [It.] (In music) lively. *(VEE-voh)*

viz. Abbreviation of **videlicet.**

vodka [Russ.] Alcoholic spirit originating in Russia and made by distilling rye. *(VOD-ka)*

vol-au-vent [Fr.] Small pie of light puff pastry filled with meat, fish, etc. *(vol-oh-vahn̄)*

Völkerwanderung [Ger.] Migration of peoples. *(FERL-ke-vahn-duh-roong)*

volkslied [Ger.] Folk-song. *(FOHLKS-leet)*

volte-face [Fr.] Complete reversal of opinion or attitude. *(volt-FAHS)*

vomitorium [Lat.] Passage for entrance and exit in ancient theatre, amphitheatre, etc. *(vom-it-OR-ium)*

voortrekker [Afrikaans] (In South Africa) pioneer. *(FOR-trek-er)*

vox et praeterea nihil [Lat.] A voice and nothing more. Empty words. *(voks et preye-TER-ay-a NI-hil)*

vox populi [Lat.] The voice of the people. Public opinion. The general verdict. *(voks POP-yoo* or *-oo-lee* or *-leye)*

vox populi, vox Dei [Lat.] The voice of the people is the voice of God. *(voks POP-yoo* or *-oo-lee* or *-leye, voks DAY-ee)*

voyeur [Fr.] One who derives sexual gratification from looking at others' sexual activities or organs. *(vwah-YUR)*

vs. Abbreviation of **versus.**

W

wadi [Arab.] Gully. Dry water-course. *(WAH-di)*

wagon-lit [Fr.] Sleeping-car on continental train. *(vag-ahn̄-lee)*

wallah [Hind.] Person concerned with, employed to deal with, or expert in, something. *(WOL-a)*

wanderlust [Ger.] Eager desire for travel or wandering. *(WON-der-lust)*

Wehrmacht [Ger.] German armed forces before and during Second World War. *(VEHR-mahkht)*

Wein [Ger.] Wine *(veye-n)*

Weinstube [Ger.] Small drinking-house. *(VEYE-n-shtoo-buh)*

Weisswein [Ger.] White wine. *(VEYE-sveye-n)*

Weltanschauung [Ger.] Philosophy of life. *(VELT-ahn-sh-ow-oong)*

Weltpolitik [Ger.] (Participation in) international politics. World politics or policy. *(VELT-poh-lee-teek)*

Weltschmerz [Ger.] World-weariness. Distress or pessimism at state of the world. Apathetic outlook on life. *(VELT-shmehrts)*

Wiegenlied [Ger.] Lullaby. *(VEE-guhn-leet)*

Wiener Schnitzel [Ger.] (In cookery) veal cutlet brushed with beaten egg and coated with breadcrumbs before being fried in butter. *(VEE-ner SHNIT-sl)*

wildebeest [Afrikaans] Gnu. *(VIL-duh-beest)*

wunderbar [Ger.] Wonderful. *(VOON-duh-bar)*

wunderkind [Ger.] Child prodigy. *(VOON-duh-kint)* Plural **wunderkinder** *(-kin-duh)*

wurst [Ger.] Sausage. *(voorst)*

Y

Yahveh, Yahweh [Heb.] Same as **Jahveh.** *(YAH-vay)*

yarmulka [Yiddish] Skull-cap worn by Jewish men. *(YAH-ml-ka)* Also **yarmulke.**

yashmak [Arab.] Veil worn in public by Moslems in some countries to conceal whole of face except eyes. *(YASH-mak)*

yen [Jap.] Japanese monetary unit. *(yen)*

yerba maté [Sp.] Same as **maté.** *(YER-ba MAH-teh)*

yeti [Tibetan] Abominable snowman: unidentified creature alleged to live above snow-line in Himalayas and known only from its tracks. *(YET-i)*

yoga [Hind.] Hindu system of meditation, asceticism and self-discipline to achieve reunion with and insight into the supreme being. *(YOH-ga)*

yoghurt, yoghourt, yogurt [Turk.] Food of milk curdled by added bacteria, usually flavoured with fruit. *(YOG-urt)*

yogi [Hind.] One who practises **yoga.** *(YOH-gi)*

Yom Kippur [Heb] Day of Atonement: annual Jewish festival of prayer and fasting. *(yom kip-OOR)*

Z

zabaglione [It.] Italian dessert of egg-yolks, sugar and wine, served warm. *(zah-bah-LYOH-neh)*

zapateado [Sp.] Stamping of feet as part of Spanish dancing. *(zah-pat-i-AH-doh)*

Zeitgeist [Ger.] Spirit of the times. *(TSEYE-tgeye-st)*

Zen [Jap.] Form of Buddhism emphasising practice of meditation. *(zen)*

zenana [Hind.] (In India, Iran, etc.) part of house where women live in seclusion. *(zen-AH-na)*

ziggurat [Assyrian] Assyrian temple in shape of pyramid. *(ZIG-ur-at)*

zingaro [It.] Gypsy. *(ZIN-ga-roh)* Plural **zingari** *(-ree)*

zloty [Pol.] Polish monetary unit. *(ZLOT-i)*

Zollverein [Ger.] Customs union. *(TSOHL-fuh-reye-n)*

zombie [African] Corpse said to be revived by witchcraft. *(ZOM-bi)* Hence, apathetic, lethargic, dull person apparently without mind of his own.

zouave [Fr.] Member of French light-infantry corps, originally formed of Algerians, and distinguished by colourful Oriental uniform. *(zoo-AHV)*

zucchetto [It.] Ecclesiastical skull-cap worn by Roman Catholic priests, the colour depending on rank. *(tsook-ET-oh)*

zwieback [Ger.] Kind of crisp biscuit or rusk. *(TSVEE-bahk)*